The Visitor's Guide
to
CORNWALL
and the
ISLES OF SCILLY

D0582471

INDEX TO 1:50 000 MAPS OF GREAT BRITAIN

Reproduced from the Ordnance Survey map with the permission of the
Controller of Her Majesty's Stationery Office, Crown copyright reserved.

THE VISITOR'S GUIDE TO CORNWALL and the ISLES OF SCILLY

Rita Tregellas Pope

MPC

HUNTER PUBLISHING INC

Published by:
Moorland Publishing Co Ltd,
Moor Farm Road West,
Ashbourne,
Derbyshire DE6 1HD
England

ISBN 0 86190 304 8

Published in the USA by:
Hunter Publishing Inc.,
300 Raritan Centre Parkway,
CN94, Edison, NJ 08818

ISBN 1 55650 589 2

British Library Cataloguing in
Publication Data:
A catalogue record for this book is
available from the British Library.

1st Edition   1983
2nd Edition (fully revised and
      redesigned)   1988
3rd Edition (revised)   1993
Reprinted   1994

Cover photograph:
Mevagissey (MPC Picture Library).

Photographs have been supplied as
follows:
R. Bishop: pp197, 182, 183; I.J. Brown:
p163; F.W. Ellis: pp122, 151 (lower),
158; F.E. Gibson: pp136-7, 139, 141,
144, 146-7; D. Hills: p82 (upper); G.
Irving: pp17, 19, 27, 33, 38, 39, 43, 50,
52, 53 (lower), 67, 71, 74, 82 (upper),
83, 130, 151 (upper), 153, 155, 166,
167, 174, 186 (upper), 187, 190, 191,
195, 200, 218; R.S. Pope: pp16, 26,
162, 175, 176, 178, 198, 199, 207, 223,
226, 228; R.T. Pope: pp217, 219, 224;
MPC Picture Library: pp30, 34-5, 42, 46,
47, 48, 51, 53 (upper), 54-5, 58-9, 60,
62, 66, 70, 75, 79, 86, 87, 95, 110, 111,
127, 186 (lower), 203, 214, 221; Ron
Scholes: p123, 142, 143; K. Skellern:
pp99, 106-7; D. Vage: pp20, 21, 78, 90,
102, 103, 114, 115, 118, 119, 126, 157,
164.

Colour and black & white
origination by:
Quad Repro Ltd, Pinxton, Notts

Printed in the Hong Kong by:
Wing King Tong Co Ltd

CONTENTS

Key to Symbols Used on Maps and in Text Margin

 Recommended walk

 Church/Ecclesiastical site

 Parkland

 Building of interest

 Archaeological site

 Castle/Fortification

 Nature reserve/Animal interest

 Museum/Art gallery

 Birdlife

 Beautiful view/Scenery, natural phenomenon

 Garden

 Other place of interest

PREFACE

Cornwall is a land of lovely beaches, magnificent cliffs and fascinating winding lanes. All are beautiful but can be dangerous. For your own safety, please observe the warnings displayed by lifeguards and coastguards and drive carefully along the lanes. Some have passing places, but not all, so be ready to reverse — sometimes quite a distance. These narrow roads began as tracks made by farm animals and offer a special relaxation for those who are willing to travel slowly and occasionally perhaps, even make time to 'stand and stare'. My wish is that you will return home relaxed, happy and above all — safe.

R.T.P.

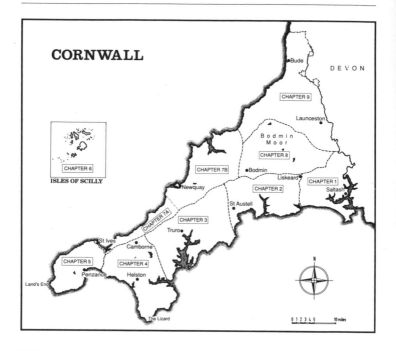

Note on the Maps

The maps drawn for each chapter, while comprehensive, are not designed to be used as route maps, but rather to locate the main towns, villages and places of interest. For exploration, visitors are recommended to use the 1:50,000 (approximately $1\frac{1}{4}$ in to the mile) Ordnance Survey 'Landranger' maps. The sheets covering the areas included in this book are shown on the frontispiece.

INTRODUCTION

THE ROYAL DUCHY OF CORNWALL

The land of King Arthur — the Cornish Riviera — the Delectable Duchy — call it what you will. Few places have as many facets as Cornwall but this is because the land west of the Tamar is not just a holiday region, it is much more. It is almost a 'nation' in its own right. Look carefully and you will find what you seek, whether it be tales of the past, pleasures of the present or even glimpses into the future.

Until the middle of the last century, few people visited Cornwall. Roads were dangerous and sea travel largely restricted to packet-ships and merchantmen. But this state of affairs ended abruptly in 1859 when Brunel's great railway bridge carried the first train over the Tamar into Cornwall. That historic event was the 'Open Sesame' for visitors. At first they came in a thin trickle, but others soon realised the attraction of the land beyond England and the era of the holidaymaker had begun.

There are, however, those who say that they can find nothing to do in Cornwall. Perhaps they have not troubled to look. The Cornish motto of 'One and All' has numerous interpretations but the right choice for this guide is 'One Place and Something for All'. S.P.B. Mais said that Cornwall has a 'diversity of riches', and as those are the very treasures which shaped its development, a brief look at the past will show how their mosaic influences have formed the region as it is today.

With the sea on three sides and the Tamar making the fourth boundary, Cornwall has always been almost an island. So when wandering tribes from Europe arrived, they were able to enjoy a life of comparative peace — scarcely disturbed by the hordes who ravaged the rest of the mainland. That is why, with only wind and weather to affect them, so many Neolithic and Bronze Age monoliths and barrows remain.

The richness of Cornwall's mineral deposits was not exploited until about 350BC when Iron Age tribes from Europe came in search of tin. The people of this fair-haired, blue-eyed race were tall and finely built, probably the originals of the 'giants' in Cornish folklore. They brought their knowledge of tin production with them as well as their culture and a completely new social structure. Evidence of this important occupation is still to be seen in hill forts, cliff castles and the 'trevs' or settlements. The area of West Penwith, beyond Penzance also retains low dry-stone walls and unique small fields — the latter having been cultivated continuously ever since Iron Age times.

The Tre-, Pol- and Pen- prefixes to family and place names which are so typical of Cornwall, also stem from that Iron Age period. For those tribes introduced the Indo-European Celtic language which, as Cornish, is the Brythonic branch. Although it seemed to die as the universally spoken tongue more than two centuries ago, it has now come out of hibernation. This revival, which began at the turn of the century, was inspired by dedicated men like Henry Jenner and Morton Nance. Today the language is studied and spoken by linguists such as the present Bishop of Leicester, the Right Reverend Richard Rutt. It is an examination subject for school children and has recently become the first language in a number of homes. Many bards are fluent Cornish speakers and at their annual Gorsedd, awards are given for literary compositions in the Cornish tongue. Weddings, baptisms and other church services are also conducted in the language.

The much-maligned Druids were Celtic priests who, far from being mere growers of mistletoe, lovers of apples and makers of bonfires, were, in fact, the most highly respected scholars of their day. Men travelled across Europe to learn from them, early Greek was indebted to them and even the great Cicero paid tribute to their knowledge. People who laugh at their customs have only heard about the more sensational aspects and would doubtless be surprised to know that these same Druids were among the first of the so-called pagans to proclaim the doctrine of immortality.

Visitors interested in Roman remains will find few here. Romans did not settle in Cornwall but their merchants came here for tin, so the Romano-Cornish association was mainly through trade.

The next arrivals were of great importance, for they led the Cornish people away from paganism to Christianity. These were holy men and women from Wales and Ireland who established their 'cells' near water — rivers, wells or streams. Many of these, previously objects of pagan worship, then became shrines and places of pilgrimage. Today about a hundred holy wells still exist, most of them pleasant places to visit, others looked upon as serving a special purpose — turning the affections of a loved one in the right direction, for example! Cornish churches (many near wells or water) are dedicated to those 'saints' and have names not seen in other English counties, such as St Gluvias, St Probus and St Petroc.

For centuries, Cornwall was entirely Celtic, but once the Anglo-Saxons had overcome England they turned to the west for further conquests. Here they met fierce resistance from Cornish chiefs or kings. One was Arthur, a Celtic ruler born in the late fifth century AD who led the last great Celtic battle against the Anglo-Saxons. The legends that grew up after his death and the medieval romances associated with his name, have so obscured the historical figure that it is now almost impossible to discover the truth about him. By the end of the seventh century the Anglo-Saxons had conquered Devon but it was not till after AD926 that King Athelstan finally conquered the Cornish. A few Anglo-Saxons settled in Cornwall, mostly along the eastern border. Some ventured further and there is evidence of this in the scattering of non-Cornish place names found elsewhere — Wicca at Zennor is a good example.

The Norman Conquest, however, did bring many changes. King William's custom of rewarding his barons with large estates held good in Cornwall — even to Land's End. The Domesday Book must have looked impressive with its accounts of groups of manors belonging to this or that Norman overlord. But many of the so-called manors were little more than small farmsteads or 'trevs' run by perhaps two people as they had been since Celtic times. In many cases, these home-steads are still farmed today — to be found almost hidden in a maze of narrow winding lanes. Here Cornwall has scarcely altered for centuries and those who would like to walk back in time need simply take the latest OS map and explore the narrow lanes of a remote parish. These lead to the very heart of Cornwall.

The castles the Normans built for defence — Launceston, Restormel and Trematon, also served to restore the sense of security the Cornish had lost since the Saxon conflicts. By the mid-twelfth century, Cornwall was Europe's largest supplier of tin, and stannary towns grew up at places where tin was tested. Royal charters for markets and fairs also encouraged trade while the building of numerous collegiate and other churches resulted in a more settled way of life. By 1337, Cornwall was therefore a fitting land for King Edward III to bestow on his heir, the Black Prince.

In the Middle Ages, however, there was less need for defensive castles so the landowners built manors with only a degree of fortification. A good example is Cotehele, overlooking the Tamar, one of Cornwall's most beautiful great houses.

At sea, as on land, Cornwall prospered. Her sailors and fishermen gained renown at home and abroad. Perhaps one of her proudest occasions was when Fowey sent forty-seven ships to help the king besiege Calais in 1346. This was nearly twice the number mustered by the City of London.

But sad times lay ahead. When the Reformation came, Cornwall's beautiful churches were stripped and most of her collegiate establishments closed. Men no longer travelled from Europe to study at Glasney Collegiate Church in Penryn and the place which might have been Cornwall's university is now remembered in a few scattered remains. The final blow came, however, when Bibles were printed in English — a language that Cornishmen did not want to understand and certainly could not read. In an effort to preserve their culture, their way of life and their long heritage, the people rebelled. Many lost their lives in the 1549 revolt, but in vain. From then on the language began to decline. There is a saying in Cornish — *An lavar goth, yu lavar gwyr.* It means: 'He who loses his tongue (his language) shall lose his land.' And that was so, for as the language faded so did the customs and the essence of the nation. But Cornwall's identity was never completely overwhelmed and is still to be found today — very easily recognised.

Prosperity returned briefly, however, in the eighteenth and nineteenth centuries when underground mining came into its own. The inventions of great Cornishmen like Richard Trevithick, Michael Loam and Goldsworthy Gurney, enabled shafts to be sunk deep into the ground and even under the sea bed so that the increasing number of engine houses transformed much of the landscape. Fortunes were made and lost almost overnight but Cornwall faced a major disaster once again when cheap surface tin was imported from Malaya. This time miners emigrated to look for work. Many settled in Canada, Australia, South Africa, Tasmania and the United States which often meant that whole families died out and Cornwall's glory faded again.

But there is much of the phoenix in this land. Its story has always been influenced by the rocks of its landscape and its coast. Granite has been the source of shelter in life and protection in death; of prosperity with tin and copper and more recently, china clay. Some feel that Cornwall's granite stones are only subjects for artists and photographers but scientists with vision have already begun to realise the great potential of this vast treasure store. The first dish scanners ever used for inter-satellite communication were built on the firm foundation of granite in the Lizard Peninsula. More recently, as a result of dry hot rock experiments made by the Camborne School of Mines at the Rosemanowes Quarry, Penryn, there is the possibility of towns and villages having their homes heated by the geo-thermal energy which is stored in Cornwall's granite wealth.

And now from the general outline of Cornwall's history to the particular — a closer look at the region. It has been divided into nine areas all with different characteristics — avoiding main roads as far as possible. In this way, it is hoped that visitors will see Cornwall's many facets and so appreciate to the full, the variety and individuality of this ancient and beautiful land.

1 IN AND AROUND SALTASH

O n the Cornwall side of the River Tamar lies **Saltash**, and visitors generally arrive either by way of the A38 or train via Plymouth. The name is a reminder of days when Romans, Anglo-Saxons and Normans used this 'passage' or 'esse' which was the meeting place of salt and fresh water. King John granted Saltash borough status and in 1270 the lords of nearby Trematon Castle owned the ferry. Soon the town held jurisdiction over the tidal reaches of both Tamar and Lynher, extending their claims on oysterage and anchorage till they controlled all tolls as far as the Calstock salmon weirs.

By 1752, traders and fishermen rebelled against the Saltash monopoly and refused to pay their tolls. The burgesses applied to parliament for confirmation of rights but were strongly opposed by James Tillie of Pentillie Castle. As he owned Halton Quay, which was a little way up river, and several trading vessels, he was considerably affected. He gained support from the governor of Plymouth and eventually won the law suit brought against him. Finally he instructed the ships' masters to pay only 1s, an act which made them free for ever 'from all encroachments of the unjust and iniquitous Saltashers.'

The town no longer sent members to parliament after 1832 and consequently declined in political importance. It kept its reputation as a great 'nursery' for sailors, however, but even more celebrated were its fisherwomen who frequently beat all comers in the four-oared gig races at various regattas.

In May, 1859, the Prince Consort opened Isambard Brunel's masterpiece, the Royal Albert Bridge and the Great Western Railway carried the first holidaymakers into Cornwall. Still an impressive sight today, the handsome structure was the first to be built in a unique combination of suspension and conventional style. It was the great engineer's last work but he was too ill to attend the ceremony. However, although he was a dying man, Brunel had an open truck

14

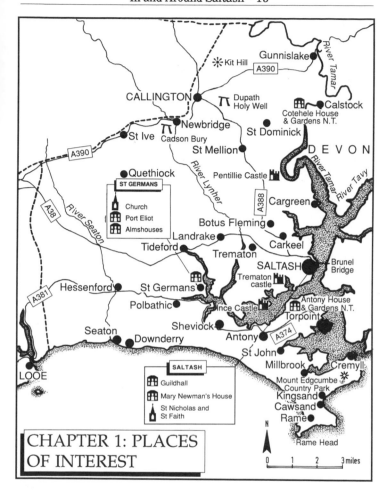

CHAPTER 1: PLACES
OF INTEREST

made especially for him and by the end of that same month travelled
in quiet triumph over the Tamar to Cornwall.

This new influx of visitors gave the town of Saltash a brief revival
but when the Admiralty bought the oyster rights in 1901, its long
maritime history came to an end. Today it is a friendly shopping centre
with a scattering of historic buildings to remind people of its past and
although the new tunnel and bypass give it the appearance of

standing alone, it is proud to know that it is still very much a part of Cornwall.

On the corner of Fore Street and Station Road is the present fine Guildhall. Over the centuries it has been market hall and town hall, now resplendent inside and out — worthy of its name. The upstairs assembly hall is used for every kind of meeting from politics to popular markets as well as the mayor-choosing ceremony. The mayoral insignia has a special local interest in that it incorporates three silver oars with maceheads. Closely associated with this building is the church of St Nicholas and St Faith. A chapel of ease until 1881, it dates from about 1225, (although the tower is earlier) while the clock — probably 1720 — is a rarity in a Cornish church (possibly because the hardness of granite made it awkward to incorporate such a feature). No visitor can overlook the sumptuous memorial to three shipwrecked Drew brothers and that, with a wall tablet, are only two of the interesting items to be found here. The tablet reads: 'This chapple was repaired in the Mayoralty of Matthew Veale, Gent., anno 1689'.

Mary Newman was born here in a small Tudor house on the steep slope of Culver Street, overlooking the Tamar. She would have seen

The Guildhall, Saltash

Brunel's Royal Albert Bridge, Saltash

many fine ships anchored in the river, but did she ever dream that one day she would be the wife of Sir Francis Drake? The Tamar Protection Society have recently restored this historic place and for a small sum it is possible to see both house and garden. Refreshments are also there for those who would like to take tea where Sir Francis Drake once lived.

Much of Saltash's history has been linked with the villages along the banks of the Tamar. On the A388 Callington Road lies **Carkeel** where an industrial estate offers work in Cornwall for local people who do not want to go to Plymouth. A right-hand turn in the centre of the village — so narrow that it can easily be missed — leads to tree-lined lanes winding round to **Botus Fleming**, set high above the Tamar. A memorial to the Symons family is in the church — an unusual wooden reredos which shows the agricultural nature of the area, with its vines, corn and various fruits. There is also a memorial brass to one of Cornwall's great engineers, Michael Loam, inventor of the 'man-engine' which saved so many lives in Cornish mines. Born in west Cornwall, he died at Moditonham House where only 12 years before, the Prince of Orange had surrendered Pendennis and Plymouth Castles. During World War II, Moditonham suffered considerable bomb damage, but the National Trust now maintains the little of the

PLACES OF INTEREST AT SALTASH

Brunel's Royal Albert Bridge
A railway bridge from Plymouth to Saltash. The last engineering achievement of Isambard Kingdom Brunel, begun in 1857, was opened by Prince Albert on 6 May 1859.

The Guildhall
Fore Street
Formerly a market house, but at the end of the eighteenth century the town hall was added. By 1890 it became the Guildhall.

Mary Newman's House
Culver Street
This little low Tudor house is the birthplace of Sir Francis Drake's first wife.

building that remains.

Lanes to **Cargreen** are warm with meadow-sweet and bright with purple vetch in summer. Linger beside the quiet quay — a pleasant place to watch the small craft. Walkers may prefer to make a bypass to Landulph church where Theodore Palaeologus was buried. He was descended from the last of the Greek Christian emperors and has achieved later fame as an ancestor of Prince Philip who, with the Queen, visited the tomb in 1962.

A handful of cottages hug Cargreen quay. The village has a lively yacht club and it is hard to realise that this was once Cornwall's Covent Garden. Market gardeners from all over the valley brought their produce here to be ferried across to Devon. Now only sailing boats and birds make the crossing — a walk beside the Tamar at low tide reveals all its beauty. It is little wonder that this riverside area is popular with both birdwatchers and naturalists while a marked increase in the number of nurserymen seems to indicate a revival in a former trade.

Motorists climb gently away from Cargreen, past Coombe Lane, where wool used to be collected from local farmers en route to a mill at Liskeard. The turning to the right, after the church, rises high above the valley again and ferny lanes give way to open views. Pentillie Castle, superbly sited to overlook a wooded sweep of the river, can be seen on the right. It was built in 1689 by James Pentillie, a steward to the Coryton family of Cornwall's Newton Ferrers. When Pentillie's great-niece married a Coryton in 1810, Wilkins, who designed

Cotehele

London's National Gallery, planned the alterations. Further work was carried out after 1965 and by 1970 the castle was almost the same as the original. Granite pillars from Kit Hill make the front look impressive while a statue of James Pentillie in the centre of the courtyard seems to register approval.

Beyond this, narrow lanes climb then dip into the strangely-named Mount Ararat woods before dropping steeply to the peace of **Halton Quay**. The Pentillie fleet ferried Hingston Down granite from here to Devon in the eighteenth century and cargoes of local fruit and flowers down river. Since the quay closed in 1926, bird lovers and fishermen have taken over so that the chapel of St Dominick beside the water is once again a place of quiet.

From here, even narrower lanes lead up past Chapel Farm to the village of **St Dominick** where there is the one remaining cherry orchard of the many which used to supply markets all over the country.

In the next valley lie the mill and riverside buildings of **Cotehele** — the manor on the hill overlooking the Tamar. This romantic medieval house, one of the least altered in the country, was built 1485–1627 and constructed round three courts on the foundations of an earlier dwelling. The furniture, tapestries and armour have always been where they are today, but if you wish to make a close inspection

Cotehele Quay with Shamrock *and the man who restored her*

of the pictures and textiles, avoid dull days early or late in the season, as certain rooms have no electric light. The valley garden has a restored medieval dovecote and on the walk through the woods to the quay is Richard Edgcumbe's chapel, built by the warring knight as a thanks offering for his survival after declaring against the Crown in 1403.

Cotehele is not a place to run away from. The whole area is ideal for a day's pleasure with walks, birdwatching and sometimes salmon fishing to watch. Picnic where you will, have refreshments in the old barn or by the river and marvel at the craftsmanship of *Shamrock* and the skill of those who restored her. She is the last surviving stone-carrying Tamar barge and a grand old lady now available for public charter on a daily basis to interested parties, societies or schools.

 Cotehele Quay on the Tamar, with its eighteenth- and nineteenth-century buildings, is an outstation of the National Maritime Museum. The former public house at Cotehele Quay is now a café and is also open to people not visiting Cotehele House. There is a signposted walk from here to Cotehele Mill where there are various features exhibited such as the blacksmith's forge, carpenter's and wheel-wright's shops, cider press and the preserved waterwheel.

For walkers and birdwatchers, there is a riverside footpath to

Calstock railway viaduct over the River Tamar

Calstock, but motorists have to follow a more narrow ferry way to this attractive village — another quiet place now but once a busy shipyard. The handsome railway viaduct brought trains to the village but destruction to its shipping. Today pleasure boats make pleasant pictures as they sail past the place where James Goss built the *Garlandstone* which was Britain's last ketch. Most river and fishing ports have always held regattas; Calstock's, which are as famous as those of Saltash, have recently been revived.

The road out of Calstock under the railway bridge is signposted to Tavistock but along the way look for a sign to Calcraft Products. Here, suits of armour are made to measure and antique pistols fashioned to your own design.

Gunnislake village climbs to an even steeper slope than Saltash and the road to the New Bridge calls for low gear and good brakes. Before stagecoaches demanded roads and not muddy byways, the approaching paths to the river went straight down the cliff side — a daunting gradient even on horseback. Piers Edgcumbe of Cotehele built this Tamar bridge in 1520 and in 1644 Sir Richard Grenville did his utmost to defend it against the Roundheads. It was then the chief pass into Cornwall, but Sir Richard's efforts were unfortunately in vain.

At this point, the Tamar 'tastes' the tide and as maritime trading interests cease, it is appropriate to turn inland again. The A390 Callington road runs at the foot of **Kit Hill** but make time to leave it and find the B3257 which takes you to the lane leading to the top. The Duchy of Cornwall preserved the 85ft stack at the summit and it remains a mining monument to the workers who won tin over so many centuries and who, with Devon men, held their Stannary Parliaments there. On a clear day the views extend to Dartmoor's Hessary Tor 12 miles (20km) away, the Eddystone Lighthouse 23 miles (37km) and west to Bodmin Moor and Roughtor, 15 miles (24km). There are old mine workings among the heather and many people, choosing their weather, enjoy a whole day here. It will be an even greater pleasure to do that when Kit Hill is fully developed into the extensive country park area that is planned for the near future. Meanwhile there should be interesting results of the work done to restore the 200-year-old water storage reservoir discovered during a survey conducted by the Cornwall Archaeological Unit.

Before entering Callington, take a minor road on the left signposted 'St Mellion'. A short way down, another lane leads to Dupath Well, a handsomely covered spring, the largest of its kind in Cornwall. When the canons of St Germans acquired property, it included 'Theu Path' and they probably had the protective building erected over the holy place. It remained in their possession until the Dissolution. The name is interesting as it is thought to mean 'The Palm of God' in old Cornish. 'Theu' changing to 'Dew' (God) and 'Path' which is a corruption of 'Palf' (palm of hand) and it then became Dupath as we know it today. Fortunately it was saved from complete disintegration by a rector of South Hill and shortly after 1936 was taken over by the Ministry of Works permanently.

The quiet town of **Callington** was once the centre of a thriving wool industry but some believe that it has an even older history and that it was originally Killiwic where King Arthur had a palace. As you drive along the short main street, notice a little lane beside the church. This was Tillie Street (now reduced to one cottage), the birthplace of John Knill, St Ives' well known and controversial mayor who will be mentioned again in Chapter 7.

The Liskeard A390 narrows immediately outside the town and is transformed into country lanes which dip to picturesque **Newbridge**.

PLACES OF INTEREST NORTH OF SALTASH

Cotehele
St Dominick, beside the Tamar.
National Trust
A romantic medieval house of
grey granite, built 1485–1627.
One of the best-preserved
examples of a squire's house and
for centuries home of the
Edgcumbes. Beautifully furnished
with original tapestries, needle-
work and armour.

Kit Hill
Two miles NE of Callington beside
the A390

An outlying eminence of granite,
the summit of Hingston Down
where King Egbert defeated
Britons and Danes in AD835.

Dupath Holy Well
About a mile from Callington
between the A388 and 390.
This is the largest well building in
Cornwall.

Pentillie Castle
Near Cargreen
Built 1689.
Not open to the public.

At this point the River Lynher is spanned by an ancient construction dating from 1478 and the cluster of cottages is typical of a Cornish 'trev' or homestead. The early settlement, however, was once high above on Cadson Bury, a prehistoric fort now owned by the National Trust. It is well worth stopping to walk up to it and enjoy the views down the lovely wooded valley.

St Ive (Eve) hamlet sits clean and fresh beside the busy road from Callington to Liskeard. The church is somewhat unusual as it is a Knights Templars foundation, dating back to 1180. There is more, too, of interest in the compact little village of **Quethiock** (Gwithick) which so many visitors do not know about. Take the narrow lane just opposite the slate-hung Butcher's Arms on the A390 and follow its twists and turns down to the church, content in the protection of the picturesque cottages guarding its history. The church is one that lovers of brass memorials should not miss. A fine example here is one crafted in 1471 for Roger Kyngdon, his wife and their sixteen children. If the church is locked there is a list of key holder's names on the porch. Look out, too, for the Maids' House before you leave. It was built in a new style of architecture not long after 1633 when a charity of poor spinsters was established. Today this remote parish of twisting lanes and secluded farmhouses leads a busy life of its own and one of the highlights is an agricultural show held in mid-July. Here the standards are good and everyone is made welcome.

From Quethiock to **St Mellion**, the lanes dip and curve in almost impossible configurations, but in high summer they are cool and delightful. It matters little whether you find the clapper bridge at Bramble Wood or take the way to Pillatonmill and climb out of the deep valley from there — both roads are rarely used. Mid-July is the time to visit St Mellion and the Cherry-Pie Feast. The Reverend and Mrs Watts revived a local tradition in 1975 and adapted it as a replacement for their summer garden party. Squire Coryton of Pentillie probably originated the feast in the last century, inviting local school children to a cherry-pie and cream tea on the lawns of his castle. Swings were set up in the 200-year-old lime trees bordering the mile-long drive from the road. Everyone enjoyed this event and were sad when it stopped in 1937.

St Mellion has another, though very different, interesting point to note. It was the birthplace of John Trevisa (1412), a Cornishman who was eager to promote the use of English. He translated the entire Bible from Latin to English but in so doing was one of the indirect causes of the eventual decline of his native tongue.

The drive round Saltash covers about 44 miles but the time cannot be assessed so closely as it would depend on how long were the stops and how deep the investigations into such items as the Kyngdon brasses and the manorial watermill at Cotehele.

The countryside which lies south of Saltash has quite different attractions from those of the Tamarside villages. A glance at the map shows that this area can be explored in two parts, but only by coming back along the same road. The information in the rest of the chapter covers the Torpoint-Rame peninsula.

Take the road from Saltash where it dips to **Forder** away from the mother church, St Stephen's. After 2 miles from the town centre there is instant countryside with Trematon Castle outlined on the far hill. In the valley, mill buildings and a cluster of old Tudor cottages huddle together watching the traffic climb sharply to the lodge gates of Trematon. This is now a private home but on two or three afternoons in the summer the grounds are open to the public and all proceeds go to charity.

Those who prefer may walk the riverside way and perhaps see the train lumbering slowly round from Saltash after carefully negotiating

Brunel's Royal Albert Bridge — the engineering triumph of its time. Today, the high granite shafts and unusual tubular arches give it a strange look, but since its opening in 1859 it has been efficient and safe, the first considerations for a railway bridge.

Train passengers, walkers and motorists all enjoy their brief sight of Trematon Castle with its romantic shape silhouetted against the sky. Possibly the most extensive in Cornwall, it has a well preserved keep which is said to be 'one of the most beautiful examples of the Norman period'. It passed into Duchy hands in the fourteenth century and later figured in a particularly distressing incident when Sir Richard and Lady Grenville were captured by treachery. Beyond the castle, where a road descends to the riverside chapel, a stumpy wayside cross marks the important part once played by this now out-of-the-way place.

Viscountess Boyd of Merton owns Ince Castle which stands beside the Lynher and if you are fortunate enough to be in Cornwall when the grounds are open you can not only wander through ornamental woods, but see the shell house and dovecote. Tea is also available on these occasions.

The architecture resembles that of a French château but the date of construction is probably early seventeenth century. It is believed that at one time the Killigrew owner kept four wives, one in each of the square towers — a picturesque story which matches the building.

There is no way for motorists across the Lynher, but the short distance along the A38 to **Tideford** is not unpleasant. This roadside village takes its name from the River Tiddy, quietly flowing down from the high moors of Caradon until it meets the salt water here. Tideford is still frequently spoken of as Tiddyford.

The riverside walk is a pleasant way to reach **St Germans** but motorists have to turn left on to the B3249. Behind the Information Centre and under the arch lies Heskyn Mill Restaurant. Once it was used for corn and flax but now it is a pleasant place to dine, perhaps before you travel further on the 3 miles to the historic but now sleepy village of picturesque cottages and flower-filled gardens. At the slope into the village notice Sir William Moyle's almshouses. Built in 1538, they were skilfully reconditioned in 1967 at the instigation of the National Association of Almshouses. Driving through this peaceful place today it is hard to believe that St Germans was once a 'rotten

Almshouses, St Germans, originally built in 1538

borough' which sent two MPs to Westminster.

The handsome parish church, formerly Cornwall's ancient cathedral, is away from the traffic, almost hidden among trees. Consecrated in 1261, the building had formerly been of importance as an Augustinian priory. Its great west doorway, Cornwall's finest, is a powerful example of Norman architecture and is constructed of elvan stone from Tartan Down near Landrake, while the church's spacious and lofty interior contains numerous interest features. Since 1974 the diocese has had a bishop suffragan at St Germans.

The Tudor gateway close by leads to Port Eliot where the Eliot family have lived for 400 years. It is probably Cornwall's largest private house but may now be visited by prior permission of the owner. Sir Thomas Elyot bought it from Cardinal Wolsey when he was selling monastery lands for Henry VIII. He was known as an astute business man, a skilled ambassador and the first person to compile an English dictionary. But perhaps the best remembered member of this family was probably Sir John, an MP and vice-admiral of Devon. Unfortunately his interest in maritime affairs proved his undoing as it led him to the Tower and an untimely death. He believed that the king's Bills

The church at St Germans

of Tonnage and Poundage would impose too great a strain on the mercantile community — a group of people with whom he worked closely. His strong feelings in the matter forced him to oppose the new proposals but he paid dearly for doing so.

In 1762, Sir Humphrey Repton redesigned the gardens and Sir John Soane made certain architectural alterations which included the addition of a splendid round room, some 40ft in diameter. The present Lord Eliot administers all 6,000 acres and sold produce from the walled garden in the Bothy Shop — unfortunately not now open. The last weekend in July was accepted as the time to visit the Port Eliot Elephant Fayre which was held in the grounds of the house. Many think that the name relates to the size of this 4-day spectacle of music, theatre, film, dance and craft but it is not so. It is simply an unusual application of the animal whose head appears on the family crest.

The view up river through the thirteen arches of the railway viaduct is a fine sight on a sunny day when seen from St Germans' quay and it is difficult to leave it for the turn to **Polbathic** nearby on the B3249. But once through that village and on to the A374 in the direction of Torpoint there are pleasures of a different kind. A whole stretch of woodland walks and picnic areas beside the St Germans (or Lynher) River, await those wanting to explore the paths to the small village of **Sheviock** and the area around Antony House. It is a part of Cornwall which has been called a miniature kingdom.

Antony House was built in the early eighteenth century and is the most distinguished classic house in Cornwall, with its central block of silver-grey Pentewan stone, and wings of red brick joined to the house by colonnades. Now owned by the National Trust it is still very much the home of the Carew-Poles, a fact that adds warmth to its elegance. The 250 acres of grounds slope gently to the Lynher — both the grounds and the house are well worth a visit. An interesting and unusual feature of this property is the Bath House — a half-mile from the main building and open only by appointment. It was built in 1784 and has recently been repaired.

Antony church is a building which should be visited. It is famous for an early brass of Lady Margery Arundell (1420) which is acknowledged to be the most spectacular in the whole of Cornwall.

Torpoint may seem a mere mass of uninteresting buildings after the elegance of Antony House but it does have its own features to offer

PLACES OF INTEREST SOUTH OF SALTASH

Trematon Castle
A mile SW of Saltash
One of a group of Norman for-
tresses, built either by Earl
Mortain or the Valletorts. Now
privately owned.

St Germans
The church — was the seat of the
Cornish bishopric from the close
of the tenth to the early eleventh
century. Its great feature is the
Norman west door.
The almshouses were built by Sir
William Moyle in 1538. They were
restored in 1967 through the Nat-
ional Association of Almshouses.

Port Eliot
St Germans
Probably Cornwall's largest
private house. Visits by private
appointment with the Eliot family
only.

Antony House
About 15 miles from Saltash
National Trust
A Carew-Pole property since the
fifteenth century, but this house
was built in the early eighteenth
century. The Bath House can be
seen on application to the secretary. Extensive grounds slope to
the River Lynher. Fine paintings
are to be seen in the house.

Antony Church
Rededicated in 1259, this church
is mainly remarkable for its spectacular early brass to Lady
Margery Arundell (1420).

Mount Edgcumbe House
Entrance at Cremyll Ferry.
Originally built in 1547–54 for Sir
Richard Edgcumbe but destroyed
in 1941 blitz. Rebuilt 1960. Home
of the present earl and open again
from 1988.

Mount Edgcumbe Country Park
Eight hundred acres of parkland
on magnificent coastline are open
all the year free.

Rame Head
Stretching into sea beyond Rame
church (St German) with expan-
sive views east and west.

Ince Castle Gardens and Grounds
(5m SW of Saltash, from A38 at
Stoketon Cross take turn signed
Trematon, Elmgate)
Five acres with lawns and ornamental woods; shell house and
dovecote.

the visitor. In 1691, William of Orange's order for the construction of
a naval dockyard across the Tamar at Cattewater was followed by
such great activity that Torpoint came into existence. According to the
comments made by Daniel Defoe, not only did the workmen need
homes but the entire operation needed 'yards, dry docks, launches

Torpoint from the Devon side of the Tamar

and conveniences of all kinds for building and repairing of ships!' There is not a vast amount of that undertaking left today but some of the old quays with their slate wharves still remain near the ferry. This has always been an important crossing and in 1793 the ferryman was obliged to keep three boats for pedestrians as well as a horse boat. His charge for everyone was one penny for the journey there and back. Today, pedestrians travel free from Torpoint but wheeled vehicles have to pay a small charge.

Instead of retracing the route use the slightly narrower road out of Torpoint which goes past the shore stations of *HMS Fisgard* and *HMS Raleigh* before cutting sharply across to **St John**. This is a quiet place of contrast, a delightful medieval cluster of narrow lanes in a fold of hills and cottages that match their surroundings. At low tide, the best way is by the road across the ford at the head of St John's Lake. This is a place to tempt birdwatchers to linger.

Walk or drive on to the little town of **Millbrook** but take care to negotiate the narrow, winding lane slowly as you pass fine Georgian houses side by side with humble but picturesque cottages. If your visit to Cornwall coincides with the early May bank holiday then stay here at Millbrook because you will be able to see and take part in a centuries-old festival. At some time in mid-morning the Flower-Boat ritual begins. A procession of dancers and singers make their way through the narrow ways of Millbrook, Kingsand and Cawsand, stopping at chosen houses and inns en route. This takes up most of the day, for they carry with them a decorated boat. Not a large one but one that is beautified with all the available spring flowers. The finale is an exciting one and when it grows dark, the boat is launched on the water, usually to the accompaniment of fireworks. This ceremony has been known in Millbrook since the fourteenth century but is thought to be pagan in origin.

The story told by an old inhabitant of Millbrook is an interesting one as it has a particular bearing on the name given to the boat — *The Black Prince*. It is well known that the son and heir of King Edward III had a great fondness for Trematon Castle, near Saltash, and whenever possible, stayed there for long periods of relaxation. He had to reach this haven by way of the ferry crossing over the Tamar from Plymouth to Saltash and apparently had a number to choose from. All those in use, however, were showing signs of wear and, according to the ideas of one of the inhabitants, were completely unsuitable to carry royalty. As a result, the Millbrook ferry disappeared one night from its usual moorings only to be seen a short distance away at Saltash. This outrageous theft caused everyone in Millbrook to declare 'war' on their neighbours and, armed with staves and pitchforks, they marched on the offenders. It was fortunate for all concerned that the Black Prince himself was there at the time for, had he not intervened, there would doubtless have been bloodshed and quite possibly a considerable loss of life. However, when he decreed that the people of Millbrook should have a new ferry — paid for by him, the tension disappeared and the militant villagers returned home quietly. Their gratitude, though, was not a light matter of a few words of thanks for they then decided that future generations should know about the generosity and kindness of the king's son. So it was agreed that the May Day Flower-Boat would always bear his name, *The Black Prince,* and although it has lapsed at times, this fascinating ceremony of so many associations, has once again taken its place with the other colourful customs in Cornwall.

An event that probably has the same roots takes place at St Ives on Good Friday — but here it is a less spectacular occasion when model yachts are brought out and sailed. And Cornwall has another story in the same vein, told of the interment of King Geraint. He is said to have been buried in a great tumulus at Carne, above the eastern side of Gerrans Bay on the Roseland Peninsula, after being rowed across the bay in a golden boat with silver oars. This particular royal leader was one of King Arthur's captains in his fifth-century battles against the Saxons and his story sounds more than legend in the light of a recent discovery at Broighter Bay in Ireland's County Derry. This was nothing less than a gold boat with silver oars.

The road to **Cremyll** goes first through Maker Heights in a steep climb and looks down on Millbrook as a toy town. Then, from the top of the world, the B3247 slides down to quiet Cremyll, a small group of houses at the crossing named the Passage of Crimela in charters of the thirteenth century. Here is a place that retains its individuality and its old houses but keeps up to date in the toll fees. Watching Drake Island and the shipping in Plymouth Sound keeps Cremyll busy all the year round and there is no objection when visitors park and join in their quiet game.

From here walk into Mount Edgcumbe Country Park, the earliest eighteenth-century landscaped garden in Cornwall and the only Grade I listed historic garden in the south-west. These 800 acres of superb parkland, bordered by 10 miles of magnificent coastline are open all the year from dawn to dusk and there is no admission charge. This park is now restored to its Edwardian splendour and the plans have been laid out with such skill that one day is scarcely long enough to encompass everything. It is a place of romance, magic and delight. If you like to be quiet, there is peace in the wooded areas and gardens full of flowers.

During the summer there are refreshments in the Orangery of the Italian Gardens with follies and a handsome conservatory not far away. The house itself, former home of the seventh Earl of Edgcumbe, was bought with the rest of the estate by Cornwall County Council and Plymouth City Council. From 1988 visitors will be allowed inside and for opening times please telephone Plymouth 822236 as they are not yet available.

Walk from here to **Rame Head** — about $2^1/_2$ miles, skirt the Park and continue through Maker parish, **Cawsand** and **Kingsand**. There are splendid distant views of Plymouth Breakwater and then across

*Gun emplacements at the Napoleonic fort,
Mount Edgcumbe Country Park*

to Heybrook Bay from Penlee Point before arriving at the headland.

Motorists have to climb again to Maker Heights before dropping down narrow lanes to Kingsand and Cawsand Bay at the water's edge. Till 1835 this area did not belong to Cornwall and there is still Boundary Cottage standing as a reminder. Few people know that a young sailor of Cawsand made history at the Battle of Trafalgar. Lieutenant John Pollard, born in 1784 was a midshipman aboard the *Victory* when Nelson was shot. He later became known as 'Nelson's Avenger' because he shot and killed the enemy sailor who fatally wounded Admiral Nelson.

Kingsand is very much a sailor's place — the streets twist like an anchor rope in a storm and the cottages cling to the cliff as seamen to the mast in rough weather. Trying to avoid leaning walls and jutting corners, most drivers miss Halfway House and find themselves in and out of Cawsand before they realise it. The *Bellerophon* set out from here under the command of Penryn-born Captain Maitland, who eventually captured Napoléon after his escape from Elba.

Once away from the villages, the road to **Rame** seems to continue for ever and, with land falling away on both sides, gives the strange sensation of driving straight into the sea. But there is a car park

Antony House

beyond the church for those who want to explore the headland. Wander down to the ancient chapel of St Michael and wonder at the piety and dedication of the hermits who lived here and kept a light burning to warn ships of the dangerous rocks below. By 1488, however, men were paid for this and they received 4d for 'Keeping of ye bekying'.

From here, the road to Seaton keeps close to the cliff top — as does the coastal path and, given fine weather, the views are superb. **Portwrinkle**'s golf course on the cliffs is almost the only sign of life till **Downderry**'s hotels appear. Beyond is **Seaton** — a place of sands and summer enjoyment for those who like crowds. A nearby attraction is the world's first protected breeding colony of Amazon woolly monkeys. They live in a sanctuary, not a zoo.

The wooded valley which leads from Seaton to **Hessenford** is quiet and magical for lovers of birds and trees. The beauty continues beyond Hessenford until the narrow winding lane opens on to the A38 just east of Tideford, and a few miles beyond is Saltash. But before the end of this 40-mile drive make the short detour into **Landrake**. It was the birthplace of Robert Jeffrye who went to London in the time of Charles Stuart. There he won fame and fortune and became Lord Mayor. He founded the Shoreditch almshouses which are now a museum but did not forget his native village. As well as establishing its first school, Robert Jeffrye also left money to help Landrake's poor. His village remembered his kindnesses and its new hall now bears the name of their benefactor.

2 LISKEARD TO ST AUSTELL

B etween Saltash and Lostwithiel lies **Liskeard**, once a prosperous town trading in tin and wool. Minerals from Caradon Hill brought a charter and subsequent wealth in 1240. Stannary privileges followed in 1307, when Liskeard became a coinage town. Later the flourishing wool trade added to the prosperity. The increasing demand for tin in the eighteenth and nineteenth centuries led to the opening of the Liskeard-Looe Canal which carried ore and stone supplies to the coast for export. Webb's Hotel in the Square was built in 1833 as a coaching inn.

The church of St Martin is the second largest in Cornwall, its history dating from the mid-thirteenth century. Stuart House in Barras Street is attractively slate-hung, as it must have been when King Charles stayed there (1644–5). Traces of the old town linger in and around Well Lane and Market Street where the Guildhall used to be. The Pipe Well, originally late sixteenth century, was restored in the early nineteenth century.

Industrial archaeologists or those interested in detective work could spend a pleasant time walking along part of the old canal bed.

Leave the town by the B3254 Looe road, first stopping in Station Road at the old industrial mill which houses Merlin Glass. This is the Pavlova Mill which once made gloves exclusively for Pavlova, the dancer. Watch craftsmen shaping their wares and buy from the shop if you wish. It is open 7 days a week.

Beyond Liskeard station follow the sign for St Keyne's Well but turn aside en route and see the Paul Corin Magnificent Music Machines. This modern wonder is housed in the family mill deep among lush, narrow lanes beside the River Looe. Spend an hour listening to instruments ranging in size from the musical box which began it all to a 20ft-high Belgian dance hall organ. An amazing collection to find anywhere but especially in the heart of the Cornish

Looe

Polperro

countryside, beside the old Liskeard-Looe Canal.

Two winding ways lead the motorist to Cornwall's most famous well, the longer passing through the hill-high village and church of **St Keyne**. Set below road level where three lanes meet, this beautifully restored well can easily be missed. In the past, newly-married

Fishing boats in the harbour at Polperro

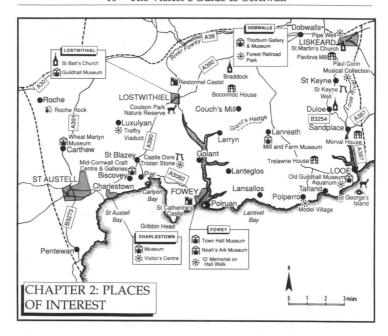

CHAPTER 2: PLACES
OF INTEREST

couples always hurried here after their wedding ceremony, believing that the first to drink the water would rule the household.

The lane dips steeply past the pleasant St Keyne Well Hotel but turn right at Badham's Farm and then take the right fork. There is no signpost here — the map says it leads through Windsor Wood — but visitors who drive along here in spring may be forgiven for thinking that the direction should be 'To Fairyland'. A grass track in the centre of the road tempts cows from their pasture and motorists must wait while they test the quality of the roadway grass, following as the animals make their leisurely way towards the next gate. Ducks, too, use this wooded valley lane and so peaceful is this place that rejoining the B3254 to Duloe seems like finding an unexpected motorway.

In fact, the village of **Duloe** is quiet and attractive, specialising in cottages with country names — fun to list them — but having its own memorable past. The church of St Cuby and St Leonard has a well preserved thirteenth-century tower and interesting associations. Signposted from the main road is a circle of eight stones, 38ft in diameter, restored in the nineteenth century.

The B3254 joins the A387 at **Sandplace** and it is worth turning east there for about a mile. Morval House, once owned by the Glynns, is a fine building, photogenic but not open to the public. The church of St Wenna, behind a rhododendron screen, is noteworthy for the fine slate memorial to Walter Coode, his wife and their twelve children. The children are represented allegorically as fruits growing out of vines trailing behind their kneeling parents. Also, the walls appear to lean outwards and a tower pinnacle seems to bend out of true. Was the church built like this or was it the scene of devil-worship as portrayed in *Bewnans Meriasek*, one of the Cornish miracle plays? Translated, the lines run:

> 'To my God Jove in his face
> I will happily offer a cat:
> There can be no better mouser.
> I bought it from Morval.
> The place where the devil was anointed.'

A meal at Polrean Country House Hotel would doubtless dispel all witchcraft as would a walk beside the River Looe. Here are birds to watch and old wooden hulks to pass by, left on the mud to rot because ill-luck is believed to come to those who break them up.

Looe's golf course is the other side of Morval at Widegates. From there, the B3253 joins the A387 just outside East Looe. The town of **Looe** had a charter as early as 1237 and much of its past is recorded in the Old Guildhall Museum. There is also, most appropriately, an excellent aquarium at the quay, open for long hours during the season.

Shark fishing, good sailing and swimming can be enjoyed from the little beach by the banjo pier (so-called because of its shape). That is seen at its best from the cliffs of West Looe. The original bridge was built in 1411, magnificent with thirteen arches and a hermitage chapel, but the present one has only seven arches and was widened in 1960.

Turn left over the bridge, pass the fourteenth-century St Nicholas church and go up the steep road which leads to Looe Bay. Beyond the rocks lies St George's Island. Once a Celtic monastery, it is now a privately owned bird sanctuary, an ideal place for a day trip. It is possible to walk along the coastal path into Polperro from here, but

Lostwithiel Bridge over the River Fowey

motorists must return to the church and turn left past the 500-year-old inn, The Jolly Sailor.

This narrow, exciting lane to **Talland Bay**, past the Measured Nautical Mile, cannot be hurried. St Tallan church stands proudly at the top of a precipitous hill leading to the beach with its strange pink-grey rocks and grey stony sand. Climb again to Sclerder Abbey, a gracious, peaceful Carmelite monastery near the A387, built by the Trelawny family.

Close by, is Trelawne, an ancient house dating back to before the Conquest and once the home of the famous Royalist Bishop Trelawny who inspired the Reverend R.S. Hawker of Morwenstow to compose *With a Good Sword and a Trusty Hand*, now almost Cornwall's national song. Trelawne was also the place where one of the first therapeutic cures was effected in the early eighteenth century by Dr Jonathan Couch, grandfather of the author Sir A. Quiller-Couch. He advised a neurotic young man staying there after a period abroad, to study the habits of the Trelawne rooks daily for a year. The detailed observations he made so absorbed the patient that after 12 months he was completely and permanently cured.

Much of the coast between Talland Bay and Polperro is National Trust property and fine views tend to offset the rough path. Motorists

The main gateway of Restormel Castle, near Lostwithiel

PLACES OF INTEREST IN AND AROUND LISKEARD

Church of St Martin
Liskeard
Second largest in Cornwall dating from mid-thirteenth century.

Pipe Well
Well Lane
Originally late sixteenth century. Restored in early nineteenth.

Merlin Glass
Pavlova Mill
Station Road
Glassmaking demonstrations. Items on sale.

Paul Corin Magnificent Music Machines
St Keyne Station, just off B3254
Amazing collection of mechanical musical instruments.

St Keyne Well
(SX 248602)
About half a mile east of the church is this famous well. Linked with legends of wedded bliss — recorded in 1541.

Morval House
Morval
Near Sandplace
Photogenic building but not open to public.

Old Guildhall Museum
East Looe
Exhibits of Looe's history.

St George's Island
Off Hannafore Point
Private bird sanctuary — visitors allowed.

Trelawne
Near Talland Bay
Ancient house dating back to before the Norman Conquest. Privately owned, but there is a holiday camp in the grounds.

Lanreath Mill and Farm Museum
Churchtown, Lanreath
Exhibits of vintage tractors and implements, granite cider press and old farmhouse kitchen.

Archibald Thorburn Museum and Gallery
Half a mile north of the A38 through Dobwalls
Unique award-winning collection of wildlife paintings.
Also **Forest Railroad Park**
(both under management of John Southern). Based on the American railroad — film shows and models.

can enter **Polperro** by the A387, but the roads were made for horses and it is preferable to park outside the village during the summer — a horsebus ride to the bottom of the hill is a pleasant mode of travel.

Small though the village is, there is a great deal to see — the unspoiled harbour sheltering behind its sturdy wall, the Pilchard Inn where fishermen once had their catch weighed and Couch House

where Jonathan Couch was born. But what was Polperro really like
before visitors came? The answer is in the Model Village, a replica
built by local craftsmen and guaranteed to set the imagination
working.

Narrow lanes lead to **Lansallos** with its fine church high above
Lantivet Bay. Unusual are the thirty-four carved bench ends, most of
them early sixteenth century. Here, too, are some fine slate-carved
memorials; and its greatest treasure, Bishop Trelawny's pastoral
staff.

To the north, the quiet hamlet of **Lanreath** seems steeped in
history — the name recalling a medieval monastery and the handsome Court Barton, once the Tudor manor home of the Grylls family.
Perhaps the famous 400-year-old Punch Bowl Inn holds the village
secrets for it has been, in turn, court house, coaching inn and
smugglers' distribution house. Artist Augustus John stayed there: the
unusual inn-sign outside is a reminder of his visit. It is much sought
after by holidaymakers who follow Egon Ronay and Ashley Courtenay recommendations. An added attraction is the fine collection of
horse brasses, many, doubtless, from places such as the Lanreath
Mill across the road, now operating as a farm museum. The past is
literally brought to life at the museum on Sundays to Fridays each
week (2–4pm) with demonstrations of forgecraft, corn dolly work and
spinning.

On the way back to Liskeard, is the Giant's Hedge, near to where
the Lanreath road joins the B3359. This prehistoric earthwork was
built by the Devil according to legend. After about 2 miles, turn right
for **Herodsfoot** — walk across country if preferred — and find the
delights of Forestry Commission nature trails in Deerpark Wood. In
this other world there are holiday cabins deep in the valley overlooking
ponds once serving an old gunpowder mill. Sailing, riding and fishing
are available for holidaymakers on this self-catering site. To see it at
bluebell time is to understand why it won the Civic Trust Award the
year after it opened.

Two more award-winning places are signposted at **Dobwalls** on
the A38 to Liskeard. A million pound memorial exhibition to Britain's
greatest wildlife artist, Archibald Thorburn and a miniature American
railroad are run by John Southern and his family. Their enthusiasm for
these hobbies has resulted in one of the country's most pleasing

Lerryn

attractions. Lovingly displayed in a friendly atmosphere, there is enough here for a day's delight.

Eleven miles west, along the A390 from Liskeard, is **Lostwithiel**.

PLACES OF INTEREST IN AND AROUND LOSTWITHIEL

Restormel Castle
(English Heritage)
A mile-and-a-half north of Lostwithiel. Impressive remains of twelfth-century castle above River Fowey. Has connections with the Black Prince.

St Bartholomew's Church
Lostwithiel
Dedicated to the patron saint of tanners, probably built in twelfth century.

Guildhall Museum
Fore Street, Lostwithiel
Built 1740, this has linenfold panelling, town insignia and photocopies of the charters.

Coulson Park
A small oasis of quiet beside the Fowey and close to Lostwithiel Station.

Boconnoc
North of Couch's Mill
Eighteenth-century house and beautiful gardens.
Park and gardens only open to public.

Lantic Bay

A quiet, welcoming place, a good touring centre where picturesque ruins and an old church are daily reminders of its importance in history from 1100 when the Normans built Restormel Castle. Today the proud shell is well cared for by English Heritage and visitors may picnic here, high above the Looe valley. The town was granted a charter of rights and port status in 1190, and a timber bridge was built to mark a crossing point which had existed since the Bronze Age. This was replaced in the fifteenth century by one of granite, still in use today. By 1272, the increasing tin trade required an assay point, so Lostwithiel's Duchy Parliament building incorporated the Stannary Court, the Hall of Exchequer and Exchange as well as the prison. The remains are still to be seen — of particular interest is the cobbled way below a fine stone arch on Fore Street, used by pack animals laden with wool or tin from Bodmin en route for the Stannary Court.

In 1337 Edward III proclaimed his seven-year-old son and heir Duke of Cornwall. When he came of age he was a just overlord, much concerned with his domain of Restormel and Lostwithiel, which he administered wisely and well and the town prospered with tin, tanning and wool trading. In 1644 Roundhead forces overcame the loyal inhabitants and desecrated St Bartholomew's church in a manner clearly described by the diarist Symonds:

Lanteglos church

'In contempt of Christianity, Religion and the Church they brought a horse to the font, and there, with their kind of ceremonies, did, as they called it, christen the horse and called him by the name of Charles in contempt of his Sacred Majesty.'

It is said, however, that when Essex's men later surrendered, the people of Lostwithiel took their revenge.

But this parish church, dedicated to the patron saint of tanners more than 300 years earlier, overcame its indignities. It is still there now for visitors to admire its unusual features, especially the spire of Breton design added at the same time as the font in the fourteenth century.

The Guildhall Museum in Fore Street is free, as is the town parking. This gives ample opportunity to explore everything — a pottery, antiques, a good bookshop and restaurants. Here, too, is The Spinners Web where Barbara Willis has brought the past to life,

spinning and weaving for all to see. She also takes orders for handspun wool, cloth and finished garments.

But Lostwithiel is not fossilised in the past; it keeps up to date with galas, fêtes and an annual regatta. If your pleasure is fishing, bird-watching, walking or simply enjoying the peace of the country, it is all here. Booklets are available to tell you where Coulson Park is and the best way to reach the Duchy Nurseries and an interesting woodland nature trail.

About 4 miles eastwards along the A390, at West Taphouse, a right-hand turn to **Braddock** dips and climbs to the church, a delight in spring but solitary beside woods where historians remember the Civil War and the Battle of Braddock Downs (1643) when Cornishmen put the Parliamentarians to rout and took 1,200 prisoners. Today the Cornish branch of the Sealed Knot re-enact this for their own pleasure and that of many onlookers.

Road and woodland paths, rich in wildlife, pass close to eight-eenth-century Boconnoc, a house whose 600 years of history include a brawling duellist, Thomas 'Diamond' Pitt (cousin to Britain's young-est Prime Minister), and a modern event, when camera crews filmed part of Winston Graham's *Poldark* series for television. The house is not open to the public but its park and garden are occasionally. The 'No Thoroughfare' road leads to the church — the key may be borrowed from the nearby estate office. It is small but interesting — more a house chapel, but nevertheless with royal arms, a wall plaque sent to a number of Cornish churches by King Charles II as a token of his thanks for the support of the congregation during the Civil War.

Narrow tree-lined lanes lead to the backwaters of **Couch's Mill** and **Lerryn**, picturesque villages beside the River Lerryn. There are wooded paths on both sides but the one north of Lerryn's sixteenth-century bridge goes to Great Wood and looks seawards along the Fowey. It became the Wild Wood in Kenneth Grahame's *Wind in the Willows*. He discovered it during one of his visits to his friend Sir Arthur Quiller-Couch at Fowey. The path reaches the point jutting into the Fowey and turns upstream to **St Winnow** a lovely, lonely church-town. The church has one of Cornwall's few surviving rood screens, Tudor bench ends and fine windows.

From Lerryn, the road, which is very narrow and between high ledges in places, climbs steeply to **St Veep** church before dipping to **Penpol**. Walkers may follow the river and climb to Haye Farm where

Bodinnick ferry

National Trust land looks across the River Fowey to Golant. Lanteglos Highway was rightly named as it runs on the spine of this largely unspoilt parish. Before taking the steep road to the Bodinnick ferry for Fowey, make a detour to **Lantivet Bay**. Park the car and walk to Pencarrow Head, where there are fine views east to Rame and west to the Lizard.

Polruan is quaint and very old but has had to give way to Fowey which now claims the first place. In 1066 it was probably the main centre of trade and population at the estuary mouth, but Fowey had a powerful feudal patron to grant and procure necessary privileges and this led, over the centuries, to Polruan's decline.

Hall Walk, where the 'Q' memorial (a memorial to author Sir Arthur Quiller-Couch) stands looking downriver, is National Trust property and covers 40 acres of cliff. A path leaves the road above the Bodinnick ferry, between the houses. It winds along the side of the hill with splendid views across to Fowey and Polruan. At the 'Q' memorial it turns east up a small creek which is crossed by a footbridge at Pont. Thereafter, the path climbs the hill before continuing to Polruan where the Polruan ferry (for foot passengers only) brings you back to Fowey. You can park at Bodinnick ferry (Fowey side) or you may prefer the larger Fowey car park which is also much closer when you leave the

Pont, on an inlet of the River Fowey, near the Hall Walk

Polruan ferry. This is a delightful walk which should not be missed. The paths are best early in the year when they are bright with a variety of spring flowers. Today Bodinnick ferry carries vehicles and has been important since the fourteenth century, forming part of the south coast route from Cremyll.

On the Fowey side of the river, coasters can be seen loading their cargoes of china clay — a different scene from the days when the Fowey Gallants sailed away to the seige of Calais in forty-seven men-o'-war.

June is a good time to visit **Fowey**. There is room then to wander at leisure through the narrow streets, which twist and turn till one would think that even a cat might lose its way. Every bend brings the past to life again: the Noah's Ark Museum, in the town's oldest house, is unfortunately no longer open to the public, the Town Hall Museum displays other treasures, the Ship Hotel remembers its days as the Rashleigh's town house (one of the many properties belonging to the family who had been prominent in most Cornish matters for at least 400 years) and even the Fowey Gallants have their name perpetuated by one of the yacht clubs. Fowey seems to offer everything: walks, swimming, sailing, fishing and a wealth of archaeological material close by.

Polruan

PLACES OF INTEREST IN AND AROUND FOWEY

'Q' Memorial on Hall Walk
Granite monolith facing down
River Fowey, beloved by Sir
Arthur Quiller-Couch who lived
there 1892–1944.

Town Hall Museum
Trafalgar Square
Town history exhibits. Possibly
guild chapel, later prison.

Tristan Stone
Beside B3269 outside town
Monolith inscribed '*Drustanus Fili
Cunomorus*' ('Tristan, Son of
Cunomorus')

Castle Dore
2¹/₂ miles north of Fowey
Possibly site of King Mark's castle,
actually a circular earthwork.

St Catherine's Castle
³/₄ mile south-west of Fowey
towards Gribbin
Remains of Henry VIII's harbour
fort.

Menabilly
Behind Polridmouth Cove, Fowey
Former home of the Rashleigh
family, and fictional setting for Du
Maurier novels. Not open to the
public.

The Tristan Stone

The beach at Polkerris

The old harbour at Pentewan

The coastal path from the town leads past St Catherine's Castle — now ruined — but once one of a chain of south coast forts built by Henry VIII. Gribbin Head is memorable with its huge red and white day mark built in 1842, providing an unmistakeable warning for shipping. Menabilly, set in the woods behind Polridmouth Cove, and formerly the home of the Rashleigh family, was used as the fictional setting for three of Daphne du Maurier's novels including *The King's General* and *Rebecca*. It is not open to the public.

Beside the B3269 out of Fowey, is the Longstone or the Tristan Stone. Its sixth-century inscription reads *Drustanus Fili Cunomorus* which is translated as 'Tristan, Son of Conomorus' (the name by which King Mark was known). Historians now think that Castle Dore, the earthwork a short way off was the site of Mark's castle, but facts have not yet verified this and students of Beroul's *Roman de Tristan* continue to puzzle over it.

At Castle Dore, a lane to the right leads to **Golant**, the quiet, sheltered waterside village with more Tristan associations. King Mark and Queen Iseult probably worshipped in the church of St Sampson, as it was near Castle and Lantyan, both connected with them. Today, these names denote farms or similar buildings but the area of **Lantyan Wood** still keeps its secrets of the lovers, silent and watchful beside the River Fowey. If you park by the riverside to explore the village or visit the adjacent pub, remember the river is tidal. The nearby youth hostel at Golant occupies a beautiful old building with associations with Garibaldi who stayed there before leaving England. Tristan's duel with Morholt possibly took place there, watched, we are told, by Cornish and Irish on opposite banks, looking like 'holm-gang' (invading Northmen). Is that perhaps how the Holmbush Inn on the A390 at St Austell came by its name?

English China Clay — the giant producer of Cornwall's kaolin, has its headquarters at **St Austell** in the heart of the 'mountains'. It is a pleasant place with old buildings, quietly enjoying the life of a medieval village in the churchtown away from the new shopping precinct and rumbling white clay lorries. Modern interests thrive at the Arts Centre and Theatre. The B3273 leads to **Pentewan** where stone from Duchy quarries was in great demand for rebuilding churches during the fifteenth century. William Cookworthy's discovery of china clay at Carloggas in the eighteenth century brought new life to this

PLACES OF INTEREST AROUND ST AUSTELL

Polkyth Recreation Centre
2 minutes drive from St Austell
Station
Squash, badminton, tennis, café,
bar, sauna, pool, etc.

Cornish Leisure World
Crinnis Beach, Carlyon Bay
3 miles E of St Austell
1¼ miles of sandy beach, with
restaurants, outdoor attractions,
miniature railway, nightclub.

**Wheal Martyn China Clay
Museum**
Carthew
Unique open-air industrial archaeology museum based on restored
clay works (dating from about
1880), with waterwheels, etc,

demonstrating this important
Cornish industry.

Treffry Viaduct
Luxulyan Valley (SX 056572)
Built for mineral railway and
aqueduct (1839), spanning valley
100ft high.

Roche Rock
Rocky outcrop south-east of
village of Roche with ruins of St
Michael's chapel, licensed 1409.

**Mid-Cornwall Craft Centre
and Galleries**
Biscovey A390
Fine collection of craft and painting in skilfully converted school.

little port. A harbour was built and waggons took their new loads down to waiting ships until tin-streaming soil and china-clay slurry caused the silting which killed it as a port. Today caravans rest on dunes beside the once prosperous harbour. The latter still contains water despite having no access to the sea these days and is well worth going to see.

A footpath goes part of the way to Black Head but joins the road where the cliff becomes too sheer for walkers. Views across St Austell Bay to Gribbin Head have a touch of mystery about them for the water shimmers with the constant presence of china clay slurry and the effects are strange and ethereal. Little wonder that Cornwall's famous historian, Dr A.L. Rowse, chose to live at Trenarren on Gerrans Point.

Charles Rashleigh began to develop the port of **Charlestown** for tin in 1791 and it continued to prosper with the growth of the china clay industry. Then J.T. Treffry of Fowey constructed the port of Par which rivalled both Pentewan and Charlestown, and it is still the main china clay port for smaller vessels although Charlestown remains active,

The old and the new at Charlestown — loading china clay on one side of

the harbour, with a sailing boat on the other

The gleaming white 'mountains' north of St Austell — waste heaps from the china clay industry

but more increasingly as a holiday place. The little beach is a pleasant place for fishing, bathing and sailing. Only half a mile along the cliff path is **Carlyon Bay** offering added attractions — the Cornish Leisure World and Polkyth Recreation Centre providing everything from table tennis to opera.

Beside the A3082, a Continental-style covered weekend market offers interest. Ralph Allen was born in a cottage only a few yards along the road towards St Blazey and a small plaque on the wall marks the place. Not many visitors to Cornwall realise that well over a hundred years before Rowland Hill invented the Penny Post, Allen had devised the first real postal system in the country. There is little of architectural interest in this area, but up the hill past Allen's birthplace is the Mid-Cornwall Craft Centre and Galleries at **Biscovey**. First class goods for sale are well displayed and it is also possible to take part in art and craft courses. It is well worth a visit.

At the top of the hill notice the Four Lords Inn — probably a unique name. The sign is attractive, depicting Elizabethan nobles in fine costume. The building marks the common meeting point of estates belonging to Edgcumbe, Rashleigh, Carlyon and Treffry — all local landowners and hence the name. Continue down the next hill to **St**

Blazey. The church dedicated to St Blaize stands slightly above the Cornish Arms at the bottom of that same hill. St Blaize is not a Cornish saint's name, but in medieval times wool was as important as tin in this area and he is the patron saint of woolcombers in the town that was once a port. Beside the Pack Horse Inn, a short distance away, a solid building standing four square to the road was the wool market. Now neither tin nor wool finds its way here, and by the traffic lights only the Shell House remains as an interesting reminder of St Blazey's great days as a port.

Par is its replacement perhaps, the port reclaimed from the sea by Joseph Austen who became Joseph Treffry. His finest achievement was the massive viaduct across the Luxulyan Valley, unbelievably beautiful in bluebell time. A left-hand turn before the St Blazey level crossing, then first right, leads to one of Cornwall's loveliest places, with walks through the woods in plenty. Even the viaduct does not detract from Luxulyan's beauty and standing proud still, though unused, this rail, road and water bridge seems almost part of the woodland scene.

The narrow lane winds to **Luxulyan** village, up and up between stone-littered fields: undoubted ploughing hazards but no disturbance to Channel Island cattle happy with the grass rich in minerals from the granite below. Overlooking Tregarden quarry, source of its building stone, Luxulyan's church centres the handsome cottages, all built to endure.

Everywhere beyond are white 'mountains' and at **Roche** (pronounced like 'poach') the scene is unparalleled. In this village the Rock (a rocky outcrop with a ruined chapel) rises like a mute guardian.

Nearby is **St Dennis**, its church set within an Iron Age encampment. The A391, off the B3374 at Stenalees, leads to **Carthew**. Here is Wheal Martyn China Clay Museum, a unique open-air museum based on a restored clay pit. Displays, artifacts, books, pottery and slide programme add to the interest. A short walk guides you past old slurry pits, waterwheels and much else, describing how the clay was obtained for this Cornish industry, which is still important today.

Restored waterwheel at the Wheal Martyn China Clay Museum

3 TRURO, FALMOUTH AND THE ROSELAND PENINSULA

The exact meaning of the name **Truro** is uncertain, though of the suggested 'settlement near water', 'three roads' and 'three rivers', possibly the last is the most feasible. The 'three rivers' were the Allen, Kenwyn and a third, long lost under Tregolls Road where the A39 enters the city from the east.

About 2,500 years ago, the first inhabitants settled here on the ridge above the water. Celts then established themselves, but not till 1140 was there any building of importance. This was a Norman castle, but only the name remains, as Castle Hill, the site of the new Crown Court.

The tin trade brought wealth to Truro and it was one of the earliest stannary towns to hold a charter, which was granted by Edward I in 1307. King John built a Coinage Hall in 1200 but this was demolished in the early nineteenth century. The Black Death (1348) halved the population, causing such poverty that the government remitted all taxes. During the Civil War, Prince Charles and Royalist troops were quartered here, and for a while Truro was also the temporary home of the Royal Mint.

In the eighteenth century, the town was as fashionable as Bath, and among the cultural activities were a Philharmonic Society, Library and Book Society. The first of these is still in existence and generally gives about thirty concerts a year.

Many gracious buildings were erected. The Assembly Rooms by the cathedral have a fine façade worthy of attention, as is Ralph Allen Daniell's Mansion House in Prince's Street. He was nephew to Ralph Allen of St Blazey (see Chapter 2), and wealthy enough to use Bath stone and have the oak specially carved by craftsmen from the local French prisoner of war camp. The date 1792 is engraved on the roof. Merchants like William Lemon built elegant houses on both sides of Lemon Street, named after him, and looking down on them is a

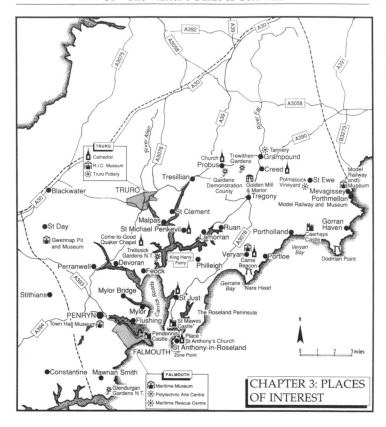

TRURO
- Cathedral
- R.I.C. Museum
- Truro Pottery

FALMOUTH
- Maritime Museum
- Polytechnic Arts Centre
- Maritime Rescue Centre

CHAPTER 3: PLACES OF INTEREST

monument to Richard Lander. He discovered the source of the River Niger and, in 1830, was the first holder of the Royal Geographical Society's Gold Medal.

The ordinary houses, too, are worth more than a passing glance. Look for strangely shaped roofs, old porticos, decorated façades, narrow, pointed windows and emotive names like Tanyard Court, Tippett's Backlet, Pydar Street and Coombes Lane — recalling the great days of Truro's wool trade. St Nicholas Street may not seem unusual, but here the merchants' houses and warehouses were cheek by jowl with the Guildhall of St Nicholas, probably extending across Boscawen Street down to Lemon Quay itself. The present car

PLACES OF INTEREST IN TRURO

Truro Cathedral
First to be built after St Paul's. Designed in Gothic style by J.L. Pearson, constructed 1880–1910, cleverly incorporating part of the former parish church. Its Willis organ is famous, and monuments include those to 'Q' and missionary Henry Martyn — also a stained glass window of John Wesley at Gwennap. The Bath stone reredos represents Christ's Sacrifice. The first bishop, Edward White Benson was translated to Canterbury after 7 years. He originated the service of Nine Lessons and Carols here in 1880.

West porch niches facing High Cross have figures of kings and bishops. Look out for the beautifully carved memorial to one of the Robartes family of Lanhydrock who died in the Great War. It is near the south-west corner.

Royal Institution of Cornwall Museum and Art Gallery
River Street
Founded 1818, this museum exhibits Cornish history, has a library of Cornish books for members and an interesting art gallery. Seasonal displays of special interest.

park is where ships anchored while waiting for their cargoes. Today at the Quay, across the A39, pleasure boats berth in the summer and run weekday boat trips down the Fal.

Most Cornish towns have narrow passages between houses. These are 'opes' — pronounced 'ops'. Truro is no exception and Squeezeguts Alley is perhaps the smallest and most awkward; Cathedral Lane is another 'ope'.

The Prince of Wales laid the foundation stone of the cathedral on 20 May 1880. It was the first to be built in Britain since St Paul's. Truro, however, had become a city in 1877 when Bishop Benson was enthroned in St Mary's parish church. This was later demolished, except for the south aisle, which was incorporated into the new building. The three-spired towers are interesting in their dedications. The central one (Victoria) was given in 1901 as a memorial to the Queen's life, and 9 years later, another local benefactor gave the two western towers — Edward and Alexandra. Altogether an unusual building, its Gothic style gives the city a continental look. Look out also for the window showing John Wesley preaching at Gwennap Pit, to the left of the Robartes memorial; the painting *Cornubia* by John Miller and St Mary's Aisle which is part of the old medieval parish church.

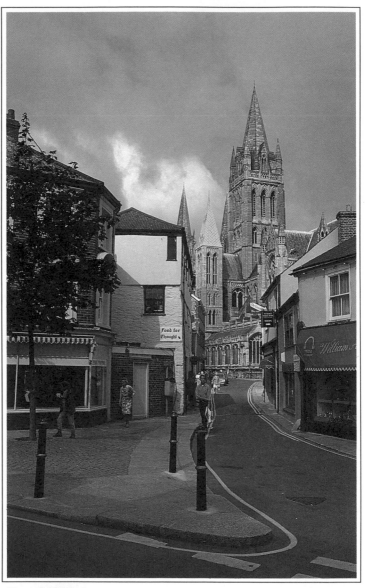

Truro Cathedral

The carved front of Truro Cathedral

There is also a cathedral bookshop for books and souvenirs and the Chapter House where you can get coffee or tea most days in the summer.

Truro is small compared with other cities, but it takes time to explore it fully. The Pannier Market is an exciting place — the cheese stall is exceptionally good and adjoining shops have their own specialities. Truro's restaurants are numerous, varied and of a high standard with the Wig and Pen, at the bottom of Castle Street, a reminder of the city's nineteenth-century cultural gatherings.

There is much to see in the Royal Institution of Cornwall which is both an art gallery and a museum. On display is a variety of material connected with life in the region since earliest times; the mining section is unusually fine. During the summer season there is generally an exhibition of special interest. A restaurant is open daily.

From the Trafalgar roundabout, a road running past Radio Cornwall, the BBC's first purpose-built local radio station, skirts a roadside bird sanctuary and follows the river to **Malpas** (Mopus).

At the end of the road there is a footpath to **St Clement**. Photographers love the old church and thatched cottages — the slate-hung upper room over the lych-gate provides added interest. From here one of the Duchy's loveliest creekside paths leads to Pencalenick, where the A39 is rejoined for **Tresillian**. At the far end of this long village is the uniquely thatched Wheel Inn. The rolled wheel is something probably not seen on any other roof. Here history was made when the Civil War ended and the Royalist Lord Hopton capitulated to Fairfax after surrendering at the bridge. Fairfax Road beside the water commemorates the occasion.

You will need more than a day to explore the **Veryan area** and to visit some of the interesting places on the way, such as the Wheel Inn. Follow the road, the A390, out of Tresillian to **Probus**, which is now a quiet village but was once an educational centre. Now only its collegiate church and a road name, College Close, are left as reminders. The fine church tower is Cornwall's highest, at $123^1/_2$ ft, lovely with its finely carved granite. Recently restored and replaced outside the church is an attractive lamp standard erected to celebrate Queen Victoria's Diamond Jubilee. Just past the village is Cornwall's Demonstration Garden and Arboretum. Keen gardeners can learn much there but it also has interesting displays and layouts in beautiful surroundings to delight the amateur. It is open throughout the year.

Just over 3 miles beyond lies **Grampound**, quietly at peace beside the rushing traffic, deceptively different from the bustling port of Norman times when the sea brought ships there. When silting began, a bridge over the Fal was built at that point and the town was given the name Grand-pont — known in 1299 as the Borough of Ponsmur, its Celtic name. Eventually maritime trading ended and the town declined slowly into the present peaceful village. Halfway up the hill almost opposite its handsome clock tower are two thatched houses, the Manor and Cornwall's only bark tannery. Visitors are welcomed at the tannery but only by appointment — this is the place which provided skin for the hull and sails of Tim Severin's curragh *St Brendan*, which weathered a force eight gale and crossed the Atlantic safely in 1976, proving the theory of the author-historian captain who believed that St Brendan made the same crossing a good thousand years before Columbus — in an identical craft.

The second turning on the right, up the hill out of Grampound, winds narrowly to **St Ewe**, beautiful and almost unspoilt. The church, enclosed by trees, has old stocks inside — both merit a close look. Follow the hill down to **Polmassick**, cross the bridge and a few yards past the chapel is another of Cornwall's unexpected delights — a vineyard where wines are available. There are walks round the vineyard and the nearby farm. Have some refreshments here and perhaps also buy a vine.

After Kestle is **Mevagissey**, one of the Duchy's oldest fishing ports. Its narrow streets and quaint shops, up the hills or by the quays, make it a captivating place. Watch the gulls and the fishing boats or go fishing. If it rains, there is always the Model Railway and Museum to enjoy. Park on the harbour quays and move for a while into a miniature world which has been featured on television. There is enjoyment here for the whole family.

The road south to **Porthmellon** hugs the cliff before dipping down to the cove famous for Percy Mitchell — the self-taught boat designer. He started his shipyard in 1924 and constructed everything from a 7ft dinghy to vessels of over 30 tons. An artist in wood, he built the *Windstar* for Sir Philip Hunloke, Sailing Master to the Queen's father as well as various boats for the Admiralty. Drive out with care along the narrow winding road — summer traffic can be dangerous here.

The coastal path to **Gorran Haven** passes Chapel Point — another place associated with Tristan. He was imprisoned in the chapel but leapt from a window to the safety of a rocky ledge — so the story goes. Views here are reward enough for walkers, even the inland lanes do not compare. Gorran Haven itself is unexpectedly small but opens out into a wide bay. Above, at **Gorran Churchtown**, Anne Treneer was born. Her book, *Schoolhouse in the Wind*, is an excellent autobiography which breathes the delights of Cornwall in the early 1920s when for her, Falmouth was a distant romantic seaport. She writes of the enchanting bareness of Cornwall and tells how she would walk to Dodman Point and 'look into the sparkling intoxicating space'.

Dodman Point, this 'noblest of Cornish headlands' is National Trust property now and there is a circular walk starting and ending at the Penare car park. At the extreme point is a huge granite cross, erected in 1896 as a mark for seamen by the Vicar of Caerhays. After dedicating the cross he kept a night's vigil beneath it, praying for the souls of shipwrecked mariners. This same promontory fascinated Sir Arthur Quiller-Couch and he used it in his first book *Dead Man's Rock*.

Hemmick Beach has no car park, only a narrow lane beside the water. It is quiet here and there is more than one stretch of sand.

Mevagissey harbour

Perilous lanes lead to it, so first gear is essential to get to **Porthluney Cove**. There is a large car park here and looking down over the beach, is John Nash's Gothic building — Caerhays Castle. A fairytale place, it is scorned by some but loved by all when the rhododendrons are in bloom. When Mr J.C. Williams owned it he cultivated fine rhododendrons, camellias and magnolias. Many species of camellia still bear his name.

The Grampound road, after climbing past Caerhays church and Tubb's Mill, turns right along more narrow winding lanes to **Creed**. William Gregor was born not far from here in 1761. During his incumbency of the parish, he discovered titanium in black sand sent to him from Manaccan. It has been called manaccanite and gregorite but is now universally accepted as titanium. In the secluded church there is a photograph of a titanium bowl and also a portrait of William Gregor.

From the Tregony road out of Creed the right-hand turn goes over the Fal to Golden Mill and Manor. This is a privately owned farm but it is possible to drive as far as the main building without trespassing. The great barn on the left still has the fine windows and sturdy walls of a medieval hall. In 1577, Francis Tregian and his family lived here and offered shelter to Cuthbert Mayne (canonised in 1974). As they were known recusants their property was searched, Mayne was

Caerhays Castle

discovered and executed, while Francis Tregian was condemned to a long period of imprisonment. Somehow he survived it all, went abroad and died there in 1608. There are elegant memorials in Probus church to the Tregians and the Wolvedons (Golden is the Cornish mutation of this name).

A different kind of country house is at **Trewithen**, nearby on the A390. It was the seventeenth-century home of the Hawkins familyand 20 acres of its grounds are now internationally famous as Trewithen Gardens, which are open to the public on summer afternoons. Shrubs are always on sale here.

The **Roseland Peninsula** includes the west side of Veryan Bay and Gerrans Bay, involving a long but very lovely drive. Take the A3078 where it turns off the A39 between Tresillian and Probus. It crosses the **Tregony** bridge where the left turn leads up to the now quiet village with its wide central street. This was once a bustling port and had a castle, a medieval market and a thriving wool factory. Even when the river silted up and trade declined, it was still a society meeting place. In the late nineteenth century, the learned Powder Book Club held meetings there for the improvement of local ladies, but

no such excitements now remain. Little is left of former glories except the fourteenth-century church of St Cuby with its slate tower and the handsome seventeenth-century clock tower which was rebuilt in 1895. Tregony is now a place of the past, recalling when ships unloaded ceramics, glass and wine then sailed away with leather, wool and tin.

From Tregony, high-banked, narrow lanes lead to **Portholland**, a

harbour of two coves, east and west. There is a fine cliff path to **Portloe** but motorists lose the view temporarily as the road takes the inland route to this tiny port more used to horse and pony transport than motorised traffic. Parking halfway down the steep hill to the beach avoids unpleasant turns, but visitors to the comfortable seventeenth-century Lugger Inn, will find a park beside it. This village loses the sun very quickly, lying in the shadow of Jacka and Manare Points, but it is a pleasant place in the sunshine. Some land here is owned by the National Trust as well as a considerable area along the cliff to Nare Head, where there is a viewing platform with a ramp for wheelchairs. One of the Trust walks is round the point from Caragloose to Camels Cove. At Kiberick Cove there is a small car park and a footpath to the

PLACES OF INTEREST IN THE VERYAN AREA

County Demonstration Garden and Arboretum
Probus
Sectional gardens are here to inspect and there is an adviser on duty each Thursday afternoon.

Grampound Tannery
Cornwall's only bark tannery. Visitors should telephone first (St Austell 882413).

Polmassick Vineyard
St Ewe
A thriving vineyard, planted on the slopes of the Luney Valley. Wines by the glass available.

Model Railway and Museum
Mevagissey
An unusual attraction offering a miniature world of nearly fifty trains. Collection of model locomotives and rolling stock.

Dodman Point
Given to National Trust in 1919; a well preserved Iron Age fort with baulk, ditch and rampart, crosses the neck of the headland. Granite cross erected as mark for seamen.

Caerhays Castle
A picturesque mansion built by John Nash for J.B. Trevanion (1808). Early spring displays of shrubs are fine. Gardens open twice in the year.

Creed Church
1 mile from Grampound
Rebuilt in 1734 and retaining some of its wagon roof. Portrait of William Gregor and photograph of a titanium bowl near organ.

Golden Mill and Manor
(SW 920469)
On private farm land is one of Cornwall's finest medieval barns. Can be seen without trespassing.

Trewithen Gardens
Grampound Road, near Truro
Privately owned, 20 acres, internationally famous for rare shrubs such as camellias and rhododendrons of special species. Plants for sale on summer afternoons.

Carne Barrow
(SW 913386)
Cornwall's largest tumulus, thought to be the burial mound of King Geraint.

secluded beach. Another walk from the same parking place is down the valley to Paradoe Cove beyond the Nare, returning via that fine headland — one of the least frequented in Cornwall.

Veryan is well known but still relatively unspoilt. The reasons for its fame are the unique roundhouses at each end of the village. Some say that a local vicar built them to keep the devil out and away from his daughters. Whatever the reason, the white, thatched cottages

One of the two Veryan roundhouses

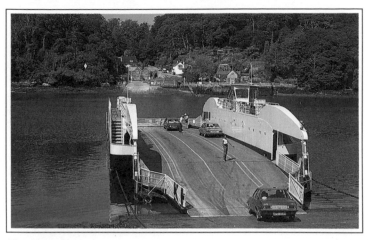

King Harry Ferry

have a charm all their own. An interesting art gallery at the north end is worth visiting. Inside the church, with its unusual dedication to St Symphorian, lies Admiral Kempe, notable for sailing round the world with Cook and scaling Quebec Heights with General Wolfe. After passing Crugillick Manor on the way to the A3078, there is a walk down the lovely wooded valley to **Pendower Beach**, another National Trust property. A disused lime-kiln is an interesting feature of this pleasant place. The great tumulus (Cornwall's largest) at nearby Carne Beacon is said to be the burial mound of King Geraint who built Dingerin Castle where the Gerrans road leaves the A3078. It is believed that his tribesmen rowed his body, in a golden boat with silver oars, across the bay to be burned and buried at Carne.

The church and art gallery at **Gerrans** village offer different, but equally good, attractions for visitors. From here is a walk of about 4 miles along the coastpath to St Anthony Head, the eastern arm of Falmouth harbour. This superb route offers unsurpassed panoramic views on every side until reaching Zone Point and the lighthouse which is open to visitors. The headland has been fortified since Napoleonic days, was under military occupation during World War II and then bought by the National Trust in 1959. There is wheelchair access to the viewpoint.

There is a splendid and easy coastal walk round the point to **Place**. Behind the privately owned manor is the church of St Anthony, wrapped in legend. Tradition says that this was once a Celtic monastery whose history is written between the two rows of dog teeth on the south door. A rough translation of it is that Christ visited this peninsula when his uncle, Joseph of Arimathea, came to trade for tin. When they were off St Anthony Head, a storm blew up and they sheltered in the little bay below Place Manor. While making the ship seaworthy again, they camped here, leaving a shrine behind them. Some years afterwards a church was built on that site. Apart from any legend, here is quiet beauty and a good place to picnic looking over to St Mawes.

A delightful walk from Bohortha Farm to picturesque **Froe** overlooks the River Percuil and, at the head of Froe inlet, the water almost makes this headland an island. The journey back to Truro along the A3078 and A39 is about 20 miles, but there are views of the Carrick Roads for most of the way which make the mileage worthwhile.

The last exploration of the Roseland Peninsula is shorter and could last either an afternoon or a day. In early July, a signpost at Tresillian Bridge invites fruit lovers to pick strawberries at Fentongollan Farm. This is a pleasant task in good weather as the farm is set high over woodlands and rolling fields. Follow the road to **St Michael Penkevil** — a handful of cottages round the church with the great gates of Tregothnan proclaiming it as private property. On certain days in early summer, Lord and Lady Falmouth open their gardens for charity. Visitors enjoy the magnificent shrubs and see some of the mansion's 365 windows.

In 1319, the church was an important archpresbytery (a college with four chaplains). An interesting feature is the second altar on the upper floor of the tower, an old tradition in churches dedicated to St Michael. Leaving the churchtown, take the first lane on the right through beautiful **Lamorran Woods** which lead to **Ruan Lanihorne**. This is a haven for birdwatchers and there is also a 4-mile walk beside the river, where ships once sailed to Tregony.

There are walks to **Philleigh** where the old Rectory, a fine early Georgian house with an attrctive slate-hung façade is worthy of more than a passing glance. Set nearby in Cornish elms is the church with its unusual dedication to St Filius.

PLACES OF INTEREST ON AND AROUND THE ROSELAND PENINSULA

St Anthony Church
Place
St Anthony-in-Roseland
Behind the Manor lies one of the first churches in Britain to be dedicated. It was then the priory and convent of St Mary-de-Valle, built on the site of an early Celtic monastery.

St Anthony Lighthouse
Built 1835 — open to visitors. Headland has been fortified since Napoleonic times.

St Michael Penkevil Church
Restored 1863–5, a handsome building. Interesting feature is the altar inside the tower's upper floor.

St Mawes Castle
Described as Henry VIII's most decorative fort. Colourful gardens and lawns to the sea. Unusual clover-leaf plan produced by a central tower with three semi-circular bastions.

Tregothnan
St Michael Penkevil
Private home of Lord and Lady Falmouth. Garden only, open on certain days in summer in aid of charity.

Trelissick
(National Trust)
Gardens only but they have fine shrubs and nature trails. Shop and barn restaurant.

Resist the temptation to drive straight to King Harry Ferry — leave that until later — but watch the last times of sailing! Go on to **St Just-in-Roseland** where the church, in its creekside setting of tropical trees, is possibly unrivalled for beauty of position. At the water's edge of St Just Pool is a workshop where ships' figureheads or specialised work for the QEII have been produced.

The A3078 eventually reaches St Mawes Castle and drops down into the village to follow the harbour round for the return journey. **St Mawes** is a sheltered place and a yachting paradise, particularly for the wealthy. St Mawes Castle, cared for by English Heritage, is a round tower, built by Henry VIII and probably enlarged by his son Edward in 1550. Its name is believed to have come from the hermit, St Mawes, St Mauditus or St Mause who effected cures with the water from a holy well. It is small but interesting with ample parking. The grounds are pleasant — an ideal place to picnic and watch the various activities on the Carrick Roads.

On the way back to King Harry Ferry, make a detour to **Turnaware**

Tolverne

Point. Here, in late summer, Cornwall's best blackberries grow abundantly. It also has historical interest as it was one of the places in Cornwall from which American troops sailed for Normandy in 1944.

Nearby, at the water's edge, **Tolverne's** thatched smuggler's cottage is interesting. Contraband was delivered here in the past, and at the end of the nineteenth century there was still a ferry to Tregothnan Deer Park. It was also another point of departure for World War II troop carriers. Ruined Tolverne chapel was built by Henry VI, who also established the crossing nearby to Trelissick, known as the King Harry Ferry.

Tales of Henry VIII riding with Ann Boleyn across this reach on their honeymoon, may be romantic but they are not true.

The latest ferry, launched in 1974, glides smoothly across the Fal to **Trelissick**, another delightful National Trust property. It is lovely in all seasons with rare shrubs and plants, extensive parklands, woods and farmland. The superb views include vistas of the Fal Estuary and Falmouth harbour. The Trust has made a 4-mile nature trail round the grounds. The gardens are open to the public from March to October, but the house is not open.

The thatched Punch Bowl and Ladle Inn at **Penelewey** dates from the eleventh century and is probably the only one with such a name.

Trelissick Gardens

Cowlands Creek and Coombe are worth a detour to enjoy the birds, the creekside walks and the famous Kea plums.

 The lane joins the A39 Falmouth to Truro road at **Calenick**, once the site of Cornwall's chief smelting house. All that remains of it is the handsome clock tower on the slate-hung Bridge House.

The great men of Truro made fortunes in tin during the eighteenth and nineteenth centuries, but it had been 'streamed' in the surrounding districts long before Truro became an important trading centre, so it is interesting to look at those old mining areas. The Truro to Falmouth A39 road down Arch Hill, goes under the track of a railway before climbing the hill to Playing Place — once the site of a theatre-in-the-round. **Carnon Downs** looks like a bungalow suburb, but hides much mining history. By the village shop a road turns left for **Come-to-Good**, a misleading name which has quite a different meaning. The thatched Quaker Meeting House of 1710 is called after its location *Cwm-ty-quite* — Cornish for 'the House of the Coombe in the Woods,' appropriate for this attractive building still in use.

Feock church has an interesting lych-gate with a slate-hung upper storey and expensive properties beyond the village straggle down to Restronguet Point beside the Carrick Roads. Before Tudor times a passenger ferry, which functioned at the turn of this century, took travellers from Truro through Mylor to Penryn and Falmouth. Across the narrow water is the thatched Pandora Inn. Originally called The Ship, it was renamed when its captain returned from sailing with Bligh of the *Bounty* to capture the mutineers. On the return voyage, the vessel — the *Pandora* — foundered and though its captain brought home some prisoners he was dismissed from the service. He then bought this inn and named it after his lost ship.

 At **Point**, Restronguet Creek is joined by the Carnon River, a bird sanctuary and a place of beauty. Once it was a prosperous mining port with a smuggling reputation as well. Tin has been streamed in the Carnon River since the days of pre-history, and in the Middle Ages, ore for export from the inland mines was brought here on mules and horses. In 1826 the Redruth and Chacewater Railway opened, the stretch from Devoran to Point still retaining horse-drawn wagons: part of this track can still be seen. Great schooners from Scandinavia anchored there, unloading timber which was taken on barges to Perran Wharf. The Norway Inn is a reminder of those days. There are

PLACES OF INTEREST IN THE MINING AREA AROUND TRURO

Quaker Chapel
Come-to-Good
Friends' Meeting House, attractively thatched, still in use.

Gwennap Pit and Methodist Museum
Carharrack, Busveal, Redruth
Each Whit Monday, Methodists gather here for a celebratory service. (Information obtainable from Mr Tom Shaw ☎ Redruth 212104)

Killiow Golf Park
Just 3 miles from Truro off A39
18-hole parkland course.
Floodlit golfdriving range.
☎ 0872 70246

Killifreth Engine House
Beside the B3298 St Day-Scorrier road
Impressive industrial building.

Two, Three and Four Burrows
Beside the narrow road S of B3277; beside A30 at junction of A30 and A390; beside A30 about 2 miles E of above, respectively Important prehistoric tumuli.

still bollards and wooden wharves at **Devoran** and the old weighbridge gate remains at the junction where the Bissoe road leaves the A39.

Beyond the Norway Inn, a road winds away to Perranwell and opposite are the buildings of Perran Foundry (1799) recalling the days when the Fox family established an industrial site there. The machinery was of high quality and European nations bought it: they supplied the world's largest steam engine to the Netherlands for draining the Haarlem Meer.

Turn right over the railway bridge at **Perranwell** and drive along Grenna Lane. There you will overlook the Carnon Valley and perhaps imagine what it was like when mining was at its peak. Then beyond Perranwell and Frogpool, **Gwennap** village lies in peaceful beech woods, deceptively quiet now, yet once the heart of a region which yielded more copper and tin than any other place in the old world. Gwennap Pit is not in the village, but is near **Busveal**, reached by turning off the A393 Falmouth to Redruth road at the Fox and Hounds, one of the many inns where a service is held and produce auctioned for charity at harvest time.

The road twists and climbs above the derelict expanse of the now silent mines: Crofthandy, Goon Gumpus, Creegbrawse, Tolgullow

Gwennap Pit

The annual Whit Monday
Methodist service at
Gwennap Pit

and others with Celtic names. The men who worked there often died
young and left widows with families. Others fell ill and were unable to
work. Wesley's message from the Pit and elsewhere brought hope to
these people because, as he wrote, 'The more I conversed with the
believers in Cornwall, the more I am convinced that they have
sustained great loss for want of hearing the doctrine of Christian
Perfection clearly and strongly enforced.' Gwennap Pit was probably
formed by the collapse of underground mining excavations. In 1806,
circular terraces were cut for seating and since 1807, an annual
service has been held there on Whit Mondays. Wesley writes of
preaching in a hollow capable of containing many thousands of
people. Gwennap Pit is certainly large and was central and ideal for

Mylor church

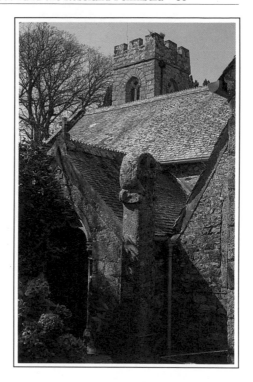

his purpose whether it held hundreds or thousands. A museum of
Cornish Methodism was opened near here in 1982.

Carharrack is a village of mining memories but **St Day** has a
different story to tell. Prosperous mine owners and captains lived
there but perhaps its real place in Cornwall's history is its role as one
of the resting places for pilgrims en route to St Michael's Mount.
Today, living precariously over a honeycomb of mines, it welcomes
modern pilgrims to the St Day Walsingham Festival in September.

Killifreth engine house, beside the B3298 St Day-Scorrier road, is
undoubtedly one of the most impressive industrial buildings remaining. It is near **Scorrier** where John Williams, the mining entrepreneur,
built his fine mansion. At nearby **Chacewater**, formerly Chasewater,
there are memories of Cornwall's first true railway. Not quite 2 miles
north-east along the A30 is **Blackwater**, the birthplace of John

Passmore Edwards who built reading rooms and institutes for all workers, especially miners. His Reading Room there stands beside the main road; and almost every town in Cornwall owes its library to him. Altogether he was responsible for fifty-three benefactions from Newlyn to Dundee.

This section of the A30 has three important tumuli beside it, Two Burrows, Three Burrows and Four Burrows and one of the Midsummer Eve Bonfire ceremonies by members of the Old Cornwall Society usually takes place at the last of these. From the A390 at Chacewater, minor roads lead to Baldhu (Black Mine) and Wheal Jane Mine, reopened in 1970 as a modern mining complex. The surrounding area is one where mineral enthusiasts can explore ochre pits, arsenic works and similar remains. From here to Truro by way of the winding lanes of Penweathers there are walks and picnic places, but few people.

Before going to Penryn and Falmouth, turn left from the A39 immediately after the Norway Inn. This leads to **Mylor,** a village much sought after by yachtsmen. The steep lane which winds away from the traffic is known locally as 'Craft and Danger', an interesting corruption of *croft an D'Angers* (D'Angers' fields). This must have described it in 1154 when that uncultivated hillside belonged to the Norman from Angers who owned the barton of Crueglew (the enclosed land by the prehistoric barrow). The wealthy mining engineer, William Lemon of Breage, bought the estate in 1749 (then called Carclew) and the house became one of the cultural centres of Cornwall. The Lemons were great benefactors to the people of Mylor: Sir Charles bought the workhouse, converted it into a school and maintained it for years. Fire unfortunately destroyed the manor house but Carclew Gardens are occasionally open to the public. The Lemon name died out and became Tremayne, but is perpetuated in the village in the Lemon Arms and Lemon Hill.

Mylor Bridge is at the head of the creek though the original settlement was the churchtown at its mouth a mile away. In the mid-nineteenth century the buildings by the pier were known as *HMS Ganges*, at that time the Royal Navy's only shore-based training centre and hospital. The ship, however, was anchored at St Just Pool across the Carrick Roads. Today it is a yachting centre but the restaurant there still bears the old name.

Almost hidden in trees, beside the water, stands St Mylor church. It is a picturesque building with a separate bell tower and Cornwall's tallest cross embedded in the ground at the south door. One of the churchyard epitaphs is unusual and visitors are always told to read about Joseph Crapp, a shipwright who died 'ye 26th of November 1770, aged 43 years.' His death is graphically described:

> Alas friend Joseph
> His end was almost sudden
> As though a mandate came
> Express from heaven
> His foot, it slip and he did fall
> Help, help he cries, and that was all.

Another gravestone is 'To the Memory of the Warriors, Women and Children, who on their return to England from the coast of Spain; unhappily perished in the Wreck of the *Queen Transport*, on Trefusis Point, Jany 14, 1814', just one of the many ships wrecked off the Cornish coast. Inside, the carved wood of the pulpit is believed to have come from Armada wrecks but the choir screen recalls more recent events. It was given in memory of those drowned in 1966 when an overloaded local pleasure boat capsized.

The writer Howard Spring found this creek so enchanting that he moved here in 1939 and used it as the background for his bestselling novel *All the Day Long*. The walk round Trefusis Point has views of Falmouth Bay which some say is the finest natural harbour in the world.

The walk ends at **Flushing**, meeting the road from Mylor. Its Celtic name was Nankersey, but when Dutch engineers arrived to build Falmouth's quays, they settled here and changed the name as a reminder of their homeland. The cottages cling to the waterside, the village is reputed to have the mildest climate in the country and flowers bloom here all the year round as if endorsing that claim. In the nineteenth century, the great days of packet-ships, it was a fashionable place to live. Lord Exmouth was born here and Lord Buckingham dined and wined with other society notables. Today sailors are there for pleasure, not national business, as were those men of former days.

No bus runs from here and the ferry across to Falmouth is the quickest way out of the village. At the head of the river is **Penryn**,

Falmouth harbour

reached either by a waterside path or inland road. These ways meet at the bottom of the steep hill beside St Gluvias, the parish church of Penryn. The town, in fact, grew from a settlement on the hill across the river. It has an interesting history, part splendid, part sad, but cherishes hopes for the future. Founded as a borough in 1216, it was granted a charter in 1236 and saw the rise and fall of Glasney collegiate church from 1265 to 1549. This establishment was a centre for religious instruction (renowned throughout Europe), growing in importance as Penryn's trade increased.

The closure of Glasney, at the Dissolution however, followed by the unexpected rise of Falmouth at the mouth of the river, led to a decline from which Penryn has never really recovered. But in 1977 its unique medieval character was recognised as rare, and Government grants were given to save old buildings, so bringing a conservation programme into being. As a result, the town whose granite is to be seen in buildings as different as London's Thames Embankment, Singapore harbour and Fastnet Lighthouse, is fast becoming a tourist attraction. A place to visit is the Town Hall Museum. It was once the gaol but now houses a variety of interesting items connected with Penryn's history. Another link with the past is Jane Laloe's falconry centre at nearby **Treluswell** — by appointment only.

Pendennis Castle

In Tudor times, the Fal River saw more shipping than any other port in the kingdom and Henry VIII, concerned about possible Spanish attacks, had Pendennis Castle built (English Heritage). It commands **Falmouth**'s best views: on one side, the holiday beaches, on the other, the docks and the town. This point is ideal for a coastguard station and one of the most modern, the Maritime Rescue Co-ordination Centre, was opened in 1981 by Prince Charles. In 1982 it was first centre in the eastern Atlantic to answer calls in the Marisat satellite system. Visitors are welcome here (a telephone call is necessary) and are told about the service that operates across the Atlantic and to the Spanish border.

In the coaching days, the Green Bank Hotel was important. In the early years of this century, Kenneth Grahame began his *Wind in the Willows* here — proof of this is framed in the lobby. Down High Street — much changed since a disastrous fire in the last century — and to the left, is the Prince of Wales Pier where the Flushing ferry disembarks its passengers. It is also the berth for numerous pleasure boats. The Moor lies above Market Strand and deceives most people with its name. From the bottom of Jacob's Ladder — (111 steps) boatmen used to ferry people over and moor outside the Seven Stars. This small building (dated 1610) is where generations of innkeepers have drawn beer from the wood, a tradition carried on today. The granite obelisk in the centre of the Moor is a memorial to men of the packet service when 'Falmouth for Orders' was the command obeyed by all captains of these ships. For over 250 years, the packets carried mail, cargoes and passengers to many parts of the world. In 1833 a wagon loaded with bullion from a packet-ship, left Killigrew Street on Monday and was in London by Saturday.

Walking through the town is a casual affair, traffic usually gives priority to pedestrians. In Church Street is the Falmouth Arts Centre, where, in the early nineteenth century, the Fox family of Quakers established the Polytechnic Society and reading rooms, setting a trend later followed throughout the country. At the far end of the town is the Georgian Custom House, handsome with its Greek Doric columns and fine façade. Beside and below, the King's Pipe, a chimney where contraband tobacco was burnt, is an interesting reminder of the manner in which contraband tobacco used to be destroyed. Off Market Street and clearly signposted to Bell's Court is the Falmouth Maritime Museum. It is a small but fascinating place housing a variety of items which illustrate Cornwall's maritime history and reflect the truly naval atmosphere of the town itself. Opposite Arwenack House is the waterside granite obelisk erected in 1738 by Martin Lister Killigrew as a memorial to his wife's family. They had lived at Arwenack and founded Falmouth, which evolved from Sir Walter Raleigh's plan to develop the harbour. He had stayed at Arwenack with the Killigrews and urged them to press forward with the project. By 1613, in spite of objections from Penryn, the town's identity had been formed and Falmouth was born.

The view over the docks from Castle Drive is one no visitor should miss. With the background of Trefusis Point and the Roseland Peninsula, this busy area is probably unique and there are hopes for a prosperous future as business people appreciate its potential.

Round the headland, the road leads to Castle Beach, Gyllyngvase and beyond to Swanpool and Maenporth. These are beautiful beaches with sands and rock pools to keep children happy for the whole holiday. Swanpool — as its name implies — is something else as well; rowing boats and canoes often share the waters with a variety of birds.

Take the road out of Falmouth which leads past the hospital to

PLACES OF INTEREST AROUND PENRYN AND FALMOUTH

Falconry Centre
Treluswell
☎ 0326 376773

Mylor Dockyard
Mylor
Now Yacht Club and sailing
centre, in 1866 it was *HMS
Ganges*, naval training dockyard.

Mylor Church
Interesting gravestones and pulpit.

**Penryn Town Hall and
Museum**
Standing centrally on Penryn's
spine road, it houses offices and
museum of local history.

**Falmouth Polytechnic Arts
Centre**
Church Street
Formed in 1833 at suggestion of
Quaker Anna Maria Fox 'to
promote useful arts'. Later copied
all over Britain.

Falmouth Maritime Museum
Bell's Court in town centre
Cornwall's maritime history.

Pendennis Castle
Falmouth
A well preserved castle built by
Henry VIII in 1539–43 shortly after
Little Dennis blockhouse below.
Enlarged by Elizabeth I and
beseiged successfully by Fairfax
during the Civil War. The old
barrack block of the castle is now
a youth hostel.

**The Maritime Rescue
Co-ordination Centre**
Pendennis Point
Purpose-built coastguard station
opened in 1981. Officials co-
ordinate search and rescue round
coastline of Great Britain and
Northern Ireland. Visitors are
welcome —
☎ Falmouth 314269 (District
Controller) first.

Penjerrick Gardens
1 mile S of Budock Vean
Large garden created by the Fox
family. With one of the largest
magnolias in existence. Famous
Cornish rhododendrons were
raised here.

Glendurgan Gardens
(National Trust)
Valley gardens of great beauty —
best seen in spring for flowering
shrubs. Runs to Durgan village on
Helford River. A maze and pool
are attractive.

Military Vehicle Museum
Lamanva
On the B3291
British and American fighting
vehicles, equipment.

Argal and College Reservoirs
B3291 Penryn-Constantine
Pleasant recreational areas, ideal
for walking.

Glendurgan Gardens

Budock, its church and the village of **Budock Water**. The church was the mother church of Falmouth and had its origins as the centre of a religious community in the sixth century. The way to **Mawnan Smith** passes Penjerrick Gardens, a Fox property now opened to the public. Springtime is best for a visit here — then the flowering shrubs are a mass of colour. From the beaches the coast path goes to Rosemullion Head but motorists are restricted to the road which ends at Mawnan church. It was built on an Iron Age site, the tower warning seamen that they were near the dreaded Manacle Rocks. Over the lych-gate an inscription in Cornish reads: *Da thym ythyn nesse the Thu* which means 'It is good for me to draw nigh unto the Lord'. Inside is a wide variety of colourful tapestry kneelers, those of the choir are patterned with medieval tunes.

Round the headland lies **Durgan**, a tiny village reached either by cliff path or road by way of Mawnan Smith. It consists of a handful of cottages, just beside the small beach. No sand here, but safe bathing and an ideal place for windsurfing. This area, together with Glendurgan, is National Trust property. Although the house is occupied, by members of the Fox family and is not open to the public, the valley garden may be visited. It is a garden of great beauty with fine trees and shrubs, walled and water gardens; a wooded valley runs down to

Durgan on the Helford River near Trebah Gardens.

Port Navas and Polwheveral Creeks between here and Constantine are rivals in beauty but the former has an added interest, being the site of the Royal Duchy Oyster Farm. There are no cliff walks here but tracks lead to the Merthen earthworks.

Constantine church, high in the village has seen continuous worship since the fifth century and is worth visiting for its brasses and 200 embroidered kneelers. It may be locked but the key is at a nearby cottage.

Beside the B3291 Penryn road is the unexpected find of a Military Vehicle Museum at **Lamanva**. There is all-weather cover here and exhibits include British and American fighting vehicles as well as badges, medals and general equipment. Nearby, the Argal and Penryn College reservoirs have much to offer.

On the right of the lanes to **Stithians** is the Rosemanowes Quarry where successful dry hot rock experiments have been carried out by the Camborne School of Mines. This village hides its church behind a screen of trees, but not the hotel, which offers excellent carvery meals. St Stythian's Feast and the Agricultural Show, are held in the second week in July. Second only to the Royal Cornwall Show, it was first held in 1834 to stimulate competition between local farmers at a time when agriculture was at a very low ebb.

From here a secondary road climbs to overlook Kennal Vale and the village of **Ponsanooth**. The sign 'Kennal Mills' is a reminder of former prosperity when the manufacture of gunpowder was an important part of industrial mining. Woollen mills were here, too, forming the basis of carpet manufacture and cloth exports. Sadly, now the river has all but dried up and could not possibly support the thirty-nine water-wheels it used to when Magdalen (Maudlin) Mine and the Perran Foundry were at peak production. These mine workings are hidden beneath undergrowth by the viaduct over the lane leaving Ponsanooth at the school and dropping to the A39 at Stickenbridge. A public footpath passes close by but there is little to show the world the tinworks that were old in Tudor times.

The A39 is at the bottom of Magdalen Lane, named after a Tudor chapel. To the right lies Falmouth, to the left, Carnon Downs and Truro.

4 HELSTON AND THE LIZARD PENINSULA

About halfway between Truro and Penzance is historic **Helston**, a town apparently oblivious of the A394 traffic which divides it. But on 8 May each year, the past takes over as old houses and twisting streets echo with Flora Day celebrations — once a pagan welcome to spring. Legend links the occasion with St Michael and the devil, who tore the lid off hell in a final effort to defeat the saint. An inaccurate aim sent the stone elsewhere and till 1783 was to be seen embedded in the courtyard of The Angel Hotel. This is an attractive building with parts dating from the sixteenth century. These include the Assembly Rooms with a minstrels' gallery. Great celebrations followed and the townsfolk adopted the saint as their patron. Whatever the truth, this annual event is worth seeing, particularly the noon dance, when couples in morning dress pick up the words of the song played by a local band and dance literally 'in and out of the houses'.

Helston's 1305 charter ruled that tinners should bring their mineral here for coinage or testing. Below the old Grammar School where Charles Kingsley was educated, Coinagehall Street is an echo of medieval days. The church at the back of the town is behind the Guildhall and the Butter Market Museum. Neither of these should be missed, particularly the latter with its emphasis on the former crafts and industries which flourished in and around Helston during the nineteenth and early twentieth centuries. It has a good display of folk history which includes Henry Trengrouse's life-saving rocket — invented after the *Anson* shipwreck on Loe Bar. Fresh fish and craft shops in Meneage Street are of above average quality as is Monday's cattle market at the lower end of the town.

The B3304 passes the boating pool on the Porthleven Road but walkers and ornithologists will want to explore the grounds of seventeenth-century Penrose beside **Loe Pool**, Cornwall's largest lake. Owned by the Rogers family since 1770, it is the main feature of their

CHAPTER 4: PLACES
OF INTEREST

gift in 1974 — some 1,600 acres altogether, the largest from Cornwall. A condition of this gift, that it be kept as a place of quiet beauty, makes it excellent for birdwatching. The house itself is not open. There is easy parking at the two entrances and the 6-mile walk taking in Loe Bar Sands will probably mean a rambling day and a picnic. The Loe is a long shingle bank dividing the freshwater lake from the sea. **Porthleven** is the birthplace of Guy Gibson, 'Dambusters' hero, and

PLACES OF INTEREST IN AND AROUND HELSTON

Angel Hotel
Coinagehall Street
Part is sixteenth century and at the end of the seventeenth, was the town house of Cornwall's great statesman, Sidney Godolphin. It later was the Excise House and has an attractive minstrels' gallery. Serves good food and is as interesting inside as it is attractive out.

Guildhall
Coinagehall Street
In 1576 a market house was built here and it incorporated the Town Hall. The classical structure seen today when erected in 1837–8, also had a corn market in part of the building, so carrying on the purpose of the original.

Butter Market Museum
In the former Market House in Church Street. It was built in 1837–8 and was composed of two buildings, one selling butter and eggs, the other meat.

Loe Pool (National Trust)
2 miles S of Helston
This freshwater lake is an unusual example of the 'drowned valleys' occurring in Devon and Cornwall. The Loe Bar formed by accumulated shingle from the Atlantic has dammed the former estuary which made the port of Helston. A 5-mile footpath runs round it. Small car parks at various points, make it ideal for a day's outing.

St Hilary Church
Near Goldsithney
On an ancient Celtic site. Despoiled in 1932 but it remains open for those who want to see its treasures.

Godolphin House
Breage
Fifteenth-century mansion, standing 3 miles from Mounts Bay on the lower slopes of Godolphin Hill. Tin mines provided the family fortune.

Tregonning Hill
Ashton
A place of pre-history with Bronze Age barrows and fortified 'rounds'. The site of St Breaca's Celtic settlement — later the church at Breage. China clay first discovered here in 1746 and in the next century the white 'signal' house was used to send messages to the ships defending Britain against Napoléon. Today a good picnic place with walks and wide views to St Michael's Mount and beyond.

Poldark Mine
Wendron
A real mine to explore. Another world of tunnels, chambers and caves where old machinery is at work. Also museum of mining ephemera, picnic areas and undercover amusements for children.

A Cornish beam engine re-erected at Poldark Mine, Wendron

a road bears his name. It is a good place for tea after wandering through its narrow streets and visiting Breageside by the harbour. This was once the heart of a thriving port — note the picturesque store built originally to hold some 7,000 tons of china clay.

Off the A394 to Penzance, running almost parallel with the coast, several lanes lead to headlands and byways. **Trewavas Head**

(Joseph Trewavas received Cornwall's first VC in 1856) and nearby **Rinsey Head** are ideal for picnics. Part of the area and the car park belong to the National Trust, who have partly restored the engine house and chimney of a disused copper mine, Wheal Prosper. **Praa (Pray) Sands**, a caravanners' haven, has a silver mile of dunes and safe beaches. Ask at the hotel for details of the West Cornwall Walking Holidays. Motorists can drive on to the privately-owned Acton Castle where Sandor Vegh began his Masterclasses. This unusual place was built at the end of the eighteenth century for John Stackhouse who originated seaweed studies here. There are footpaths only for **Cudden Point** with its unusual view of St Michael's Mount. Walkers will enjoy Prussia Cove and Betsy's Cove, both haunts of John Carter, eighteenth-century smuggler and self-styled 'King of Prussia'.

The great inland mining area is reached via **Goldsithney**, a busy place in coaching days, now a quiet village. The main building of St Hilary church dates from 1854 but the tower dates from the thirteenth century, while an inscribed stone in the churchyard is probably sixth century. The unusual pictures on the inside walls are reminders of the despoilation of the church in the 1930s when violent protests were made against the vicar, Fr. Bernard Walke who had introduced Anglo-Catholic services. It was originally whitewashed and served as a landmark for ships in St Ives and Mounts Bay. Its broached spire is one of the few in Cornwall.

Off the B3280, a turn to the village of **Godolphin Cross** comes after the hamlets of **Relubbus** and **Bosence**, both busy, lively places in Roman times. Relubbus had the tide at its feet and Roman remains at Bosence prove its trading capabilities. Deep in woodland lies Godolphin, a house which deserves a book to itself. This fifteenth-century mansion, was built with wealth from nearby mines. Sir Sidney Godolphin, Elizabeth I's great High Treasurer, and the famed Godolphin Arab stallion are only part of the history associated with this property.

The whole area of Godolphin and Tregonning is ideal for walks and picnics are made more pleasant by easy roadside parking. Chief Conin's dwelling, **Tregonning**, is a hill of ancient settlements and of more recent interest for William Cookworthy's discovery of china clay there in 1746. His subsequent findings at Carloggas near St Austell eventually led to the formation of Cornwall's most modern industry.

Before returning to Helston, stop at **Breage** (pronounced like 'vague') church. It has Margaret Godolphin's coffin plate, a Roman milestone and some fine murals among its other features.

Three miles north of Helston, along the B3297, is **Wendron** and the Poldark Mine. Here you can go safely underground and experience for yourself something of the past. Tin lodes, working machinery, and even dripping water help to recreate the mining age, with some of Richard Trevithick's instruments on display. Ample picnic space inside or out is available and there are entertainments for the children. Allow plenty of time here.

North once more, the bleak **Carnmenellis Moor** emphasises the mining atmosphere and a short climb to Hangman's Barrow and the Nine Maidens stone circle adds still more. This, too, is a place of many walks. Nearby, Stithians Reservoir is a must for ornithologists, but for access to the hide they should first obtain permission from the Cornwall Bird Watching and Preservation Society.

The village of **Carnkie**'s disused engine houses have a melancholy beauty best viewed from the centre of the village and then in panorama from **Carn Brea**. Here is another place to visit whether you are artist, historian, birdlover or gourmet. Good coffee with home baking and full meals are served at the unique recently-restored Carn Brea Castle (except Mondays). An experience not to be missed. Come when gorse and heather are out, explore the top of the Brea, where you can sit and relax and, while admiring the view, perhaps wonder about the Neolithic families who once lived here. Then find the path downhill to **St Euny**, Redruth Churchtown. Nearby Reswythen Bridge was made unstable in 1301 by the mining operations of Ralph Wenna and John de Treveyngy and their goods were confiscated to pay for the damage. In **Redruth** itself, in Cross Street, William Murdoch used his invention of gaslight for the first time in 1792. Murdoch House has been restored as a memorial to him.

Sir Richard Tangye (1833–1905) was born at **Illogan** and became a national benefactor and a brilliant engineer. He instituted the Saturday half-holiday and also built machinery to raise Cleopatra's Needle on the London Embankment. He was inspired by a fellow-countryman, the neglected genius, Richard Trevithick (1771–1833).

If you come to **Camborne** near to 26 April you might be fortunate enough to join in the Trevithick Day celebrations — held close to that day — when people remember one of Cornwall's most colourful characters. The son of a mining engineer, he followed his own ways even while he was at school, paying little attention to lessons because he was absorbed in his own diagrams and calculations. He would not even learn to spell yet could produce the correct answer to any mathematical problem six times faster than any adult. When he left school officially, Trevithick refused to have anything to do with the mine administration affairs in his father's office and wandered about the underground workings, examining and studying everything. The miners appreciated his knowledge of the machinery and his skill as a wrestler made him a popular figure. His invention — the high-pressure engine — so impressed the wealthy Cornishman, Davies Gilbert (later President of The Royal Society) that they grew to be close friends. On Christmas Eve 1801 Trevithick frightened the local people with his 'puffing devil' which carried ten or more passengers even uphill. (The model he made in 1797 is now in the Science Museum in London). Two years later he took a similar engine to London but had to bring it home because of financial difficulties.

There is no room here to tell more about the extraordinary career of this great man except to say that his high pressure locomotive predated Stephenson's *Rocket* by 12 years. Among his other inventions were the blast pipe, a ship propeller, screw propeller and central heating, yet the government flatly refused him any remuneration for his brilliant work. In desperation he turned to the New World but there met similar ups and down of fortune. Eventually he went to London and died while working at Dartford in Kent. Because of his penniless state he was buried in an unmarked grave but there is a tablet to his memory in the parish church, and windows in Westminster Abbey record his main achievements. His statue outside Camborne Library faces the street where he first put his theories into practice.

✳ **Pool** has a fine Leisure Centre and it is a good place to spend a day enjoying sport or relaxing — sometimes plays are performed ✳ here, too. Beside the main road at Pool is a restored Cornish 'whim' engine or steam winding engine, while just north of this is a huge Cornish beam engine. The whim raised copper ore from the East Pool Mine to the surface, while the beam engine pumped water out of the workings. These two engines are now in the care of the National Trust.

The Helford River

The internationally famous Camborne School of Mines, housing a museum, is on the A3047, while just off the B3303 at **Penponds** is the cottage — now National Trust — where Trevithick lived for a great part of his life and perfected most of his inventions.

Barriper (from Beau Repaire) road was once part of the pilgrims' route to St Michael's Mount and the whole area is so peaceful that it is difficult to imagine it as a prosperous industrial locality. The un-Cornish name of **Leedstown** is a reminder of the time in 1740 when the youngest daughter of mining magnate Sir Francis Godolphin married the Duke of Leeds. The new Mineral Tramways Project is much in evidence, being the largest and most important heritage and environment scheme of its kind in Europe, Recreations are based on history and Carn Brea is being promoted as a World Heritage Site.

William Oliver lived at Truthall, a fine privately-owned manor in **Sithney** parish. He later moved to Bath and made famous the biscuits which bear his name and portrait, Bath Olivers. The church has a fine collection of glass medallions believed to be thirteenth century.

From Helston, the **Lizard Peninsula** can be explored by turning off the A394 Falmouth road past Trewennack to **Gweek**. Pleasant high-hedged lanes lead to Boskenwyn Downs and open on to a straight road probably constructed by the Romans to take tin from

PLACES OF INTEREST AROUND REDRUTH

Nine Maidens/Hangman's Barrow
Near junction of B3297 Wendron road and B3280 Praze-an-Beeble to Redruth road
Megalithic standing stones.

Stithians Reservoir
A centre for birdwatching, sailing, boardsailing, canoeing, rowing, water-skiing and natural trout fishing. For permits apply to the SWWA.

Carn Brea Castle
Carnkie, Redruth
Restored medieval castle now a restaurant. Walks along the heather and gorse-clad spine of the ridge — once a prehistoric settlement. The 90ft granite monolith is a memorial to Francis, Lord de Dunstanville and Basset of Tehidy, erected 1837.

William Murdoch's House
Redruth
Not far from the Buller's Arms this renowned house is tucked away in a Redruth back street. Here gas-lighting was invented. (Under repair and currently not open.)

Cornish Beam Engines
Pool
Splendid working winding engine alongside the old A30 half-way between Camborne and Redruth. Nearby and also open is the pumping engine house at Taylor's Shaft with its enormous 90in cylinder. (National Trust)

Camborne School of Mines Museum
On the A3047 midway between Camborne and Redruth, internationally famous School of Mines houses a fine collection of minerals and rocks from Cornwall and many other parts of the world.

Carn Brae Leisure Centre
Station Road, Pool
Swimming pool, sports, sauna.

Peloe Dairy Farm
Near Praze-an-Beeble
Farm video, assault course, trail, displays. Refreshments.

Richard Trevithick's Cottage
Lower Penponds, Camborne
Not open to the public but it is interesting to see this thatched cottage down the lane at Lower Penponds. Here the engineer lived for over 30 years and perfected many of his inventions in the outhouse. (National Trust)

Crowan Reservoirs
Beside the B3280 Redruth-Hayle road.

Grambla to the port. Gweek's unusual name comes from the Latin *Vicus* which confirms the Roman presence. Since very early times the valleys all round have been streamed for tin, and careful observers may still discover ancient tin moulds built into the quay walls. In 1201 Gweek was important enough to warrant a merchant guild as well as

burgess privileges. The creek is now silted up but beside it is the
Cornish Seal Sanctuary; the Marine Animal Rescue Centre. It was
established in 1957 and is the largest in Europe. Over the years the
objectives of this conservation centre have been expanded and it now
cares for all marine animals. It also shows how everyone can help.

The B3292 to St Keverne runs between a thatched tollhouse and
the water — a pretty road affording occasional glimpses of the creek
and walks through the woods. But a narrower primrose-clad lane on
the far side of the house offers rewards for brave motorists. It is narrow
and steep, winding up past an ancient earthwork, dipping through
beech and elm woods before crossing the B3293 to wander up and
down into the valley where **Mawgan-in-Meneage** lies. The whole
parish of Monks (Meneage or Menaig seems to come from Cornish
managh or monk) is full of beauty and history — its church provides
something of both. Look for the seventeenth-century sundial, a dog
door and an unusual brass memorial to the unknown Hannibal Basset
with the words 'Shall we all die'.

Keep to the Manaccan road through wooded lanes until a signpost
to Kestle is reached. This lane leads to the unbelievably beautiful
haven of **Frenchman's Creek**, which Daphne du Maurier saw, loved
and made famous in her book of the same name. It has rightly been
described as a place of 'distinct, eerie charm', and access to it is close
by the farm. Over 35 acres along the south bank are National Trust
property and footpaths go to Tremayne Quay and Helford.

Motorists should return to the Manaccan road for **Helford** to see
its thatched beauty, stop at the old Shipwrights' Arms and cross the
river at Monks' Passage to the Ferryboat Inn. The road to **Manaccan**
is a delight. So is the village, perched saucily on a hillside. Geologists
will remember that William Gregor discovered titanium from here and
all should note that ill luck befalls those who pick figs from the tree in
the church wall. Few, however, may know that Bligh of the *Bounty*
came here to survey for the Admiralty, was mistaken for a French spy
and promptly arrested. The centuries-old New Inn provides a wide
variety of good food — beside a log fire.

St Anthony church on the beach at **Gillan** harbour is as beautiful
as its surroundings. This was a busy port in medieval times, with ships
sailing to Southampton loaded with fish, fish oil, hides, slate and tin.
Today, the charm of his quiet corner of the Lizard lies in its remotenes

Near Frenchman's Creek, on the Helford River

and not in trade. The lonely village across the water is protected by a difficult access road so walkers may follow the coastal path, as motorists have to turn inland again. The wild cliffs and fierce rocks explain the need for a coastguard and the lifeboat that was stationed here from 1869–1945, rescuing ships from the dreaded Manacles. **Porthoustock** (P'roustock) is a somewhat calmer place today as local men find quarrying roadstone safer than fishing.

    St Keverne church has reminders of shipwrecks and has rightly been called the 'church of heartbreak'. A plaque on the churchyard wall is in memory of Michael Josef an Gof, the blacksmith who led the Cornish army to Blackheath with Thomas Flamank of Bodmin. This was the first rebellion of 1497 and he paid for this fight with his life. However, before his grim death at London's Tyburn, he told the crowd that both his name and fame would not be forgotten. His words came true for his memory and deed lives still in the hearts of all Cornishmen.

    At this point some may wish to return to Helston, wandering quietly through the narrow lanes. If so, look for Trelowarren, between the villages of **St Martin's** and **Garras**. For 500 years it has been home to the Vyvyan family and the handsome house is now used for conferences and retreats. One of the most secluded caravan parks in Cornwall takes a small part of the extensive grounds and a cluster of

St Anthony-in-Meneage

former barns and outhouses have their own attractions. A small pottery and an excellent restaurant will tempt most people while others may like to buy Trelowarren herb plants or visit one of the variety of craft exhibitions held throughout the summer.

There is even more to see and enjoy on the western side of the Lizard so allow plenty of time for this. Immediately outside Helston, along the A3803, is the Royal Naval Air Station at **Culdrose**. It is Europe's largest helicopter base and has recently celebrated its 40th birthday, marking the date by enlarging its public viewing area.

A very different kind of entertainment is to be found just off that same road in the Cornwall Aero Park and Flambards Victorian Village. All-weather family amusements are set out here and include a life-size layout model of the London blitz.

The B3293 from here will lead you to **Goonhilly Downs** and the startling sight of a group of futuristic-looking dishes. This is the Goonhilly Earth Station, now British Telecom International, where the enormous aerials turn to the sky like creatures of science fiction. They were sited in this particular area because only the depth of granite found here was strong enough to bear the weight of these impressive structures. July 1987 saw the first quarter century of these satellite communications. The first commercially funded satellite was known

PLACES OF INTEREST ON THE LIZARD PENINSULA

Cornish Seal Sanctuary
Gweek

Started in 1958, now devoted to seal rescue and care. Baby seals are in the hospital from September to March, but others are always on view. Two safari trains are available for transport from the car park to the main points beside the lovely Gweek River.

Gweek Quay Maritime Centre
Large collection of rare and historic boats. Working boatyard, chandlery, café.
David Pask, blacksmith nearby usually works shop hours and welcomes visitors.
☎ Mawgan 710

Trelowarren House and Craft Centre
Mawgan-in-Meneage
Probably first owned by Earl Harold before Domesday. Home of Vyvyan family since 1426. Elizabethan-style Stuart building with a Victorian interior. Crafts exhibition (July and August), book shop, craft shop, coffee bar. Caravan sites. Good restaurant.

Royal Naval Air Station
Culdrose
This is beside the A3083 Helston-Lizard road. It is one of Europe's largest stations and machines are always on standby. Public viewing enclosure is close to the B3291.

Cornwall Aero Park and Flambards Victorian Village
Flambards
Aeroplanes, helicopter flights in high season. Victorian village with lifesize reconstructions. Also 'Britain in the Blitz' — recreation of a wartime street.

Goonhilly Earth Station
Beside the B3293 are the huge dish scanners of the British Telecom Earth Station. There is a public viewing enclosure and a new visitor centre.

Lizard Lighthouse
Built in 1751 but altered in 1903. Squat building with white walls, cowls and foghorns. Today it has one of the most powerful beams in the world and visitors are welcomed every day except Sunday.

Marconi Memorial
Poldhu
The first radio signals across the Atlantic were sent from here by Guglielmo Marconi. Spot marked by a small obelisk on the golf course.

as *Telstar*. There is a very fine centre for visitors. Here you can study working models of both dishes and satellites and enjoy the well presented audio-visual explanation of the mystery of modern telecommunications. There is also a restaurant of first-class quality.

From July to October the barren downs which surround the Earth Station are brilliant with white-pink and deep lilac Cornish heather which is rarely found anywhere else in Britain. A walk round the adjoining National Nature Reserve affords the chance to see some of the Lizard's unique flora.

About 4 miles farther along the B3294 is **Coverack**, a picturesque village, still mainly Cornish in character, with an appeal for those who enjoy sea views and a safe beach. The local lifeboat station is a particular place of interest.

There are numerous cliff walks in this area, the one leading to **Kennack Sands** ends in a safe beach for swimming in fine weather. The motorist, however, must return to the B3293 and turn left at Traboe Cross in order to reach the National Trust **Poltesco Cove**. It is reached by scrambling down beside a trout stream, but is well worth the effort, and for energetic walkers, there are nature trails to follow.

Cadgwith is a very 'picture-postcard' village which is a little sad because it has lost most of its former fishing activities, although it still attracts artists and photographers. Serpentine can be found around these parts, and inland from Cadgwith, great blocks of it can be seen in the church towers of **St Ruan** and **Grade** — the latter to be found at the end of a cart track.

All the cliff walks round here offer spectacular views at **Lizard** **Point** but the motorist has to go inland a short way from Landewednack and Grade to reach **Lizard village** which is little more than a cluster of souvenir shops with serpentine goods in great variety. At the end of the road is a lifeboat station and Britain's most southerly beacon with interesting historical points to note. It was from here, about 400 years ago, in the summer of 1588, that the ships of the Spanish Armada were first sighted.

The first guiding light on this headland was built in 1619 by Sir John Killigrew of Falmouth who needed money and planned to collect the dues from passing ships. So many vessels passed by without paying, however, that he was forced to give up his scheme as it was too expensive to maintain. In the mid-eighteenth century, two towers were built here to house a coal-fired warning light, but that produced so many problems that the idea was abandoned until oil lamps were installed in 1812. 1840 saw the first fog signals, and in 1878, a steam-driven generator powered two electric arc lamps which gave good service until 1903 when they were replaced by a single 12 million candlepower beam. The light that shines from the Lizard today is one of the most powerful in the world.

Cliff walkers will have no problem in finding the lovely places along the western coast of the Lizard Peninsula — **Kynance**, **Mullion** and **Gunwalloe** — before the return to Helston. Perhaps this is one of Cornwall's finest cliff walks because, not only are there attractive villages to see en route, but all the time there is a

view of St Michael's Mount, topped by its fairytale castle and looking different at every turn.

Motorists will need to watch for signpost directions along the Lizard-Helston A3083, watching particularly for the turn to Cury and Poldhu. On the cliffs of **Pol-dhu Cove** is Guglielmo Marconi's

memorial, a granite column, now the only reminder of the momentous events which took place on

these high cliffs overlooking Mount's Bay, for the historic buildings were dismantled in 1937. In 1900, Marconi chose to erect on this site, a wireless station of a size never before believed possible and on 12 December 1901, Poldhu was revealed as the cradle of the radio age when signals sent from here bridged the Atlantic and were received by Marconi at St John, Newfoundland. So wireless telegraphy was born here and, in time, played a vital part in World War I. Later, in 1924, the Marconi-Franklin beam system was also transmitted from here and revolutionised long-range radio communication. Short-wave beam systems followed and it is also interesting to note that the

Mullion Harbour

coaxial cable, which is an integral feature of every home television installation, was devised in the course of research done at Poldhu.

So, although the Lizard Peninsula may seem small in relation to the rest of Cornwall it has been, and will continue to be, responsible for events that make vital contributions to the progress of world science. A thought to remember on the return to Helston.

5 WEST PENWITH, PENZANCE AND LAND'S END

Rail travellers have always thought of **Penzance** as the place of journey's end. It is certainly the rail terminus in the west but the locals say that it is in fact where Cornwall begins. Before exploring the area of West Penwith (*Penwyth* is the Cornish for extremity) to discover the truth of this statement, there is much to enjoy in the town of Penzance itself, for it is a place of surprises.

Beautiful still, with its high, stone-stepped pavement is Market Jew Street, the main thoroughfare which greets pedestrians, motorists and rail travellers who have left the station at the bottom of the hill. The long road leads to the handsome granite Town Hall, before which stands the statue of Sir Humphry Davy. He was born in a house close by and there, too, began the experiments which eventually brought him fame. He was knighted in 1812 for his contributions to science and was later created baronet for his invention of the miner's safety lamp. It is perhaps not surprising that Davy, one of the foremost European chemists of the nineteenth century, was the one who realised and encouraged the talents of Michael Faraday. Davy's wide range of interests also touched on poetry, as well as the natural sciences. President of The Royal Society at 41, founder of the Athenaeum Club and the London Zoo, this man of Penzance was worthy to be called a genius.

The road behind the former town hall, now the Market Hall, turns left towards the harbour and the Barbican Aquarium down Chapel Street. This once bustled with mule trains laden with their copper ore for ships' cargoes. Now it is a backwater of memories, many of them lingering in the Union Hotel where the Battle of Trafalgar victory was first announced from the minstrel's gallery. Local fishermen had learnt it from the ship racing up-channel to Falmouth with the news. Such was local pride in this 'first' that Penzance men made the Nelson banner (now in Madron church) which has ever since been carried in

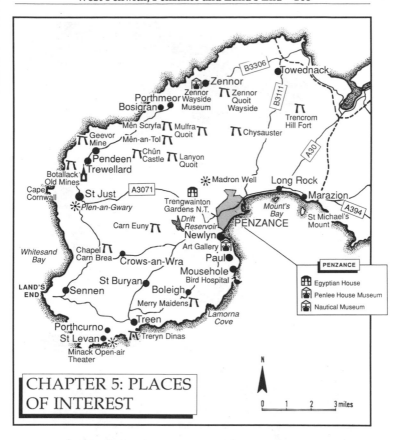

CHAPTER 5: PLACES
OF INTEREST

(map labels:)

B3306
Towednack
Zennor
Porthmeor
Zennor Wayside Museum
Zennor Quoit Wayside
Bosigran
B3111
Mên Scryfa
Mulfra Quoit
Trencrom Hill Fort
Geevor Mine
Mên-an-Tol
Chysauster
A30
Pendeen
Chûn Castle
Lanyon Quoit
Trewellard
Madron Well
Long Rock
Botallack Old Mines
Cape Cornwall
St Just
A3071
Trengwainton Gardens N.T.
Marazion
A394
Plen-an-Gwary
Mount's Bay
St Michael's Mount
Carn Euny
Drift Reservoir
PENZANCE
Newlyn
Whitesand Bay
Chapel Carn Brea
Crows-an-Wra
Art Gallery
Paul
LAND'S END
Sennen
St Buryan
Boleigh
Mousehole
Bird Hospital
Merry Maidens
Treen
Lamorna Cove
Porthcurno
St Levan
Treryn Dinas
Minack Open-air Theater

PENZANCE
 Egyptian House
 Penlee House Museum
 Nautical Museum

N

0   1   2   3 miles

procession on the Sunday nearest to Trafalgar Day. At the back of this historic building there is the shell of a Georgian theatre, opened in 1789: restoration work has begun. Here miners sought relaxation in the performances of Edmund Keen, Grossmith and other well known actors.

Number 25 Chapel Street claims different honours. It was the home of Maria Branwell who married in Yorkshire and became mother to Charlotte, Emily, Anne and Branwell Brontë. She never lost her love for Cornwall, remembering it even on her death bed when she begged the nurse to raise her up so that she could watch her clear the grate because 'she did it as it was done in Cornwall.' The house is not

The Egyptian House, Chapel Street, Penzance

The chapel on
St Michael's Mount

St Michael's Mount

open to the public.

The National Trust's Egyptian House with its flamboyant façade,
also in Chapel Street, is of unusual interest. Restored by the Landmark Trust, part of the ground floor is now taken up by a National Trust
shop. The Admiral Benbow Restaurant and Nautical Museum are at
the sea end of this old-fashioned street and are also worth a visit.

There are many side ways and shop-lined lanes to explore in this
most western of Cornish towns. Each has something to offer, but
beyond Market Jew Street, the road leads on to Alverton, with St
John's Hall whose handsome granite façade houses the Town Clerk's
office.

Not far away is the Penlee House Museum in Morrab Road — a
place of many treasures standing in subtropical gardens where
camellias bloom at Christmas above the long promenade stretching
from Newlyn to the memorial at the end of Chapel Street. If you are
a walker, telephone Penzance 69409 for details of guided walks

PLACES OF INTEREST IN PENZANCE

The Egyptian House
Chapel Street
Worth seeing for the unusual
Egyptian-style façade. Built in
about 1830. Part of it is let as
holiday flats but part is a National
Trust shop.

Nautical Museum
Chapel Street
Varied, interesting, appropriate
exhibits for this maritime place,
with many items recovered by
divers investigating historic
wrecks.

The Barbican Aquarium
Harbour
A fine aquarium and craft
workshops are among the
attractions here. Fishing trips can
also be arranged in this place.

No 25 Chapel Street
One-time home of Maria Branwell,
mother of the Brontës. Not open to
the public.

Penlee House Museum
Morrab Road
Entirely local display reflecting the
history and environment of
Penzance.

round the Penwith beyond Penzance.

From here, the road follows the vast, magnificent sweep of Mount's Bay past the Heliport (for the Isles of Scilly) and Long Rock to **Marazion**. This place is a delight, with its view of St Michael's Mount (acknowledged to be the earliest identifiable place in Britain). Its golden sands and safe bathing are ideal for children while the marshes nearby attract birdwatchers. Marazion was a thriving port as long ago as the Bronze Age as it was on one of the main overland routes for merchants taking Irish gold to Brittany.

Marazion is usually interpreted as meaning 'Little Market' but probably 'Small Sea' is a better meaning of the interesting name: 'mara' meaning sea and 'zion' comes from *vyghan* or small. The latter describes perfectly the narrow strip of water between the village and the Mount, which can perhaps be seen to better advantage from the higher villages inland.

Ordnance Survey maps mark **Long Rock** just offshore and the houses along the main road take their name from it. Near the bypass is **Tolver Water** where the Mount's Bay Vineyard is to be found — a place not to be missed.

Legend relates that St Michael appeared to some hermits, sup-
posedly on a large rock, which has ever since been known as St
Michael's Chair, while history tells us that it was Edward the Confessor who established a Benedictine chapel on **St Michael's Mount**.
The monks' domestic buildings are now incorporated in the fourteenth-century castle on the rock summit but the abbot's kitchen is
well preserved and stands apart. Even grey skies cannot dim the
magical quality of the Mount, which was given by Lord St Levan to the
National Trust in 1954. His son, the fourth baron, now lives here.
Visitors reach it by foot across a causeway or ferry from Marazion.
Apart from the situation of this spectacular retreat, there is interest
here for all. The harbour and village may always be visited, but visitors
should check for opening days of the castle beforehand. In any case
it would be easy to spend a whole day here thinking of the past:
perhaps of 1497 when Perkin Warbeck left his wife on the Mount to
make an abortive claim for England's throne, or of 1549 when the
owners of the castle were involved in the Prayer Book Rebellion, or
possibly even of 1642–3 when the future King Charles II was given
sanctuary en route for the Isles of Scilly — a plaque proclaiming this
is on the wall of a house in Marazion.

In 1981, an unusual scheme was proposed by Lord St Levan. He
decided to reconstruct a twelfth-century monastic herb garden. His
idea was to grow medicinal plants used by the Benedictines, especially those for the relief of toothache as they were much sought after
by pilgrims. This interesting herbaceous border may be seen between
the ticket kiosk and the dairy.

Ludgvan (Lugian) is a quiet churchtown set well above the bay
amidst narrow, twisting lanes. Dr William Borlase, born at Pendeen in
1695, was village rector for 52 years and published several books including *The Natural History of Cornwall* in 1758, 31 years before
Gilbert White's well-known *Natural History of Selborne*. This energetic clergyman was the first archaeologist to detail the heritage of
Beaker Age monuments and his work in this field is still unsurpassed.

From the steep B3309 below the church towards Crowlas, the
second lane on the left leads to the exciting Penwith countryside,
studied by Borlase. A lane curves round the foot of **Trencrom Hill** —
a National Trust area that is ideal for views, walks and picnics. It

The prehistoric stones of Men-an-Tol

consists of 64 acres of gorse-covered hill, overlooking an expanse of both land and sea. Here are numerous well-preserved antiquities — an Iron Age stone-walled hill fort enclosing several hut circles. Legend says that Giant Trecobben used to throw 'pebbles' at his brother Cormorran who lived on the Mount: the gigantic Bowl Rock beside the Lelant-Towednack road to the north, given to the Trust in 1962, has the notice 'thrown by a giant'! The café at the foot of the hill has leaflets about this unusual archaeological site.

Further along that same road is **Trink** — once reputed to be the home of another giant but now a delightful place for holidaymakers. North-east from here, a turning off the B3311 leads to lonely **Towednack** church. A strange story lingers in its history which is remembered on 28 April when the Towednack Cuckoo Feast is celebrated. Here the event recalls the time when a local farmer caught a cuckoo which flew from a log he was burning during a party. Perhaps the villagers hope to hold and preserve the spirit of spring in this way. (Most Cornish churches hold their feasts to commemorate the arrival of their patron saint.)

The way to Castle-an-Dinas and Chysauster is down the Nancledra valley where tin has been streamed since earliest times. The former is one of the chain of hill forts across the country, the latter

Lanyon Quoit — the remains of a Neolithic burial chamber

(along a pleasant lane off the B3311) probably one of the best preserved beehive hut circles in Great Britain. It was an Iron Age village from about the second century BC to the third century AD and consists now of a series of stone houses, each containing a number of rooms. Partial excavations have been made here and the walls of the buildings are still clearly visible. Not far away is Mulfra Quoit, a close group of standing stones on the site of an ancient settlement at Mulfra Hill, which gives substantial evidence to the theory of ancient ley lines.

Also in the same area is the Men-an-Tol, the Men Scryfa (Inscribed Stone) and the Nine Maidens Stone Circle. Were these stones really girls who had danced on the Sabbath and had been turned to stone for their sin? That is what the legend says. The Men Scryfa, however, is thought to be closer to reality — some think it was the grave of a giant warrior, others consider it another ley marker and there are those who think it could be the gravestone of the noble Rialobran (Royal Raven) who lived between the fifth and sixth centuries BC on nearby Carn Galver.

Beside the lonely secondary road which runs from Morvah to Madron stands Lanyon Quoit — probably Cornwall's most famous monument and the only known example of the remains of a long barrow. It was originally 90ft long and its capstone so high that Dr Borlase rode his horse under it. Storm damage accounts for the present lower height.

Madron village is where this road joins the B3312 into Penzance. It is high over the port and has a huddle of cottages pleasantly grouped near the church which is named after a sixth-century holy man from Brittany, Maddern. It is the mother church of Penzance and, acknowledged to be one of Cornwall's finest, is well worth a visit. The pew ends are unusually fine, there is the Nelson banner (mentioned earlier) and the great bell from the famous Ding-Dong Mine, whose ruined engine house is silhouetted starkly on the high land ridge behind the village. A short distance away is Madron's famous wishing well and those who care to walk about half a mile down a damp ferny lane will probably see rags hanging from the surrounding bushes — offerings still made to St Maddern, possibly for happiness in love or simply to placate the invisible spirits and hope for their protection.

The lovely Trengwainton Gardens, a National Trust property, lies beside the A3071 below Madron. There has been a house here since the sixteenth century, but it is now privately owned. In 1814, Rose Price, the son of a rich West Indian sugar planter, bought the house and estate and began to develop it along the lines seen today. He enlarged the original house, gave it a granite façade, built the lodge, planned the walled gardens and planted the magnificent woods of beech and sycamore which are so greatly admired today. The 98 acres of park and garden were given to the National Trust in 1961 by Lieutenant Colonel Sir Edward Bolitho and it is interesting to learn that today's beauty has been created mainly over the last 40 years with help from three great Cornish gardeners — Mr J.C. Williams of Caerhays, Mr P.D. Williams of Lanarth and Canon Boscawen of Ludgvan. The walled gardens contain many tender plants which cannot be grown in the open anywhere else in Britain, and although Trengwainton is always lovely it is perhaps only fair to say that it is at its best in the spring.

Brenda Wootton, Cornwall's popular folk singer, has a song called *My Yesterday Town*. It is about **Newlyn** where she was born and looks back sadly to former times when it was an important fishing harbour before artists and visitors poured in to intrude on the intimacy of its community life. Then it was a village with five bridges, five pubs, one church and cottages tip-tilting down the hill to the sea, their livelihood, their joy and their sorrow. Memories of sadness are still retained in the name Mount Misery, high above the bay. This was where anxious wives and sweethearts watched during storms, fearful that their men might not return. The fisherman's world is no longer the same, but the charm of the old cottages remains and there is still the fine quality of clear light which later on attracted Stanhope Forbes and other artists who exhibited in the Newlyn Orion Art Gallery at the turn of the twentieth century. Eden Phillpotts, the prolific novelist, began his career while staying in this area.

The name **Penlee** reverberated round the land like the tolling of a funeral bell at the end of 1981 when storms off this coast caused a lifeboat tragedy. Penlee Point is on the coast road to **Mousehole** (Mouzel), the prettiest fishing village according to many visitors, and which, with Penzance and Newlyn, was burned by the Spaniards in July 1595 and almost destroyed. Its delightful cluster of cottages hugging the harbour appeals to artists, photographers and most holidaymakers. Others enjoy visiting the Bird Hospital on Raginnis Hill, founded by the Yglesias sisters, now a registered charity.

The village of **Paul** clusters round its church, another guide for shipping. The church is high above Mousehole and on the churchyard wall is a memorial to Dolly Pentreath whom some consider to be the last traditional speaker of Cornish. She was buried there under her married name of Jeffery in 1777.

Only 2 miles along the cliff path, but further by road past the Roman encampment of Castallack, lies the fertile and lovely **Lamorna valley**. A bubbling trout stream and colourful gardens tempt visitors down to the little harbour or cove, justly known as one of Cornwall's loveliest, enticing them to linger. The artist Samuel John Birch could not leave, added Lamorna to his name, and gained fame as S.J. Lamorna Birch R.A.

The 10-mile cliff walk from here to Land's End is one that should not be hurried. There are flowers, birds and views sufficient to satisfy everyone, but few people know the story of how the famous Marconi met and fell in love with Betty Paynter on the Lamorna cliffs. She was then the fifteen-year-old daughter of Colonel Paynter of nearby Boskenna House, but the vast difference in age did not stop the engineer. He installed a radio receiver in her schoolroom at home,

Lamorna Cove

sent diamond bracelets to her at school and sailed his yacht into Bournemouth almost every weekend in the hope of a meeting. A story in the best romantic tradition, but one that did not end according to the Cinderella pattern. After 3 years of fun and friendship, the schoolgirl, then grown up, realised that the love was all on his side and refused him for the last time.

Above Lamorna Cove, past Trewoofe (Troove) is **Boleigh**, site of the last battle between the Cornish and the English, which took place in AD935. To celebrate his victory, King Athelstan gave a charter to found a collegiate church at **St Buryan**. The two immense megaliths known as 'the Pipers' are believed to have been erected by the king as peace stones to seal the treaty. On the other side of the road is another group of stones — the Merry Maidens. It consists of nineteen stones, is about 75ft in diameter and is one of the places where the Cornish Gorsedd is sometimes held. (This gathering is an annual event at which new bards are admitted to the Gorsedd, or College of Bards, an organisation unique to Celtic communities enshrining their common cultural heritage.)

St Buryan is a handsome church of the late fifteenth century with a fine rood screen and a 92ft granite tower. Further along the B3283 lies the village of **Treen**, once the heart of a busy tin-streaming area

Penberth

now only a cluster of houses in the beautiful wooded valley leading to the National Trust properties of Penberth Cove and part of Treryn Dinas. The cove is a reminder, perhaps, of the way of life once common in many Cornish fishing communities where wives and children grew violets and narcissi for the London market — now you can buy wines there. The old trade developed considerably after the opening of Brunel's Royal Albert Bridge in 1859. The valley, cove and headland passed to the National Trust in 1957, many of the small gardens are still cultivated and inshore fishermen are as active as their forefathers were.

The fine jagged headland of **Treryn** (Treen) **Dinas** forms one side of **Porthcurno**, a bay of startling blues and greens with the Minack Open-air Theatre on its other side. Treryn Fort consists of 36 acres and incorporates a complex of defensive ditches dating from the Iron Age. Here is the famous Logan Rock, once moved ill-advisedly by Oliver Goldsmith's nephew for a prank. It weighs 66 tons and the over-enthusiastic young man had to replace it at his own expense. Space is limited on this headland so visitors must leave their cars above the bridge over the stream and walk the last quarter of a mile.

Motorists who leave the B3315 to drive to Porthcurno Beach and on to the Minack Theatre must be prepared for narrow and winding

PLACES OF INTEREST
NORTH AND EAST OF PENZANCE

St Michael's Mount
(National Trust)
Originally the site of a Benedictine chapel probably established by Edward the Confessor. The spectacular castle dates from the fourteenth century and from its walls there are fine views towards Land's End and the Lizard across Mount's Bay. When the approach causeway is covered there is a ferry service from Marazion. Owing to the quick tidal movement visitors will probably walk back so return tickets should not be taken. The small chapel is unusual in size and location. It is open on Sunday at 10.30 for Divine Service which begins at 11. Café and National Trust shop.

Mount's Bay Vineyard
Tolver Water, Long Rock
Wines and a shop restaurant, all of high quality.
(☎ Penzance 60774.)

Trencrom Hill
(SW 518362)
National Trust
Between St Michael's Mount and

St Ives, this hill fort has fine views over the narrowest part of Cornwall and it forms part of the granite backbone of West Penwith with well preserved Iron Age remains at the summit. The soil here is good and Channel Island herds thrive in the area. The site was given to the National Trust by Colonel G.L. Tyringham of Lelant in memory of the men and women in Cornwall who gave their lives in the two World Wars.

Chysauster
2¹/₂ miles NW of Gulval
An Iron Age village. It consists of a series of stone houses, each containing a number of rooms. Parking and toilet facilities.
(English Heritage)

Mulfra Quoit
At the head of the Trevaylor valley, towering over the Penwith Peninsula. Three of the four original uprights still stand and support a partially displaced capstone. Traces of a circular barrow about 40ft in diameter, the original covering of the chamber.

lanes. The road passes the Cable and Wireless Training School before the car park nearest to the beach. Theatregoers have to drive up the steep road beyond to reach their destination, but it is a place not to be missed. It is unique. In 1932, Miss Rowena Cade and her gardener began the task of creating an amphitheatre out of the natural rock on the cliff edge for a performance of *The Tempest*. Stone seats now replace the original grassy ledges, sound and lighting and dressing-room accommodation are of the best, but the

PLACES OF INTEREST
NORTH AND EAST OF PENZANCE — Continued

Men-an-Tol
A fascinating monument with numerous legends. In 1749 Dr Borlase learnt that local people still crept through the hole to cure their rheumatism while children who suffered from rickets were passed through it at certain times of the year. Later, Sir Norman Lockyer wrote that this megalith was an astronomical instrument for the observation of certain sunrises and sunsets.

Men Scryfa
3 miles NW of Madron
Up a side lane beside the Morvah-Madron road is an 8ft tall inscribed stone. *Rialobranus Cunovali Fili* is the Roman inscription and could be translated as 'Son of Chief Royal Raven'.

Lanyon Quoit
4 miles NW of Penzance, via B3312
A huge granite capstone (18 x 9ft) on three upright stones, the most famous of Cornish antiquities as well as the most restored. Re-erected by public subscription in 1824 after a violent storm (1815) broke one of its four stone supports.

Nine Maidens Stone Circle
On high ground near the Men-an-Tol and Men Scryfa. There is another at Wendron.

Madron Well and Baptistry
B3212
Water from here said to have effected many miracle cures. Reached down a marshy path where there is also the restored fourteenth-century baptistry of St Madron.

Trengwainton Gardens
A3071
(National Trust)
The proximity of the Gulf Stream affords almost complete frost-free gardening here and Sir Edward Bolitho's gardener took advantage of this. Rare plants from Burma and Assam. A garden of exotic delight, probably at its best in spring time.

original magic remains. No matter what the play or the players, the setting makes every performance one of individual delight — the sight of the moon rising over the backcloth of ocean is a never-to-be-forgotten experience.

The church of **St Levan** and its holy well lies beyond the Minack, and there the road stops, so motorists must return to the B3315 for **Land's End**. The walk along the coast from here would take most people about 2¹/₂ hours. On a fine day the views are unrivalled. Here

The cliffs at Land's End

is another place for a whole day's exploration; photographers, bota-
nists, poets and holidaymakers of all ages will find something here to
please them. Longships Lighthouse lies due west of the last group of
rocks while 7 or 8 miles beyond is Wolf Rock. This was the place used
by Trinity House for their experiments in airlifting supplies to lighthouse crews. The results were completely successful and now the
men on Bishop Rock Lighthouse, Scilly, are among those who enjoy
the benefit of food and mail delivered on time as well as being able to
leave when their spell of duty has finished.

About a mile to the north lies **Sennen**, near the Mayon and
Trevescan Cliffs, both National Trust properties. Mayon Cliff is topped
with a good example of a Cornish cliff castle (Mayon meaning *maen*
or stone) with sheer drops to the sea and a view of basking sharks
cruising off the rocks in summer. Above Sennen Cove, which continues on to Whitesand Bay, is the ancient church of St Sennen, the
westernmost church in Britain. It is small and low, as befits its site and
was reconsecrated in 1440.

Before the village of **Crows-an-Wra** (Witch's Cross) several paths
leave the main road and climb to Chapel Carn Brea (not to be
confused with Carn Brea at Redruth) which also belongs to the
National Trust. It is the first and last hill in Britain and is reputed to have

the widest sea view from the mainland of the British Isles. Two Bronze Age barrows and the remains of a medieval chapel dedicated to St Michael may be seen after a gentle climb to the top, where in 1907, one of Cornwall's largest Bronze Age urns was found (it is now in the Truro Museum). Today at this place, members of St Just Old Cornwall Society light the first in the chain of forty bonfires which illuminate Cornwall on Midsummer Eve from Land's End to the Tamar. This is a particularly festive occasion. Songs and prayers (usually in Cornish) accompany the 'sacrifice' of herbs and flowers thrown in the flames by the Lady of the Flowers to propitiate the sun god. In other words a plea, shared by all visitors, for summer sunshine.

The whole area is good for picnics and walks and for exploring the many nearby antiquities. Carn Euny is an ancient Iron Age village now cared for by English Heritage. The remains are said to rival those of Chysauster and there is the added attraction of a fine 60ft-long fougou or underground chamber. The Blind Fiddler Stone — source of many legends — stands beside the A30, and down a farm lane opposite is Boscawen-noon, an isolated stone circle with a central heel stone or altar. Henry Jenner, who revived the Cornish Gorsedd in 1928, chose this place for its first assembly.

Carn Euny Iron Age village

PLACES OF INTEREST WEST OF PENZANCE

Newlyn Orion Art Gallery
24 New Road
Donated to artists and the community in 1895 by Passmore Edwards.

Mousehole Bird Hospital
Opened as a bird sanctuary by the Yglesias sisters (1928) when they cared for an injured jackdaw found in a drainpipe. Visitors are welcome but a telephone call is advisable.

Merry Maidens
B3315 Newlyn-Treen road
Best known stone circle stands in meadow and is sometimes the site for the Cornish Gorsedd.

Treryn Dinas
Porthcurno
(National Trust)
198 acres with Iron Age promontory fort.

Minack Open-air Theatre
Porthcurno
A unique open-air theatre fashioned from natural rock amphitheatre.

Chapel Carn Brea
Near Land's End
Covers 53 acres and is Britain's 'first and last' hill. Medieval chapel remains and Bronze Age barrows on summit.

Carn Euny Ancient Village
Sancreed
A notable Iron Age village with a 60ft fougou.

Drift Reservoir
Pleasant for walks and picnics.

Land's End
Site open daily throughout the year. Exhibitions open daily March–November. Craft workshops, shop, picnic areas, refreshments. (☎ Penzance 87501)

Nearby **Sancreed** church is worth looking at. There is a good rood screen, original barrel roofing and five crosses in the churchyard. One which has lilies on it is said to be noteworthy. Half hidden in trees in a field close by is the Sancreed holy well and baptistry possessing an exceptional air of mystery and sanctity.

The road runs past Drift Reservoir to join the A30, but old mingles with new here, for **Drift** village is mentioned in Cornwall's best known folk tale — John of Chyannor. He left Treen when mining was at a low ebb and went to look for work in the east. That to him was not land overseas, but a farm a few miles east of Marazion. This particular story is especially interesting as it names all the places John visited in his wanderings, something which does not often occur in folk tales.

Deep in the valley of Buryas Bridge there is a cross inscribed with symbols of the Cretan mysteries — another link with the strange past of West Penwith. These insignia appear to relate to the famous Cretan labyrinth where the Minotaur lurked, but no-one has yet provided a real explanation for the designs.

To see the best of the northern part of this peninsula follow the A3071 out of Penzance. It passes Castle Horneck shortly after leav- ing the edge of the town, a splendid place for a youth hostel and once the home of the Levelis or Lovell family. They owned much of the land in this area in early medieval times and were greatly involved in the Crusades. A well-known Cornish Christmas song, *The Mistletoe Bough*, is based on a tragic incident in the Lovell family. A young bride hid from her husband in an old oak chest and was entombed there, trapped by an unseen spring lock.

The countryside around **St Just** is almost other-worldly; its small fields and dry-stone walls bringing to mind the first men who ever settled here many centuries ago. The tower of the church though low, can be seen from quite a distance as it has stood in granite solidity since the fifteenth century. Near the clock tower a grassy arena is used today for the ceremony of choosing St Just's Carnival Queen. It is, in fact, a *plen-an-gwary* (Cornish for 'playing place') where medieval mystery plays were performed.

Decisions may have to be made here because walkers and historians will probably want to explore the **Tinners' Way** — in Cornish, *Forth an Stenoryon* — while others enjoy the views from the car. Only recently has this ancient trackway been brought to the notice of the public, the person responsible being a past Grand Bard, Hugh Miners (a Grand Bard is the elected titular head of the College of Bards in each of the Celtic countries). He lives at Carnyorth, between St Just and Pendeen and will either act as your guide or tell you more of the history of this ridgeway. For the experience of a lifetime join his night group at the full moon nearest to Midsummer Day and you will always remember your walk in the steps of the tin traders.

No-one knows the exact age of this moorland path but it was certainly used by tinners more than 2,000 years ago while ornaments and ingots made by Bronze Age goldsmiths found close to the trackway go back another 1,500 years. Stone axes which had been quarried from the Kenidjack cliff have been discovered throughout

On the North Cornwall Coast Path between St Ives and Zennor

southern Britain and such discoveries lead to the logical conclusion that West Penwith's Tinners' Way was originally part of a nationwide network for trade in Neolithic times.

To explore the area yourself, take a 1:50,000 Ordnance Survey map and walk the route on your own. Although it consists mainly of rough tracks and paths, no part of it is particularly difficult and when you reach the harbour at St Ives you will have the satisfaction of knowing that you have travelled over many centuries of history. Begin by walking down the church path away from St Just until Nancherrow Bridge where the way turns up towards Carn Kenidjack. This is often called the 'Hooting Carn' and is associated with many tales of haunting but as you climb, the colourful moorland surroundings of barrows, holed stones and chamber tombs will more than hold your attention. The B3218 crosses the path now but the ancient route carries on, skirting Woon Gumpus Common towards Chun Quoit and Chun Castle. The latter is the remains of an exceptionally large and strongly built Iron Age fortress with 12ft-thick walls which, until about 100 years ago were still 12ft high.

Before reaching Bosullow Common note that the map shows the site of a settlement. This was, in fact, the Iron Age village of Bosullow Trehyllys where its inhabitants were comparatively secure with Chun

Ruined engine house at Botallack Mine, perched precariously on the cliffs

Castle in the vicinity. Beyond this, a modern road again crosses the trackway which rises to Watch Croft, Penwith's highest hill (827ft). From here it is possible to make a slight detour and wander to look at Men Scryfa and the famous Men-an-Tol. Many people are sceptical about the tales told of cures at the latter site but they are said to still happen today. The ruined engine house of Ding-Dong Mine is easily visible from here. Tradition says that the famous tin mine was worked in Roman times. It re-started in 1814 but finally closed in 1928.

It is peaceful and lovely along here where the track runs high and almost parallel to the coast road to Zennor and St Ives, crossing the minor road from Treen to New Mill. Try Valley is marked on the map but not Try Round, said by tradition to have been a corral for mules. Further on, the old way near Lady Downs branches off along the hill above Chysauster, passes the Castle-an-Dinas hill fort and eventually reaches Mount's Bay. Historians believe this to be the route referred to by Pytheas, the Greek geographer, who wrote that the people of West Penwith took their melted tin in wagons to export it from Iktis (St Michael's Mount).

For a short distance a metalled road now overlays the ancient track at Embla and Almaveor, names which go far back in history. They only occur elsewhere in Cornwall, north of Wadebridge at Chapel Amble. As with so many Cornish place names, these have been distorted over the centuries but their origins can still be recognised. *Amal* is Cornish for slope, boundary or ledge, and its plural *emlow* is Embla today and walkers who reach this area will be well able to confirm the existence of numerous slopes in the proximity.

After Coldharbour Moor, the track passes that now lonely church of Towednack, which was mentioned earlier. Its closeness to the Tinners' Way probably indicates that it is a place where the Celtic holy man or 'saint' who lived there would welcome weary travellers with rest and refreshment.

Road and pathway now run together down Rosewall Hill with the ivy-clad ruin of an engine-house reminding the world of the presence of tin. The ancient route ends at St Ives, through the part called Stennack (*sten* is Cornish for tin).

Return to St Just to explore the Penwith coast with perhaps less effort. A good place to start would be at Cape Cornwall Street which leads from the Square to **Cape Cornwall**, now a National Trust

PLACES OF INTEREST NORTH-WEST OF PENZANCE

St Just *Plen-an-gwary*
An open, grassy area once used for medieval miracle plays — till 1600. Gorsedd held here on occasions.

Botallack Mine
Romantic ruins on the lower cliff below the Count House.

Chun Castle and Cromlech
1 mile Morvah
Both antiquities are important, the castle is an outstanding hill fort, the only stone one in Cornwall.

Geevor Mine
Pendeen
Ruins of famous tin and copper mine. Future uncertain. The site incorporates the Levant Mine, scene of Cornwall's worst mining disaster, when thirty-one miners were killed. Preserved beam engine can be visited only on certain days.

Pendeen Watch Lighthouse
Built by Trinity House in 1900. Its light gives four white flashes every second while the fog signal blasts 7 seconds every minute.

Pendeen Manor
Sixteenth-century farmhouse. Not open to the public.

Wayside Museum
Zennor
On the St Ives to Land's End coastal road the exhibits include tools and implements connected with the mining, agricultural, quarrying and domestic life of Zennor. Admission free.

property. Many people find it pleasant to spend a day here, taking advantage of the numerous walks, picnic places and advantageous locations for birdwatching. The towering nineteenth-century chimney at the summit of Cape Cornwall is a reminder of the many mines once busy in this district. There is an extensive view from this height although Priest's Cove to the south is probably hidden. It was once a medieval landing beach but now has a different character, and is very popular with local swimmers.

Beyond Land's End is the Longships Lighthouse while in the other direction are the picturesque cliff-edge ruins of the Three Crowns Mine at **Botallack**. In 1865, the Prince and Princess of Wales (later King Edward VII and Queen Alexandra) came here and descended the mine. This profitable mine caught the imagination because it produced riches from beneath the very sea bed itself. Tunnels 7ft by

The lighthouse at Pendeen

4ft were cut into a rich copper lode and men worked there each day at a depth of 1,360ft below sea level and half a mile from shore. When the quarterly accounts were produced, owners and mine managers would celebrate their gains with a feast at the Count House, now a restaurant with an excellent reputation.

The coastal path, like the road, goes towards **Trewellard**, an old mining village with a unique church. The Reverend Robert Aitken designed it himself and by 1851 it was finished, built entirely by the local miners. Some may think little of the plain, bleak place of worship but no-one can deny that it suits the surroundings and reflects the comfortless life which was the lot of most people who lived at Trewellard in those days.

Pendeen Manor, an attractive sixteenth-century farmhouse, was the birthplace of Dr Borlase, the father of Cornish archaeology. In the yard there is a fougou or underground passage which runs for 23ft in one direction and 33ft in another. At the angle of these is another chamber. There has been much speculation as to the original use of these constructions — Cornwall has several of them. Archaeologists have not yet been able to agree on a satisfactory reason for their existence so no-one can say whether the fougous were built for storage, defence or even primitive housing. The most recent thought on the subject is that they might have been designed for worship.

Past the manor, the road leads to Pendeen Watch, a lighthouse open every day except Sunday. Perched on a cliff edge, it is surrounded by open land where there are birds and flowers in plenty. Also at **Pendeen**, is Geevor Mine. Tin and copper were once brought up from the deep workings of this spectacularly-situated mine, but now no-one knows what its future is to be. It was registered as a limited company in 1911 and incorporated the old mines of Wheal Stennack and the ill-fated Levant. Tragedy struck in the latter in 1919 when the man-engine, carrying its full complement of men and boys to the surface, broke, crashed in ruins to the bottom of the shaft and killed thirty-one miners. The deeper workings were then abandoned, work ceased altogether from 1930 and the sea took possession of them. Fortunately the Cornish Engine Preservation Society (now the Trevithick Society) saved the beam engine in 1935 and in 1967 handed it to the National Trust. They then restored both engine and engine house which may be visited on certain days in the summer, a sad reminder of the prosperous times of 1870 when the area supported about twenty mines. Now only their ruins remain, picturesque and sad, along the cliffs, slowly but surely weathering away.

From here to Zennor, the coast road is particularly interesting, especially at **Bosigran** beyond Morvah on the National Trust cliffs. These are wild and exposed but man has learnt how to survive here from prehistoric times, sheltering his crops and animals in tiny fields surrounded by their stone hedges which remain from the Iron Age. The adventurous will probably enjoy the circular walk westwards from Porthmeor Cove to the Iron Age ruins of Bosigran Castle, along the spur path past the Climbers' Club hut and back to Porthmeor Cove along the main road. Adjoining Bosigran is more Trust property with a rather special history. Here, during World War II, commandos trained (the western side of the valley is, in fact, named 'Commando Ridge'). Here, too, Lord John Hunt and Sherpa Tensing climbed together to celebrate the tenth anniversary of the ascent of Everest. Never before had Tensing seen the sea and it was his first experience of cliff climbing. Cars can be parked by the road here and access to the coast is by the spur path previously mentioned.

The village of **Porthmeor** is missed by most people, who, not unnaturally, are eager to reach Zennor. It is, however, worth asking at Borthpennis for permission to cross the private land and look at the Iron Age village courtyard house here. It is similar in many respects to Chysauster but in addition has its own fortification and gatehouse and is one of the best of the numerous ancient monuments scattered on the downs above the B3306.

Today, **Zennor** is a picturesque miniature village lying in the slight shelter of Trewey Hill. It has, however, a long and interesting history. Isolated as it was by the natural features of land and sea, Zennor remained almost inaccessible for centuries which is why the presence of the past is still so strong in and around it. The small fields of middle and late Bronze Age settlements are still to be seen at Trewey and Wicca. Some tools and farm implements used for agricultural work down the years are among the exhibits in the small Wayside Museum, close to the car park. Whether mining is quite as old as farming here no-one knows, but it is said that tin-streaming has thoroughly worked almost every area of the Foage valley. Tools used for this are another feature of the museum. Both these industries were quite local but Zennor's stone-workers were once famous far beyond their homes. Tradition tells that the granite for St Ives' church was brought by sea from here, boats sometimes having to wait for weeks in order to take advantage of a spell of rare fine weather. Great cubes of Zennor rock were also used in the construction of Falmouth harbour and some also went to London for pavement edging.

The square church tower is not high but it stands as a clear marker of the centre of Zennor life. On the outside wall of the church just inside the gate is John Davey's memorial stone. He was a man of history who died in 1891 and was said to have been the last one to speak the traditional Cornish language — more than a century later than Dolly Pentreath, mentioned earlier. There are only two old bench ends in the church but one of them is especially interesting. It portrays a finely carved mermaid and recalls the story of the beautiful sea-creature whose charms were the downfall of Matthew Trewhella. Opposite is the Tinner's Arms, so old that its origins are unknown.

Behind the inn, the path which runs parallel to a trout stream flowing into Pendour (Mermaid) Cove leads down to Zennor Head. This is part of the 84 acres owned by the National Trust along the cliff, enabling walkers to enjoy the delights of thyme-scented springy turf all the way to Wicca Pool, an Anglo-Saxon name, so out of place in this essentially Cornish area.

There is a great deal to see in this little valley. Another Logan Stone, Zennor Quoit, Giant's Rock and the very fine views from the gorse-covered slopes. Little wonder that D.H. Lawrence loved it here and that Virginia Woolf, who spent childhood summers in St Ives, wrote that Cornwall's cliffs and seas had endowed her with riches beyond price.

Nearby, Boswednack Manor is a centre for special interest holi- days.

The quickest way back to Penzance by car is up Trewey Hill, climbing away from Zennor and on to moorland which tempts many to a last walk and picnic above the magnificent cliffs of Penwith's north coast.

6 THE ISLES OF SCILLY

T he Scillies consist of more than 300 islands but only six are inhabited. These are St Mary's, Tresco, St Martin's, St Agnes, Bryher and Gugh and they have a total acreage of only 4,400. St Agnes, though almost the smallest, has the special distinction of being the most southerly inhabited point in Great Britain. Situated about 26 miles west of Land's End, this interesting geographical grouping is unique in its relationship to the mainland. Though associated with Cornwall, the people are not part of it, as any true Scillonian will stoutly maintain. Nor do they belong to the rest of England, in spite of the imposition of taxes that would make it appear so.

For a considerable saving of time, most visitors prefer to travel from the mainland by air, from Newquay, Penzance or perhaps St Just, while, although the crossing can be extremely rough, even in summer, others enjoy the sea journey. The vessel will probably be the *Scillonian III*, a comparatively new ship launched by Prince Charles in 1977.

The first sight of the islands seems to contradict the various names given to them over the centuries — Isles of the Blest, Paradise Islands and the Lotus Isles. The immediate impression is of rocky outcrops with scarcely any vegetation in sight, but soon the unusual peace and quiet, which is part of Scilly's charm, takes over and the almost complete absence of vehicles makes itself felt. As a result, it is easy to relax and enjoy the startling blue of the sea, silver sands on empty beaches with birds and flowers that are so different, not to mention the stone 'library' of prehistory which consists of more than 150 Bronze Age relics. The fact that all the inhabited islands have maintained their reputation as a lifeline to tranquility is largely the result of extremely careful administration by their owners, the Duchy of Cornwall and their tenants, the Island Council, who have prevented any development that might spoil the unique beauty of the Scillies.

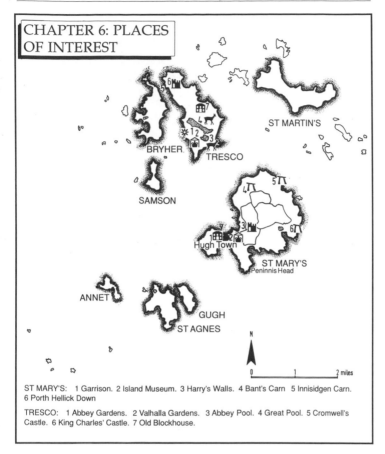

CHAPTER 6: PLACES OF INTEREST

ST MARY'S: 1 Garrison. 2 Island Museum. 3 Harry's Walls. 4 Bant's Carn 5 Innisidgen Carn.
6 Porth Hellick Down

TRESCO: 1 Abbey Gardens. 2 Valhalla Gardens. 3 Abbey Pool. 4 Great Pool. 5 Cromwell's
Castle. 6 King Charles' Castle. 7 Old Blockhouse.

Unlike anywhere else in the British Isles, Scilly, with its exceptionally soft climate, is the ideal place for open-air holidaymakers to visit in late February or early March. This is the time when the flower harvest is at its height and the fields of floral 'sunshine' rival even the brilliance of the sun. The atmosphere is different from that of the summer season and visitors enjoy being part of the concentration on flower exporting which pervades the islands in early spring. The flower show, which takes place in March is, of course, connected with the seasonal business but it is no ordinary one and claims to be the

The harbour, St Mary's

oldest in the country, because Scillonian growers were among the first to promote the growing of flowers as an industry. It began here in a somewhat strange manner when one William Trevillick, who farmed on Rocky Hill, St Mary's, packed a few blooms in his Aunt Ellen's hatbox and, as an experiment, sent them to Covent Garden. The date of that inspired idea is thought to be as early as 1867, but it makes little difference. What is important is that it came at a time when the islanders were desperate for a new source of income.

Old industries had gone — kelp-making, which ended with the introduction of synthetic iodine in 1835, was superseded by boat-building. But this, in its turn, ended in about 1870 when sail gave way to steam; so the flower industry which resulted from Trevillick's brain child was greeted with considerable enthusiasm. It was encouraged by Augustus Smith of Herefordshire who leased the islands between 1835 and 1872 and became, in fact, a self-appointed lord of the Isles and benevolent landlord, using all his resources for the good of the community. Not only did he help the incipient flower industry, but fostered the potato trade and brought Guernsey cattle over to improve the quality of the milk. He is also acknowledged to be the one who

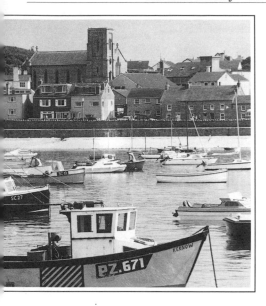

pioneered compulsory education here long before it appeared on the mainland — altogether a remarkable man whose enthusiasm and foresight undoubtedly saved the Isles of Scilly from the fate suffered by some Scottish islands where inhabitants were forced to leave their homes for lack of employment. But the flower growing industry, too, is unfortunately in decline, although many of the fields are still golden in the spring. Today's industry is tourism.

St Mary's is the main island. **Hugh Town** — that rather grand name for such a small 'capital' — is built on the isthmus which separates the Garrison area from the main part. It is here that many visitors stay after their arrival at the air terminal near Old Town or at the harbour of Hugh Town. In this small capital there are numerous shops, two banks, the main post office and three churches, each of a different denomination. The Town Hall serves a dual purpose as it shares its officialdom with performances of concerts and plays during the season. The Isles of Scilly Museum has a variety of interesting displays which cover the archaeology, wildlife and history of Scilly. Its central feature is a fully-rigged pilot gig (a Scillonian speciality) and there are also an appropriate number of wreck relics.

PLACES OF INTEREST ON ST MARY'S

The Garrison and Star Castle
Garrison Gate was built in 1742 as part of the garrison wall extending round the promontory. Today there are batteries, a park and promenade. Star Castle was a fortress erected by Elizabeth I and has walls projecting at eight salient angles. The inner building had two upper storeys and a bellcote.18ft-thick ramparts and a dry moat surround it. Since 1933 it has been an hotel, its first guest, the then Prince of Wales. The dungeons are now a bar.

Isles of Scilly Museum
Church Street
Hugh Town
Built in 1967, it displays all facets of past and present life on the islands.

Porth Hellick Down
The beach is rich in seashells, Sir Cloudesley Shovel's monument is at the eastern end of the bay. Here also are an early hill fort and the rock formation, Loaded Camel. Nearby is a burial chamber.

Harry's Walls
Begun about 50 years before Star Castle. Originally square with four bastions.

Bant's Carn
This burial chamber was probably built about 2000BC. It remained in use for 500 years.

Innisidgen Carn
There are two monuments, upper and lower. The former a mound about 26ft in diameter.

Naturally there is a considerable amount of boating and fishing here, and from St Mary's Quay, the popular sport of gig-racing can be watched and enjoyed every week during the summer. The history of these unique craft apparently began in 1790 when 'a gentleman in holy orders' placed an order for one to be built at the Peters boatyard of St Mawes. He specified a six-oared boat that could be used for saving life on the treacherous north coast of Cornwall. Tradition has it that this vessel was the first Padstow lifeboat and members of the old shipbuilding fraternity there say that a six-oared gig would certainly fill the role.

But these fast, slim boats had other uses too. The *Klondike* for example, which is now in the museum at St Mary's, usually went out on coastguard duty and was the vessel involved in the changeover of crewmen on the Bishop Rock Lighthouse. Another one, however, had a much more romantic task — to transport wedding parties and this pleasant work carried on till 1929 when the last bride to travel to her

The granite rocks at Peninnis,
with Hugh Town, St Mary's in the background

wedding by gig went to Tresco from her home on Bryher.

There are numerous dramatic accounts, too, of gig crews, employed in work on salvage operations, who returned with unusual cargoes. On one particular occasion, goods listed after a wreck were stated as 'lard, frozen geese, turkeys and two hundred fat bullocks'. Not the romantic kind of underwater treasure that most people envisage in these circumstances but nevertheless there must have been a profit for someone. With their capacity for greater speed than most vessels, it is only to be expected that when smuggling was part of life, these gigs should have been used for illegal purposes. And this was indeed the case, for records show that trips involving contraband goods were made regularly from Scilly to the port of Roscoff in Brittany.

But this specially designed island craft also suited local pilots who were more interested in legitimate business and they would race their boats out into the Channel, each hoping to gain the fee by being the first to reach any sailing ship needing guidance through the dangerous coastal waters. And from that, the idea of racing for fun evolved, especially when the prize was more golden guineas than the crew could earn in a week as pilots. Sometimes the men would row many miles, even after work, to take part in one of the many regattas which were held all round the Cornish coast in the last century. These lapsed after World War I, however, and no more gigs were built. It was not till the 1950s that gigs were seen again: a Newquay man decided to encourage the revival of building these special vessels and eventually there were four gigs from Scilly fully restored. In the early 1960s, races began on the island and are now a familiar part of the summer scene. It is good to know, too, that the knowledge of gig-building has not disappeared and that the skills are being passed on at Cornwall College in Falmouth.

St Mary's Quay is also the point of departure for inter-island boat trips. These are particularly delightful in the spring when the seabird sanctuaries can be seen at close quarters. (The Island of Annet is closed to all visitors from mid-April to late August so that nesting birds may be protected.) Atlantic grey seals can also be seen easily from these inter-island launches. Some of the boats will take visitors out as far as Bishop Rock Lighthouse, 7 miles to the west and the most fortunate may be able to see the relief by helicopter of the lighthouse keepers. Trinity House experimented with this method of exchanging crews on the Wolf Rock Light off Land's End in 1973. It was such a success that the idea was adopted and the men of Bishop Rock now reap the benefit of that experiment. It is easy to understand why some visitors consider these particular boat trips to be the highlight of their holiday on Scilly.

Perhaps one of the greatest attractions of the Isles of Scilly is the seclusion of its sandy beaches. They are all safe for bathing and even in high summer remain uncrowded. There are, however, two danger spots. The sand bars connecting St Mary's with Toll's Island and St Agnes with Gugh are unsafe when the water flows over the two bars, but that is only at high tide. The clear waters attract skin-divers particularly, on account of the marine life and the numerous wrecks. The authorities, who know the swell conditions and tidal streams, recommend divers to operate in groups under supervision, particularly as the nearest decompression chamber is at Plymouth, some 120 miles away.

If the weather is right, visitors usually take a short circular walk around the Garrison walls on their first evening as the fine sunsets over Samson are not to be missed. This is when they begin to

*Hugh Town and the Old Quay, St Mary's,
with St Agnes and the Western Rocks in the distance*

appreciate the wisdom of the local council ruling: 'Caravans, motorised caravans and similar vehicles MAY NOT be brought to the islands. PRIVATE CARS ARE MOST UNWELCOME AND ARE QUITE UNNECESSARY FOR THE ENJOYMENT OF A HOLIDAY IN THE ISLANDS (there are approximately 9 miles of road on St Mary's).' Taxis and bus services cater for all necessary transport.

Garrison Gate was not built till 1742 although Star Castle (an hotel since 1933) was constructed in 1593 at the top of the hill as a defence against possible Spanish attack. The population then moved from Old Town to greater safety near the castle.

There is a coast path here as elsewhere on the island, but another leads straight down to Woolpack Point where two rusty old cannons still point seawards as if awaiting the enemy. From here, if the weather is good, there is a fine view across St Mary's Sound to the islands of St Agnes and Gugh, but it is a place to be avoided during a northwesterly gale. Returning to Hugh Town, the road passes the Duchy of Cornwall's Land Steward's impressive granite offices. They over-

Prehistoric burial chamber at Porth Hellick, St Mary's

look Porth Cressa, St Mary's central and most popular beach.

The exploration of the main part of the island begins at **Peninnis Head**. The shorter way leads to the church, begun by King William IV and finished in 1837 by Augustus Smith. Past the vicarage is the island power station, skilfully built in an old quarry, and at the top of the hill is Buzza Tower. This was constructed in 1821 as an old Spanish-style windmill to grind corn; after which it was converted into a tower to commemorate King Edward VII's visit in 1902. It now has an even more useful role as a landmark for shipping. A bumpy track between a granite-walled lane leads eventually to Peninnis Head, a magnificent, rugged promontory at this southern extremity of St Mary's. Here, even the granite has been smoothed and weathered by storms; the resulting shapes deserving names such as the Tuskless Elephant, the Toastrack and the Kettle and Pans (where shrimps are plentiful).

The path to **Old Town** and its bay passes the medieval church, now only fragmentary remains of a once large cruciform building. The churchyard is full of memorials to Scillonians and other seamen wrecked off this coast. Some of the men were from Sir Cloudesley Shovel's ill-fated fleet, notably Henry Trelawny, son of the famous bishop from Pelynt, near Looe, captain of one of the ships. Here, too, the victims of the *HMS Schiller* disaster (1851) are buried. A memorial for those who died in both World Wars and a monument to Augustus Smith are also to be found in the cemetery.

From Hugh Town the road goes past the lifeboat slips and turns right at Parting Carn for Porth Hellick. The coast path also reaches this point too. Here is the quartz monument to Sir Cloudesley Shovel whose flagship *Association* was wrecked in 1707, and the most valuable underwater treasure ever located round the British Isles, which belonged to it, was discovered in 1967. Since then the *Romney*, *Eagle* and *Firebrand* have been found, the last-named as recently as 1981. The admiral's personal plate alone would be worth a small fortune today, but the hazardous diving conditions have clearly hindered rescue operations, although divers still persevere.

On these downs is a group of five chambered tombs, all very close together. Most of these 4,000-year-old passage graves are crumbling, the best preserved is maintained by English Heritage.

The coastal path carries on to **Pelistry Bay** where the sand is especially beautiful (felspar and quartz) and the sea views hard to beat. This is where swimmers need to avoid bathing when the sea covers the bar. Inland is Holy Vale, believed to have been the site of

Bant's Carn burial chamber, St Mary's

Yucca in flower at Tresco Gardens

Cromwell's Castle, Tresco, with Hangman's Isle and Bryher in the background

either a convent or a monastic cell and the path continues to picturesque **Watermill Bay**, past coastal indentations, before returning to Hugh Town.

Telegraph Walk, in Hugh Town, as it is called, starts at the lifeboat slips and leads to Porthmellon and **Porth Harry**. Here are the uncompleted sixteenth-century fortifications known as Harry's Walls. Visitors can enjoy the facilities of the golf course beyond Porthloo Beach, but coastguards at Telegraph Tower are always on watch and

PLACES OF INTEREST ON TRESCO

Tresco Abbey Gardens
A delightful place where an immense number of varied plants are grown. The whole atmosphere is charming and laid out to delight all visitors — whether or not they are gardeners. In the spring, arum lilies, camellias and azaleas begin the main flowering season. By the old pump, the Pump Garden leads to the ruins of the old priory, inside which are graves dating from the Dissolution of 1539, to 1820. There is also a small stone under the archway which suggests that it was a Christian tombstone of the fifth or sixth century AD. Pebble Gardens, Neptune's Steps and terraces are other delights in the Tresco Abbey Gardens.

Abbey Pool
A 12-acre area populated with geese and ducks. It is popular with bird lovers.

Great Pool
A similar place to the above.

Valhalla Gardens
A museum for the preservation of carved, wooden figureheads from over seventy ships wrecked in Scilly. It is housed in a building especially constructed by Augustus Smith about 1860.

Cromwell's Castle
It was built in 1651 by Admiral Blake of the Republican forces and consists of a 60ft circular tower and granite platform to command the channel between Bryher and Tresco. It is well preserved and finely situated. The entrance is high up and must be reached by ladders. On the roof are six gun ports. Free access.

King Charles' Castle
This earthwork is of similar design to others in the period. A pentagonal fort was added in the Civil War. Free access.

The Old Blockhouse
This was built at the end of the sixteenth century as an artillery battery. It is above Old Grimsby.

also send meteorological readings to the London Air Ministry for weather forecasting. On the rough cliff slopes near Bant's Carn, is another English Heritage property. This encompasses a prehistoric burial chamber and village of the Roman period.

At the pine-fringed northern tip of St Mary's lies **Bar Point** where there is some of the best bathing. Here are two more English Heritage monuments, the Innisidgen prehistoric burial chambers.

Before leaving St Mary's, Scilly's main island, there is an interesting point to consider about the western lighthouses. Eight of them can

The rugged western side of St Agnes

be seen from here on a clear night. Bishop Rock, Peninnis Head, Sevenstones and Round Island are in the locality. Further away are Wolf Rock and Longships off Land's End, while on Cornwall's mainland, Pendeen and the Lizard are also visible.

The 750 acres of **Tresco** might well be considered a complete nature reserve, the population living mainly in a line of hamlets across the central neck of the area. It differs from the other islands as it is leased privately from the Duchy. There are no cars, caravans or motor cycles, nor is camping allowed. The beauty of this place, and probably the conservation of the entire group, is due to the vision of Augustus Smith. In 1834 he lived first on Tresco and built a huge Victorian house there before emigrating to St Mary's. This extraordinary man with the very ordinary name was a far-sighted visionary from Hereford who gave the islands new life simply by rooting out the cause of their deterioration — an ancient system of land tenure.

These old ways had resulted in serious unemployment caused by a surplus population so he put the men to work building roads and the wall boundaries which were the beginning of the famous Tresco Abbey botanical gardens. Smith created them on the site of a tenth-century Benedictine abbey and in the equable climate and natural shelter of Tresco, made the barren island blossom with sub-tropical plants sheltered by Californian and Monterey pines.

South from Timothy's Corner at **New Grimsby**, the path leads past the Bulb Farm (picking starts here before Christmas) and skirts **Appletree Bay**. At low water it is possible to walk across the flats to Samson though speed is essential to avoid being cut off. Here, above the road, stands a granite monument to Augustus Smith and his successors. He designed it, intending it to stand beside his grave at St Buryan in West Penwith, but there was insufficient space so it remains here.

Inland lies the Great Pool which, with the smaller Abbey Pool, occupies about 46 acres. A great concentration of bird life on these waters attracts bird lovers, who come especially to see the rare migrants that breed here. About fifty species nest in the island and probably more are seen here than anywhere else in Europe.

Through the beauty of Abbey Wood there is a way to the Abbey Gardens themselves. It is impossible to describe such a place briefly for it is unique. But there are more than 5,000 species of plants from a hundred countries and from every climatic region in the world — many brought by Scillonian seamen returning home from their voyages.

Yet within this paradise is another — the Valhalla Gardens. It is an appropriate name for the collection of figureheads and other relics washed ashore from over seventy ships wrecked in the area. This place is strange and eerie but it should not be overlooked.

The northern part of Tresco has cliff walks on heather, ling and short springy grass which lead to Cromwell's Castle. This substantially built round tower with its 12ft-thick walls was erected in 1651 as a defence against the Dutch. There is King Charles' Castle, too; a long, low oblong fort but so badly sited that the guns could not operate. **Castle Downs** has early tin-workings, and on the headland at **Piper's Hole** there is evidence of three more. Intrepid and agile visitors may scramble down this gully and find a large freshwater lake. Candlelight turns this unexpected discovery into a miniature fairyland, but it is only for experienced climbers. Old Blockhouse, an old artillery battery, is nearby.

Samson consists only of two hills joined by an isthmus. It has become famous as the setting Sir Walter Besant used in his novel *Armorel of Lyonesse*. There is also a kistvaen or burial chamber here.

Bryher has been called 'the pearl of Scilly', but it is wild and untamed with lovely views but little else. People visit the outer islands for bird-watching — **St Agnes**, **Gugh** and **Annet** which is a bird sanctuary.

With so much of nature at peace it is small wonder that these rocky outcrops have been called the Lotus Isles.

7 THE NORTH COAST

Legends cannot be avoided when telling the story of Cornwall, but the one particularly associated with **St Ives** is usually shrugged off in disbelief, for it is said that the holy St Ia, who was the first to come to this part of the coast, sailed across the water on a leaf! The idea is very picturesque but seems too extreme to be at all possible — that is, until one remembers the comparatively recent cross-Atlantic voyage which successfully re-enacted the journey undertaken by St Brendan many centuries ago. A replica of the saint's small craft was made, a mere wooden framework covered with hide and surely as close as could be to the 'leaf' of St Ia.

Apparently St Ia eventually established a settlement here and it later became the attractive fishing port of St Ives, but as miraculous leaves are in short supply today, people who want to see the town in comfort should leave their cars at Lelant Saltings if they are only staying a few hours. This avoids parking problems and adds another pleasure, for, if the weather is fine, there can be fewer railway journeys more delightful than the small local train which runs from St Erth to St Ives and collects passengers on the way. There is ample parking space at Lelant and the ride takes a little over 10 minutes, which most people say is all too short because it is probably one of the country's loveliest coastal routes. From the Saltings, with its bird hide and interesting estuary scenery, the friendly train takes its passengers along the cliffside to give a clear view of the famous 5-mile stretch of the golden sands which edge the coast from St Ives to Godrevy Point. Vehicular access to the town is restricted during the season, though buses are available from Trenwith car park on the outskirts, so it is both wiser and more pleasant to arrive on the local train.

The steep, winding cobbled streets of this 'picturesque seaside town par excellence', as it has been called, do much to retain its Cornishness. Looking over the water at Westcott's Quay where the

149

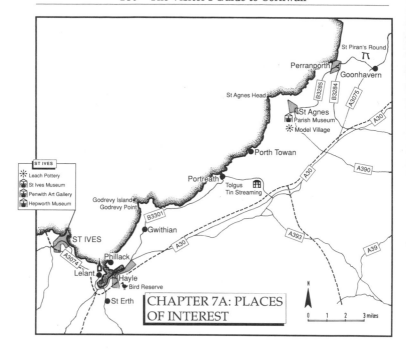

CHAPTER 7A: PLACES OF INTEREST

Warren turns into Pednolva Walk, it is easy to understand why the St Ives Art Club decided to hold meetings in that wharfside fishing cellar — the view from there is so characteristic of the whole place. Turner was probably the first artist to come here and paint scenes of the town. That was in 1811, but it was Whistler and Sickert who, in 1884, actually established the art colony there. Today's artists exhibit their work in the Penwith Galleries.

Later, in 1927, another group formed, the Society of Artists, which was wider-ranging and included people like Sir Alfred Munnings, Lamorna Birch, Barbara Hepworth and Bernard Leach. Leach, a potter, designed the tiled stone round the grave of Alfred Wallis, the self-taught primitive painter who is buried in Barnoon cemetery beside the car park. In 1920, Leach established a workshop at **Higher Stennack** on the B3306; it is still there and examples of his work are always on display. Stennack comes from *sten* (Cornish for tin) and the whole valley was once a profitable mining area. The most notable of

The harbour, St Ives

St Ives beach, harbour and St Ives Head

the workings was probably Wheal Trenwith as it produced not only tin but also copper, pitchblende and the radium used by Madame Curie in her experiments.

Barbara Hepworth lived and worked near the harbour just behind

PLACES OF INTEREST IN AND AROUND ST IVES

Penwith Galleries
Back Street West
St Ives
Here is the place to see work of
the St Ives Society of Artists —
originated by Sir Alfred Munnings.

Leach Pottery
Higher Stennack
Established by Bernard Leach in
1920. Still used as a pottery. His
work is also on display.

St Ives Museum
Wheal Dream
A comprehensive, local maritime
exhibition with excellent displays.

**Barbara Hepworth Museum and
Sculpture Garden**
Barnoon Hill
Administered by the Tate Gallery,
all in the sculptor's former home.

Lelant Bird Reserve
Quay House
Overlooking the Hayle estuary an
open hide is available in the
grounds of Quay House.

Paradise Park
Hayle
Collection of the world's rarest
birds, otter sanctuary.

 the parish church. Many of her sculptures and paintings are on exhibition permanently since the Tate Gallery bought her studio and garden and now administer the museum.

Since World War II other artists went to St Ives and produced work which greatly influenced the development of painting in Britain. As a result a new museum, The Tate Gallery St Ives, has opened. Managed by the Tate Gallety it displays local artist's work.

 On the island beside St Nicholas' chapel, a huer's hut looks down on the harbour and Smeaton's Pier. In former days, the look-out posted there would watch for pilchards and then cry 'Hevva!' to the waiting fishermen. After a good catch the toast in the town would be to 'Fish, Tin and Copper'. Today, Cornish cooks remember the hey-day of Cornwall's fishing industry when they make their 'heavy cake'. When the men were on the beach waiting anxiously for the shout that would send them out to their nets, their wives stood beside them. Then when the welcome call announced the approach of a shoal, the women ran home to bake something good for their husbands to eat after toiling with their heavy nets. And it was the 'heavy' — or 'hevva' cake that took just the right time to prepare and cook, being ready, with

Smeaton's Light, St Ives

its criss-cross net pattern on the top, to eat with a piping hot 'dish o' tay' when the weary fisherman returned home.

   Those times can be recalled in a visit to the nearby St Ives Museum, a building with a history that is interesting on its own account. This site was originally Wheal Dream copper mine but it was unsuccessful like many others, so it was used as a store to cure and pack pilchards for exporting to Italy in the mid-nineteenth century. Afterwards the Bible Christian sect took it over, then it became a laundry and later a cinema. The first floor, however, continued to have a maritime connection when a British Sailors Society Mission used it to house shipwrecked mariners who were waiting to be repatriated.

It is strange to see animal traps on show but one could trap three mice inside at once and this is a strong clue to the reason for the local preference for cats. St Ives is known for two types of cat. One is short-backed and stubby-legged, the other a large, contented animal resembling Alice in Wonderland's Cheshire cat. It was no doubt the local interest in cats that probably accounted for the nursery rhyme that helps many youngsters learn to count, 'As I was going to St Ives'.

A large part of the main room is devoted to exhibits connected with John Knill (1733–1811), perhaps the most memorable of all St Ives' citizens. Customs officer, mayor, lawyer and lovable wealthy eccentric, Knill was at one time private secretary to the Earl of Buckingham and a trustee of his estate. Rumour has it that he was also a privateer, and he did have plenty of opportunity for this. On his instructions John Smeaton built the harbour pier which provided such necessary shelter for shipping and Knill built the Steeple monument just outside the town. He intended this to be his final resting place but he was buried in London. In his will he laid down that every 5 years there was to be a ceremony held on 25 July when ten girls and two widows should dance round the Steeple. A strange request but one which has kept his memory alive.

Five splendid sandy beaches which can accommodate many people, form a golden crescent round the town. On one of them — or perhaps all — Virginia Woolf played when she was on holiday at Talland House and later brought these early memories of Godrevy into *To The Lighthouse.* Today St Ives, with its cliff walks, windsurfing, fishing and sailing, still welcomes visitors to the essential Cornish atmosphere which people so enjoy.

The train returns from a small station above Porthminster Beach and as it moves away, Tregenna Castle Hotel, Cornwall's finest, with its castellated turrets, may be glimpsed high above on the cliff top. The next stop is Carbis Bay which has such fine, smooth sands that it is perhaps the most popular of all the local beaches. This is in sharp contrast to the appearance it had in the last century when it was used as a dump for mining waste.

Lelant is an unexpected place with a quiet individuality that has to

The Hayle estuary and the wide sweep of St Ives Bay

be searched for. This probably stems from the knowledge that it was a thriving seaport in the Middle Ages, long before St Ives achieved popularity. The church lies behind the Saltings in a village of old-world charm. It is dedicated to St Uny and was the parish church for St Ives as well until 1826. Inside are interesting memorials to members of the Praed family from Trevethoe, the mansion at the foot of Trencrom. William Praed (1620) and his family are remembered in a slate carving, with kneeling figures, flowers, sand-glass and skull. His famous descendants are Mackworth (whose portrait is in the St Ives Museum) and William. The former was the eminent engineer who planned England's canal system, the latter, the banker after whom London's Praed Street is named. Another building of the past is the abbey in Lower Lelant, a long, low sixteenth-century construction, and L-shaped as befits the period. Neither Trevethoe nor the abbey are open to the public.

Quay House — reminiscent of former days — stands beside the Saltings where the A3074 joins the A30. It is an ideal place for bird lovers to study the numerous species to be seen so the RSPB have built an open hide in the grounds. It is available for anyone to use at any time without obtaining permission from a warden.

The St Ives branch line ends at **St Erth** which is another example of a once proud and busy place. The Star Inn was there in the seventeenth century when the Trewinnards startled everyone by introducing the first private coach to Cornwall. Truro Museum now has that same vehicle in its safe keeping.

Most drivers hurry through **Hayle**, glad when they are beyond it, but its present dullness does, in fact, hide one of Cornwall's oldest ports. This particular estuary has been important since Bronze Age times when copper and gold were sent from Ireland to Brittany via St Michael's Mount. Centuries later, when the Industrial Revolution demanded the best in engineering, this part of the world provided it. The old wharves, still visible near the railway bridge, were once part of the great foundry and engineering business belonging to Harvey's — known throughout the world simply as 'Harvey's of Hayle'. Beside the B3302, which leads out of the square and up Foundry Hill, are some remains of this once extensive complex — the hammer mill and the old mill pond can still be found. Those who designed the town's modern purpose-built library were (fortunately) determined that Hayle's great past should not entirely be forgotten and now for all to see on its gable are three original wood patterns for gear wheels for mining machines made in Harvey's foundry in the late 1880s.

Today that secondary road makes its way to a more modern concept — Paradise Park. Here is a fine collection of the world's rarest and most beautiful birds, including flamingoes, toucans and free-flying parrots. Within the grounds there is also the new Cornish otter sanctuary, an ambitious conservation scheme to help restore the otter to the local countryside. Another project, probably even closer to Cornish hearts, is 'Operation Chough'. Launched here in 1987 it is one stage in a 3-year study into the possibility of re-establishing the chough in selected locations on the coast. This rare bird which, with its red beak and legs, was once a familiar sight on Cornwall's rugged cliffs, is associated with King Arthur and so synonymous with Cornwall that it appears on the County Council's coat of arms. Detailed research has been done in other Celtic parts of Britain and results already show that the chough's decline is closely linked to the disappearance of the Large Blue butterfly.

It would be wrong to leave Hayle without remembering a person who was born in the town and whose name is as internationally famous today as Harvey's was in the last century. She was Florence

Godrevy Island and Lighthouse

Nightingale Graham, born in 1884, one of the three children of a chemist who encouraged her experiments with cosmetics. The Graham family anticipated the collapse of Cornish mining and in 1908 emigrated to Canada. Young Florence soon moved to New York, became a partner in a beauty salon business but before long, opened her own beauty parlour on Fifth Avenue. She took the name of Elizabeth Arden from the novels, *Elizabeth and her German Garden* and *Enoch Arden*. In 1915 she introduced mascara and eye-shadow and eventually extended her business to thirty-five countries. She also achieved another first when she opened her health farms. In 1966 she died but the company she founded continues to thrive.

Copperhouse, now an extension of Hayle, has only the Copperhouse Inn sign and, by the old quay, walls built of dark green copperslag blocks, to serve as a reminder of its former importance as a copper smelting site. Across the Hayle Canal, the romantically named church at **Phillack** (St Felicitas) overlooks the water and nearby is Riviere House where Compton Mackenzie and his sister, the actress, Fay Compton, spent many happy childhood holidays.

The huge stretch of towans (sand dunes) which forms part of St Ives Bay is ideal for holidaymakers to walk, swim, or laze, although all lifeguard's warnings must be observed. **Connor Downs** is a sprawl-

The cliffs at Hell's Mouth

ing development beside the A30 above Gwithian and many historians think it possible that the ancient city of Connor (Irish for 'haven') lies there beneath the dunes.

 Gwithian itself is a small village with a low-towered fifteenth-century church. The unusual sight of thatch here makes the whole of it an artist's delight: animal lovers, however, take pleasure in watching the seals which are sometimes seen at Navax Point (belonging to the National Trust) beyond Godrevy Lighthouse. The cliffs all round here are turfy and good for walking but bathers will find that the water is often stained by the Red River which collects tin waste on its way to the sea.

In 1649, **Godrevy Island** was the scene of a notable shipwreck. After the execution of King Charles I, many loyal subjects tried to save some of his lace-trimmed garments and other possessions and sent them abroad for safe keeping. Unfortunately the ship carrying them was wrecked and only a few of the royal clothes were washed ashore — together with the only survivors, a man, a boy and a dog.

In July and early August, the cliffs of **Reskajeage Down** between the B3301 and the sea, are brilliant with gorse and heather. Once past the fearful Hell's Mouth, however, the coastal footpath is easier and safer. The views along the coast towards St Agnes Head and St Agnes Beacon are really spectacular on a bright day; the colours

PLACES OF INTEREST
IN AND AROUND ST AGNES

St Agnes Beacon
(National Trust)
A delightful area of brilliant
heathers, extensive views and
ruined engine houses standing
high on the cliffs.

St Agnes Parish Museum
Well displayed collection of
exhibits connected with local
history.

Harmony Cot
Birthplace of John Opie, famous
painter. Privately owned and not
open to the public.

Tehidy Country Park
Best approached from B3301 at
North Cliffs/Reskajeage Downs.
Free access

**St Agnes Model Village and
Leisure Park**
On edge of village on B3277
Café, shooting gallery, gifts,
gardens.

Perranzabuloe Folk Museum
Ponsmere Road, Perranporth
Museum exhibits include photographs, displays, a replica Cornish
kitchen and costumes. Craftsmen
at work, offering holiday courses.

St Piran's Round
Beside the B3285, an Iron Age
fortification, adapted in medieval
times for performances of miracle
plays. Today the Gorsedd ceremony is sometimes held here.

sometimes appear almost too brilliant to be real.

Most of the land between Carvannel Downs and the A30 was once the vast Tehidy estate and belonged to the Basset family until about 1921. Their mansion is now a hospital but in 1983 the local council bought the estate's 250 woodland acres and restoration work has been in hand ever since. The whole area has been used to encourage the public in matters of environmental conservation as well as offering them a variety of recreational facilities. An events programme is published each year and includes bird watches, bird surrvey oppor-tunities, etc. The Country Park was officially opened in 1987.

Those interested in gardening are no longer able to visit the Experimental Horticultural Station at Reskadinnick near **Rosewarne** as it has closed down. But quite close by is Magor Farm and it was here that remains of a Roman villa were discovered, something very unusual in Cornwall.

From these roads, and for miles around, can be seen the Carn Brea monument at Carnkie, Redruth, which was erected to the memory of Francis Basset de Dunstanville, a great local benefactor. His main concern was to improve the lot of the numerous poor, especially those who risked their lives gathering the succulent herb that grew in dangerous places on Samphire Island. He built **Portreath** harbour in 1760 and this not only afforded protection to the ships, but also facilitated the loading and unloading of copper ore. Before that, the ships had to be loaded from the beach, a very irksome task. This was, and still is, a coast of storms, so the landmark known as the Pepperpot was a much-needed guide for ships to berth safely. This white conical tower was built in the last century as a daymark, but at night a small tidal light was shown from the hill, still in use in 1918. By 1840, when mining was at its peak, the population of this area was about 30,000 with people at work in mining as well as all the ancillary industries connected with it.

Inland, pleasant minor roads afford a quiet drive towards either Portreath or St Agnes while the section of the north coast path between Portreath and St Agnes has been described as the finest walk in Cornwall. **Porth Towan** and **Chapel Porth** have fine sandy beaches, but the undertow of currents and lifeguards' warnings must always be heeded. All round the National Trust's land at Chapel Porth and inland for some way, there are derelict mine buildings in profusion. The heathery slopes of the cliffs still only partly cover the great heaps of arsenic waste that have been there for so long. In the mid- and late nineteenth century, **St Agnes** parish was one of Cornwall's most active mining areas and those who worked here boasted that *Sten Sen Agnes an gwella yn Kernow* ('St Agnes' tin is the best in Cornwall'.) All these little porths or landing places have been used since very early times and foundations of the chapel traditionally dedicated to St Agnes can still be seen in the cliffs at Chapel Porth.

On the edge of St Agnes you will find the Parish Museum, the Leisure Park and the Model Village. The latter is such a successful Cornwall in miniature that some say that it is like standing in the middle of Cornwall and seeing all the beauty spots at once. Models include mining scenes, a small cathedral, Penzance Heliport, the Come-to-Good Meeting House, the new County Hall and numerous others, all in a landscaped setting and complete with the Tamar

Bridge carrying its load of cars.

The handsome Miners' Mechanics' Institute in the centre of the village is a different reminder of the past. Built in 1893, it was one of the first of many gifts from the Cornish philanthropist, Passmore Edwards, who was anxious to help the men educate themselves. It is now a club, but inside there are some interesting old mining records.

The fine old church lies low beneath the road beyond the Institute and opposite is St Agnes Bakery with a name for good bread and if you can park here it is worth buying something from this shop. Carrying on down the hill go slowly and notice the picturesque miners' cottages at Stippy Stappy along the left side which overlook the area of Peterville. Here you will find, on the upper floor of a carefully restored old building, the Saffron Art Gallery which has a varied range of the best local paintings not often seen in such a small place. Also in the Saffron Gallery is a framing studio. This is not only an appropriate feature but one which is proving very popular. A coffee shop complete the arrangements upstairs, which with the fascinating gift shop on the ground floor belongs to 'Images of Cornwall'. Only quality goods are sold here.

Leave the car here and walk the short distance along a narrow lane to **Trevaunance Cove** which is possibly the real heart of St Agnes and once a busy port from which ships sailed with their cargoes of tin and copper. A glance at the cliffs would make anyone wonder how an important harbour could ever have been built in such a place, but success was only achieved after several efforts. The final attempt of 1793 resulted in completion in 1797 but then stagings had to be constructed on the cliffs so that cargoes could be transferred by means of a horse-whim — a satisfactory arrangement which made Trevaunance Cove the scene of a very lucrative trade.

The north coast route continues along the B3285 towards Perran-porth but it is worthwhile making a detour down the first lane on the right after Barkla Shop. This is narrow and steep and motorists need to travel slowly so that they do not miss the thatched cottage called 'Harmony Cot', birthplace of the famous painter, John Opie, who is buried in St Paul's Cathedral. Beyond the ford over the Silver River, so named because of its trout, the lane climbs towards the B3284. On the left, before the railway bridge, is Ferndale, a bird rescue station where visitors can see the work being done. In the Agnes Clarke Bird

A miniature Cornish copper and tin mine at the St Agnes Model Village

Care section, anything from a starling with a broken wing to a puffin which has been blown off course, is looked after.

On the coastal side of the B3285 are the headquarters of the Cornwall Gliding Club, just beyond Cligga Head, an ideal place for birdwatching. Views from these cliffs rival the Mediterranean in the varied colours of the sea, sand and rock formation. The beauty of **Perranporth**'s beaches (which are in sight) is deceptive and many lives have been lost here by those foolish enough to disregard the red flag warnings. Currents, quicksands and the massive power of incoming waves are the dangers, but surfers who take the right precautions can enjoy the 3-mile stretch of glorious Atlantic rollers. Away from the dangers, children are catered for with bathing pools, a model yacht boat pond and various other amusements.

Halfway along the short main street is a turning to the left. It can easily be missed but to do so would mean losing the opportunity of seeing the Perranzabuloe Folk Museum. Housed in a handsome Victorian building, this small but fascinating collection of exhibits includes material which depicts life in the parish from prehistoric times. In the same building there are also craftsmen at work and it is also possible to make arrangements to participate in a holiday workshop. Goods made here are on sale in the craft shop.

The ruins of the real thing — Wheal Coates near St Agnes Beacon

The Gannel, Newquay

Beyond Gear Holiday Camp on the north side is a stretch of sand dunes, once visited by pilgrims from many lands. They came to pay homage to St Piran, patron saint of tinners whose chapel, as old as that of Iona, is now protected by concrete because inroads by the sea had despoiled most of the ancient building. The sands at the extreme end of Perran Beach are now used by the military so all visitors can only reach Newquay by inland routes from here.

The B3285 climbs out of Perranporth, passing St Piran's Round, an impressive Iron Age fortification, adapted in the Middle Ages as a *plen-an-gwary* (playing place) where religious instruction was given in the form of miracle plays. This open-air theatre has an amphitheatre that is 50yd across with circular terraces for the audience. In 1969 and 1973 productions of the Cornish medieval plays were performed here — the first time for many centuries.

Goonhavern village, at the crossing of the B3285 and the A3075, is where potters made the commemorative Royal Wedding Cream Churn for the firm of A.E. Rodda and Son who produce Cornish cream, famous since 1890 and sold on many airlines and railways.

About 5 miles along the A3075 is **Newquay** — a lively town with something for everyone in all weathers and voted first among Cornwall's holiday resorts for its magnificent beaches. At low tide

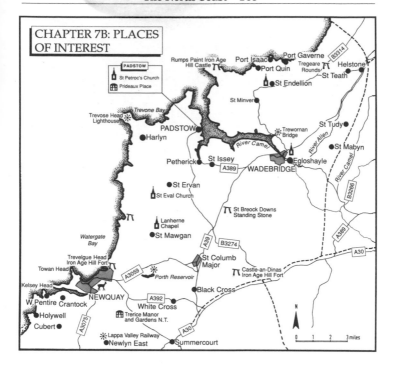

CHAPTER 7B: PLACES OF INTEREST

PADSTOW
St Petroc's Church
Prideaux Place

Rumps Paint Iron Age Hill Castle
Port Isaac
Port Gaverne
Port Quin
Tregeare Rounds
Helstone
St Teath
St Endellion
St Minver
Trevose Head Lighthouse
Trevone Bay
St Tudy
PADSTOW
Treworman Bridge
River Camel
St Mabyn
Harlyn
River Allen
Petherick
St Issey
Egloshayle
WADEBRIDGE
A389
River Camel
St Ervan
St Eval Church
B3266
St Breock Downs Standing Stone
Lanherne Chapel
St Mawgan
A39
Watergate Bay
B3274
A389
A30
Trevelgue Head Iron Age Hill Fort
St Columb Major
Castle-an-Dinas Iron Age Hill Fort
Towan Head
A3059
Porth Reservoir
Kelsey Head
NEWQUAY
Black Cross
W. Pentire Crantock
A392
White Cross
Holywell
Trerice Manor and Gardens N.T.
Cubert
A3075
Lappa Valley Railway
A30
Newlyn East
Summercourt

N

0 1 2 3 miles

these become one bay but each has a different character when the tide comes in.

Newquay existed as a port in the mid-fifteenth century and the export of pilchards to the Mediterranean was extremely profitable during the seventeenth and eighteenth centuries when the huer's hut below the Atlantic Hotel came into its own. In 1838, Joseph Treffry of Fowey decided to use the shelter of this harbour for his china clay exports so he built a new quay. For 40 years cargoes came and went until Par was developed and usurped Newquay's usefulness.

The list of attractions here covers everything holidaymakers expect at a popular resort. Some surprise visitors — particularly the pleasantly situated zoo and leisure park set in 8 acres of landscaped gardens, 5 minutes away from the town centre. One or two days could well be spent here during a Newquay holiday.

The surfing facilities and cliff walks are perhaps Newquay's

Pentire Point

specialities; each rocky promontory — as with the bays — is of interest. **Towan Head**, which stretches out to sea past the huer's hut and the golf course, boasts a small castellated tower and private chapel belonging to the Molesworth family and from here Cornwall offers another fine two-way expanse of distant coastline. Pentire Point East at the opposite arm of Fistral Bay has good views too and the vantage point was appreciated by prehistoric man as well: tumuli remains have been found to prove this.

There are numerous places of interest near Newquay, including Porth Reservoir off the A3059 to St Columb Major. Along the coast road there are prehistoric round barrows on Trevelgue Head which lies beyond the bay of Porth on the B3276.

On high ground behind **Watergate Bay** lies RAF St Mawgan, formally affiliated to the parish of St Columb Major, the first local authority to be so linked. Come here in August for the International Air Day. The date varies but details can be found in local papers.

Further north, the smallness of **Mawgan Porth** is delightful. The discovery of an extensive Dark Age settlement on the nearby cliffs was of great interest to historians. It was not fortified and excavations show several courtyard houses, grouped as a Cornish 'trev' or hamlet where the land sloped to the stream flowing into the bay. Drifting

Trerice Manor House

sands apparently forced the inhabitants inland to St Mawgan but they preserved an unusual quantity of remains for archaeologists. Domestic details were comparatively easy to establish. Pottery finds were significant because, being of north European type, they indicated Cornwall's break with Mediterranean cultures, the result of Arab domination over old sea routes. The remains of the small church or anchorite's cell indicate that this particular settlement had been an important place.

The tranquil Lanherne valley is little known though very lovely. Halfway up the valley and in the shelter of long-established trees **St Mawgan** village hides its charms. The church has Cornwall's best collection of brasses, mainly of the Arundells whose former home was Lanherne, the nearby manor house. It has been a Carmelite monastery since 1794 and the small chapel is open to the public.

The creeper-clad inn opposite seems to have an out-of-place name, The Falcon. Nevertheless it is particularly apt as, during the persecution of Roman Catholics in Reformation days priests celebrated Mass in secret and the signal to the faithful that it was about to begin would be the freeing of that particular bird.

The road climbs through leafy lanes to another village which has been important in the past — **St Columb Major**, even considered a possible site for Cornwall's cathedral but best known now perhaps for the Shrove Tuesday Hurling Contest when a ball of silver-coated applewood is used in the Town versus Country game. This custom was once a feature of most village feast days and is believed to have originated as a pagan festival in honour of spring. The handsome church dominates the houses around and, proud of its fourteenth-century foundation, plays host to a popular annual music festival. The Ring o' Bells inn across the road is a secular reminder of the fine tradition of bell-ringing associated with this church. And a mere few hundred yards away is the Red Lion, proud of a former landlord, James Polkinghorne, also Cornwall's most famous wrestler. An unusual memorial on the roadside wall depicts him in action.

Over the roundabout at the beginning of the bypass there is a sign to Castle-an-Dinas, about 2 miles along the road. There is only pedestrian access across private land but it is worth the climb for the panoramic view beyond Goss Moor to the china clay country. These remains of a massive Iron Age fort are some 700ft above sea level and composed of three concentric rings, hedges and ditches. The single entrance emphasises the wisdom of prehistoric builders.

The hamlet of **Ruthvoes** was the birthplace of a man little remembered here. He was Deadwood Dick, folk hero of many Wild West stories. Born in 1847, Richard Bullock started work in the clay industry then, emigrating to South Dakota became a bullion guard for the Homestake Mine owned by Senator Hearst. Richard's expert marksmanship earned him the nickname 'Deadwood Dick', but in spite of many hazardous journeys on duty, he died peaceably at the good age of seventy-three.

Black Cross and **White Cross**, which lie between Castle-an-Dinas and Quintrell Downs, could have been named as important stations for pilgrims to Holywell. Or perhaps they were depots for the black and white tin from the moorland. In either case **Summercourt** September Fair, one of Cornwall's oldest, would have been involved.

On the A3058 Summercourt to Newquay road, Dairyland offers an unusual look at country life. It is a working farm with 'space-age milking on a merry-go-round' where 160 cows are milked to music in one of Europe's most up-to-date modern rotary parlours. The mu-seum of rural exhibits in another part of the farm displays tools and instruments used on farms in the past.

PLACES OF INTEREST
IN AND AROUND NEWQUAY

Newquay Zoo and Leisure Park
Trenance
Newquay
Animals, boating lake, sports, miniature railway.

Porth Reservoir
Off the A3059 Newquay-Wade-bridge road — permission for use from South-West Water Authority.

Trevelgue Head
A promontory fort with a seven-line defence composed of banks and ditches.

Lanherne Chapel
St Mawgan-in-Pydar
The entire property once be-longed to the Arundells. Since 1794 it has been a Carmelite monastery. Open to the public.

Castle-an-Dinas
2 miles ESE of St Columb Major

An approximately circular fort high above the clay tips and Goss Moor.

Dairyland
On A3058 Summercourt-Newquay road
Working farm and museum.

Trerice Manor
SE of Newquay
A very attractive National Trust property — this small manor house was rebuilt in 1571. It has contemporary fireplaces and plaster ceilings.

Lappa Valley Railway
St Newlyn East, near Newquay
Steam train carries visitors along part of GWR Newquay-Chace-water line. Leisure park and East Wheal Rose (engine house and tall chimney stack) at end of journey.

At **Kestle Mill** hamlet on the same road in the Newquay direction, a narrow lane winds steeply up to the charming National Trust prop-erty of Trerice Manor. Protecting trees stand round this popular Eliza-bethan house which is small enough to be a home, yet retains the quality and character of the Royalist Arundells who rebuilt it in 1571. This secluded manor house contains fine fireplaces and plaster ceil-ings, oak and walnut furniture, and tapestries; a small museum in the barn traces the development of the lawn mower! A summer garden has some unusual plants and there is an orchard of Cornish fruit trees.

The Lappa Valley Railway at **St Newlyn East** takes visitors in a miniature steam train along part of the original GWR Newquay to Chacewater track. At the end of the short ride to a leisure park with various attractions, the historic engine house and stack of the disused East Wheal Rose can be seen here. This was Cornwall's richest lead-producing works until a cloudburst brought disaster to the miners and closure to the mine. The handsome ruin is all that remains.

The road from St Newlyn East to **Cubert** and **Holywell** is so straight that it probably follows an ancient pilgrim way. The well which gives the latter place its name is, in fact, not on the beach but about a quarter of a mile away at Trevornick Farm. This lies behind the extensive dunes set in a wide area of National Trust and Ministry of Defence land — footpaths are clearly defined. The Trust path leads to Kelsey Head and West Pentire on the Newquay side of Porth Joke and is strangely remote though so near to the busy holiday resort. Here the cliff flowers are specially delightful in spring and early summer while the little cove is ideal for families who want to avoid crowds. Porth Joke's unusual name comes from the fact that it was once the haunt of choughs — *chogha* being Cornish and the plural of jackdaw to which family the chough belongs.

Crantock is an attractive village centred on the Round Garden, the little orchard in the middle belonging to the National Trust. Its ancient collegiate church is on a hill overlooking the Gannel, a sandy estuary. St Carantoc and St Cubert are thought to have been missionary 'saints' who, like others of their kind, travelled in pairs and then settled near each other. The former founded a monastery here and the monks prospered by controlling the estuary trade. It was famed for its learning and had a library long before the days of Caxton. A house in the village — Great Weston — was named after one of the prebendaries who taught here in the collegiate days. In the late sixteenth century it was recorded that Crantock had seven churchyards and seven other parishes to administer. Some historians, however, believe that Langarroc was its original name and a legend of a wicked city buried beneath the sands may perhaps have some foundation here.

It is pleasant to walk from here to Cubert Common, one of the few enclosed commons in the country, now National Trust land. Another path to take follows the line of the Gannel to Trevemper and Newquay, and, though the beach of this inlet is good for children, it can be dangerous, as the river runs swiftly in under the cliffs of East Pentire. A short and different way back to Newquay at this point is by passenger ferry from West Pentire.

Padstow is the next holiday centre along this north coast and rests quietly on past memories. Buildings here date from the Middle Ages and are still relatively unspoiled, with slate-hung and stone cottages and their colourful sheltered gardens edging the one-way route to the harbour. Today, small coasters from the Continent berth next to gaily-rigged yachts, some built locally at Brabyn's Yard and it all looks so peaceful — a very different kind of activity from the scenes of several hundred years ago when Sir Walter Raleigh, then Lord Warden of the Stanneries, presided in the sixteenth-century courthouse on south quay.

As you look across the harbour you will be standing at the start of an ancient 26-mile track across Cornwall now known as the 'Saints' Way'. It was, however, originally used by Bronze and Iron Age traders who preferred the land route to Fowey rather than risk the dangerous waters at Land's End when they made the long journey to Brittany from Ireland and Wales. Many centuries later, Celtic Christians also travelled overland and followed the same way but they stopped to build churches, erect granite crosses and open up holy wells. It is in remembrance of them that this long walk has now been established as the 'Saints' Way'. These 26 miles could well be the central point of an entire holiday because along the way there are so many different aspects of the Cornish scene to be enjoyed.

The name of Thomas Martyn means little to most people but we should all be lost without the modern 1 inch maps he originated. Born in Gwennap in 1695, he came to Padstow to teach and pass on his scientific skills. After this he was employed to make surveys of large Cornish estates such as the manors of St Ewe and Tolverne and his work was so accurate that he was eventually prevailed upon to undertake a similar task for the whole of Cornwall. By 1748 he issued his 1 inch to 1 mile map which was not only accurate but beautiful and sold for three guineas each, long preceding any similar publication.

St Petroc, Cornwall's chief saint, settled here in the sixth century and the church dedicated to him is still mostly unrestored from the building which dates from the fifteenth century. Notice its unusual font of blue-black Catacleuse stone from the nearby quarries at Harlyn Bay. The name can also be spelt Cataclew's, as seen on the map at Cataclew Point. The rock here is Palaeozoic but variable in character — dark grey or blue and sometimes even yellowish.

Behind the church and screened from the road by a castellated wall is Prideaux Place, one of the few Cornish manor houses still occupied by the family for whose ancestors it was built. In July 1987 it was opened to the public for the first time in 400 years and visitors can now wander round the 20-acre deer park and marvel at the great chamber inside the house, gazing up at the embossed plaster ceiling which depicts scenes from the Bible. That dates from about 1585. But there is one special day — 1 May — when all the world seems to come to Prideaux Place. That is when the 'Obby 'Oss festival takes place and the doors here are opened to the blue horse who dances in the staircase hall to the music of an old traditional tune.

Parking is not easy in Padstow during the season and on May Day it is impossible, especially with crowds lining the narrow streets waiting for the procession of this unique folk festival. It takes the form of a dance struggle between 'Oss and Teazer and is thought to represent the conflict between winter and summer or even good and evil, as seen in the story of St George and the dragon. A short distance from the town a spring dedicated to the saint is believed to have gushed forth from the rock immediately he set foot there. But whatever lies behind the old custom, the procession of horse, teazer, dancers, singers and musicians still makes its way annually between houses decked with flags and greenery.

North of Padstow, above Brabyn's Yard, the public footpath leads to St George's Well and on to Stepper Point where the spectacular cliff scenery remains unspoilt. There are tracks all round past **Trevone Bay** to Trevose Head. Motorists have to shuttle to and from these coastal points as there is no connecting road. The fine farmstead at the entrance to the hamlet of **Treator** on the B3276 is the birthplace of Sir Goldsworthy Gurney, another great Cornish engineer.

After Trevone Bay, with its clean sand, where rock eddies can be dangerous, is **Harlyn**. It is interesting historically because of the gold lunulae and the many prehistoric remains discovered there early in the twentieth century when workmen, digging foundations for a house, uncovered a Neolithic cemetery. Some of the antiquities are to be seen in the museum at Truro.

The toll charged to drive to the point at **Trevose Head** is little enough to pay for some of Cornwall's wildest and roughest coastal views. The lighthouse, the last to be run on compressed air and paraffin, is open daily except Sunday.

Few golf courses can be as well sited as the links at Trevose. Open to the headland, with more than ten beaches and the ruins of the chapel where St Petroc converted Prince Constantine close by, they must be unique.

The coastal footpath is difficult to negotiate along these very exposed cliffs, and agile walkers who venture down the steep path to **Fox Cove** will find a delightful place of retreat even at the busiest times. The National Trust have saved the cliffs at Porthcothan and in 1966 also acquired 220 acres. That land stretches from Porth Mear, past several fine small coves, a fine rock arch and beyond Park Head to Diggory's Island at the north end of Bedruthan Steps. These rock stairs became eroded to danger point but have recently been re-stored. There is an information centre, shop, tea-room and car park near this justly famous beauty spot with its spectacular cliff scenery.

Arable fields are under cultivation right to the cliff edge and flocks of sheep are surprisingly numerous. Tamarisk hedges which are un-usual in Cornwall are planted here not for their beauty but because they afford the most effective protection from salt spray blown off the sea during gales.

After the pleasures of Padstow and its nearby coast, visitors will find it strange to be directed to a disused aerodrome. But it is a pity to miss the church at **St Eval** (pronounced as in 'ever') standing lonely and surrounded by dreary concrete flats, once busy runways. On the way there is a sign to St Eval Leather Crafts — a cottage industry housed in a neat homestead with a variety of high quality goods.

The rather severe exterior of St Eval church belies its character. It is, in fact, one of the most friendly in Cornwall, with open doors for visitors. During World War II, squadrons of Coastal Command flew from St Eval station; their badge incorporated a likeness of the church. In March 1959, 205 Squadron presented their standard to this place of worship, where it still hangs. The handsome font cover is an additional remembrance of that occasion. Today, padre and vicar share services as the congregation is drawn from RAF St Mawgan and the civilian homes in this scattered parish.

In complete contrast, **St Ervan** church is hidden in the wooded seclusion of its churchtown at the end of a narrow lane between sections of the old aerodrome. It is built on a circular Celtic site high

Bedruthan Steps

above a lush valley and a golden angel at the door — perhaps it is the saint himself — invites you to enter. Inside, there is the Lord's Prayer in Cornish, a friendly letter of welcome from the vicar and some fine old slate headstones on the walls.

From here the lanes wind through Rumford and over the B3274 to the parish of **St Issey**. The rich brown and red-brown stone quarried nearby is used locally, its warm colours reflected from the walls of cottages whose bright gardens border on the road. Where the lane joins the A389 Padstow Road, there is another Ring o' Bells.

Little Petherick takes up a considerable amount of the A389 from here to Padstow, but it is such a delightful village that no one complains. Old slate-hung houses lean towards the mill stream as if sharing a secret. The church is small and very Anglo-Catholic since the beginning of the twentieth century. There is little left of the tiny church that was here 600 years before — only two bells, some bench ends, a font and the thirteenth-century marble slab to Sir Roger Lemporu, unusually decorated with a human head and a foliated cross. Athelstan Riley became patron here in 1898 and restored building, furniture and vestments to former High Church traditions.

Wadebridge is interesting for several reasons — its name, its position, its bridge and its own pleasant character. Historians believe

Wadebridge

The Bridge on Wool inn sign, illustrating the popular story of the bridge

that 'Wade' indicates that it had probably been used by the Romans who crossed the River Camel at that point because of the *vadum* or ford there. In the Middle Ages, before the bridge was built, there was so much traffic at this fording point that chapels were erected to greet travellers and pilgrims. St Michael's at the St Breock end was licensed as early as 1382 and about 1468 a bridge was built between it and the King's Chapel at the eastern end. They were both sold for secular purposes by Queen Elizabeth I in 1591. So many tales exist about the construction of what Carew called 'the longest, strongest and fairest bridge that the Shire can muster' that more needs to be said about it. In 1538, Leland gave the following interesting account:

> Wadebridge wher ther was a fery 80 yeres syns and menne sumtyme passing over by horse stoode often in great jeopardie, then one Lovebone, Vicar of Wadebridge, movid with pitie began the bridge and with great paine and studie, good people putting their help thereto finished it with xvij fair and great uniforme arches of stone. One told me that the foundation of certein of th' arches was first sette on so quick sandy ground that Lovebone almost despaired to performe the bridge ontyl such tyme as he layed pakkes of wolle for fundation.

The Bridge on Wool inn sign agrees with this report and so do those who appreciate that wool solidifies when wet and compressed. Others believe that money to build the bridge came from wealthy sheep farmers in the area, especially those from Bodmin Moor.

The slate quays and stone wharves which can still be seen in places beside the river are, however, little more than ghostly reminders of the great trading days of the town, situated where the old pilgrims' way to the Mount crosses the trade route from Ireland to Europe. Eventually, railways brought a different kind of traffic — holidaymakers and goods to Wadebridge and Padstow, but the line beside the Camel estuary is now only for pedestrians. It provides a quiet 2 hours of walking — the new raised swan nesting mounds are of special interest. Buses run from Padstow for those returning by road.

Inland, on the A389 Bodmin road, another old railway line at Sladesbridge offers more quiet walking. This, however, extends very much further over the St Kew Highway and on towards Delabole, Camelford and north Cornwall.

To the south of Wadebridge, an extensive showground lies on high ground beside the A39 from St Columb. The Royal Cornwall Show is held here in June when Cornish talents compete in every

Hingham Mill

PLACES OF INTEREST IN AND AROUND PADSTOW AND WADEBRIDGE

Prideaux Place
Padstow
An Elizabethan house (and deer park) with a magnificent embossed ceiling. Public viewing for the first time in 400 years.

Trevose Head Lighthouse
3 miles W of Padstow
This Trinity House establishment on a rocky promontory near Padstow is reached via a toll road. Open daily except Sundays.

St Eval Church
On a disused airfield about 3 miles from Mawgan Porth Dedicated to St Uvelus, the building is solitary on a high plateau north of the Vale of Lanherne. It has such a prominent tower that in 1724–7 Bristol merchants rebuilt it for use as a landmark.

St Eval Leather Crafts
A cottage industry with high quality goods for sale.

St Breock Standing Stone
Near Wadebridge
(SW 968683)
An historical monument in the care of English Heritage — a long stone of prehistoric date, probably once about 16ft high.

field. Vintage car rallies and all the many other events taking place here are well advertised. The St Breock standing stone is also on these, the St Breock Downs.

Wadebridge's parish church of St Breock lies in a tree-encircled valley a little out of the town. It rests peacefully away from the traffic.

To explore the area north of Wadebridge, begin at **Egloshayle** (estuary church) on the A389 Bodmin road. The church itself lies on the corner of a lane but is impressive with its 80ft high tower. Inside there is a door which commemorates the fact that Vicar Loveybond (Elizabethan variant of Lovebone) gave both the tower and a grand east window of five lights. The dedication is thought to be to St Conan which is unusual in Cornwall.

The lane climbs and twists away to Above Town, turns left, then right at the next junction where it meets unexpected country and one of the few corn mills still working. The bridge over the River Allen is scarcely a car's width which indicates the narrowness of the way ahead to **St Mabyn**, a village of many footpaths — all worth exploring.

Three miles beyond lies well kept **St Tudy**, where there is much of interest. Born and buried here was Richard Lower, the first to

*Memorial on the wall of
St Tudy church to
Charles Bligh*

perform an operation of blood transfusion direct from one animal into the vein of another and then from man to man. He became the most noted physician in London and was in attendance on Charles II. Unfortunately his interest in politics was ill-timed and the Titus Oates affair caused him to lose everything — his position, his practice, his credit and his Fellowship of The Royal Society. He died at the age of sixty in 1691. There is a monument to Charles Bligh, a member of this St Tudy family, on the wall of St Tudy church, and Captain W. Bligh of *Bounty* fame was born here.

North from here along the B3266 the village of **Michaelstow** shelters in a valley where the blue and white of wild bluebells and garlic make the churchyard a lovely sight in early summer. High above this protected community the Iron Age earthwork is named on the map as Helsbury Castle. Within it is the ruin of a chapel and not far away is Helsbury Farm and Helstone, recalling the possibility of an original

Port Gaverne

cult which worshipped the sun (*howl* in Cornish). When Christianity came to the area, a chapel was built to exorcise the pagan associations and was dedicated to St Michael, whose name was also given to the place where people had settled in the valley below.

It does not matter which of the narrow lanes you take from here to cross the A39 and reach **St Teath**. This is another village which has long since lost its former importance. The church, which is in the centre, was built within a circular Celtic site and so follows the worshipping tradition of centuries but there is now no trace of the collegiate institution once established here. Better remembered, perhaps, is Ann Jefferies who was born in the early seventeenth century when witch hunts were beginning. She entered the service of Moses Pitt, a man unexpectedly well educated for those times. From him she learnt about the healing powers of herbs and helped many with her knowledge. Unfortunately, one of the harsh Tregeagles was jealous of her popularity and had her committed to Bodmin Gaol as a witch. But, though she was deprived of food, she survived her ordeal and was eventually released. Then she married a Padstow man and carried on with her work of healing until she died.

The countryside picture changes now with open land much more in evidence as the byways join the B3314 and climb to Tregeare Rounds where the lane before Pendoggett turns sharply towards the sea. As the road nears the coast, the number of footpaths increases — all leading down the valleys and along the cliffs towards Port Gaverne, Port Isaac and Port Quin.

Each of these places has a different history, and has been important in its own way since before Tudor times. **Port Gaverne** used to support a thriving pilchard industry which brought prosperity to the small community even as late as the nineteenth century. The National Trust now owns the beach and two groups of cellars where fishermen used to make and store their pots, nets, sails and gear as well as process their catch.

The name of **Port Isaac** often puzzles those unfamiliar with the Cornish language. It means simply the 'corn port' (*porthysow*) — although it once had additional trade in pilchards and supported a good trade in slate. Now its narrow, twisting streets tumble down to the postage-stamp beach where visitors pay to park their cars in season. It is a place popular with artists, lovers of small buidings like doll's houses and those who like walking — a special attraction in the very heart of it is 'The Birdcage', a delightful, high, narrow house, recently acquired by the National Trust.

From here the coastal footpath keeps faithfully to the cliffs but motorists have to run inland through **St Endellion**. The church is another of the various collegiate establishments in Cornwall and has both an interesting history and specially fine bench ends. The ringers' rhyme in the tower is noteworthy as it was written by Nicholas Roscarrock, a recusant whose manor, Tresungers, still retains its former Tudor grandeur and is considered by some to be Cornwall's finest seventeenth-century building. Today, however, most visitors go to St Endellion to enjoy the annual festival of music and drama which is held at the end of July.

Port Quin is a sad, beautiful place — a place of tragedy. It now belongs to the National Trust who have adapted the fishermen's cottages, and the tiny cove, once again, has a cared-for look. In the last century this hamlet was home to fishermen and others employed at the Doyden antimony mine. But eventually it failed and the miners

PLACES OF INTEREST NORTH OF THE CAMEL ESTUARY

Tregeare Rounds
2 miles NNE of St Kew
A site with a curious slope to the ramparts, suggesting a cattle enclosure rather than defence.

Doyden Castle
Port Quin
Can be seen on a cliff walk from Port Quin to Rumps. Let as a holiday home.

Helsbury Castle
Michaelstow
Iron Age earthwork and ruined chapel.

Tresungers Manor
St Endellion
Seventeenth century. Privately owned and not open to the public.

The Rumps
Pentire Point
(National Trust)
A fine example of an Iron Age cliff castle, one of the best in Cornwall.

Trewornan Bridge
(B3314)
A deceptive bridge, apparently medieval but in fact Georgian.

emigrated to Canada. At a later date all the remaining men of the little port sailed out together to fish, were caught in a storm and none survived. Small wonder that Port Quin is known as the village that died, for that is exactly what it did do and is only slowly coming to life again now.

Doyden Castle which looks down from the cliffs edging the cove was built as a gambling retreat in 1839 by a colourful character called Samuel Symons whose home was near Wadebridge. The National Trust bought it and so it is kept in good order.

Seven hundred acres of the land from Trevan Point to **The Rumps** and Polzeath Beach belong to the National Trust. Saved from bungalow development by popular appeal in 1935, this fine historic promontory might be considered a poet's memorial. Lawrence Binyon sat on this headland and found inspiration for his famous poem *For The Fallen*, with the words that are quoted on Remembrance Day throughout Britain:

'They shall grow not old, as we that are left grow old
Age shall not weary them, nor the years condemn.
At the going down of the sun and in the morning
We will remember them.'

Port Isaac

 May is the best time to come here for the flowers are specially lovely then and this is one of the few places where pillow-lava — a volcanic rock which looks like pumice-stone — reaches the surface. Still quite visible are the ruins of an Iron Age cliff castle.

Just below lies Polzeath Beach, fine for surfing and consequently very popular. The Doom Bar opposite Daymer Bay is composed of sand which is especially good for fertilising and has its own legend. The story goes that a mermaid had once guarded the port of Padstow, but after being mortally wounded by a young man who was tired of her advances, she cursed the place, withdrew her protection and caused the sand to pile up and hinder shipping. It still does, but has now become a blessing as its benefits to farmers are a partial compensation for the loss of shipping revenue.

Rock has wide and beautiful sands and is an estuary beloved by both artists and yachtsmen because of its rare combination of colour and sheltered freedom. It is also a place for sportsmen who tire of the sea — **St Enodoc** has a golf course nearby. The little chapel at St Enodoc was buried in the sands but dug out and restored in 1863. It

The entrance to the harbour, Port Quin

is mainly Norman but both tower and spire are unusual in Cornwall —
the latter dating from the thirteenth century. Sir John Betjeman, the
Poet Laureate who died in 1983, chose to be buried here because he
loved Cornwall dearly and the area of the Camel estuary best of all.

The road back to Wadebridge lies through **St Minver**, another
village famous for its bellringers. Like St Endellion, the church has a
painted ringers' rhyme and, like Lostwithiel, a broached spire.

Trewarnon Bridge which takes the traffic over the River Amble is
of particular interest as it is perhaps the only one built after the Reformation that is worth looking at. It has all the appearance of a medieval
design with similar pointed arches, but it is, in fact, little more than a
century old and was built by the Georgian squires who found riches
under the ground and controlled the destinies of Cornwall through
their wealth.

8   BODMIN & THE MOOR

The town of **Bodmin**, Cornwall's geographical centre, stands on the Moor beside the River Camel where the twentieth-century A30 (bypassed in 1976) crosses the ancient trade route from Ireland to Europe. Its name means 'abode of monks' for the town grew up around the priory which had been built by St Petroc's followers who settled here in the fifth century. In 1086, Bodmin was Cornwall's only town and has since been a coinage centre, a meeting place for the Assize Courts (which have now been moved to Truro) and the home of Cornwall's Infantry Regiment. But when Truro became the cathedral city, Bodmin's importance rapidly declined and an air of regret for what might have been still seems to linger in the town.

There are, however, a number of interesting places to visit both in and around Bodmin. St Petroc's is an imposing building and the largest parish church in Cornwall. Under lock and key in an ivory casket, the relics of the saint are preserved — so precious that when a jeweller was asked to value them he said he could not because they were beyond all price. In 1177 these same relics were stolen by an Augustinian monk but were later recovered by Prior Roger of Bodmin after some brilliant religious detective work. Each year, at the annual mayoral elections, the treasures are taken out of the church and carried in procession through the town. At the lower end of the churchyard, down Priory Road, is St Guron's Well set in the wall at the roundabout. This is believed to be named after a little-known Celtic saint who came here even before Petroc.

A few hundred yards up Turf Street is Mount Folly, probably the old friary garden, as Folly is a corruption of a Cornish word with that meaning. The Great Hall used to be the Assize Court and in the nearby Guildhall are two relics from the past. One is a bell, the other a stone corn measure inscribed 'However ye sell - BF 1563 - your measure fyll'; perhaps a warning that the local Weights and Measures

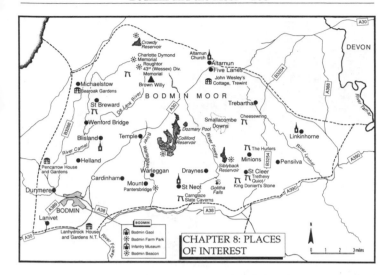

CHAPTER 8: PLACES
OF INTEREST

official was keeping watch for cheats. Close by is the Turret Clock, a reminder of what happened after the 1549 Prayer Book Rebellion. It was here that the mayor of Bodmin, Nicholas Boyer, was hanged for his part in the uprising.

Today the names of Belling and Quiller-Couch are probably better remembered than that of Boyer. John Belling (1680–1761) was a burgess and clockmaker in the town. Today his descendants manufacture electrical equipment used throughout the world. Sir Arthur Quiller-Couch (1863–1944), known as 'Q' was the internationally accepted author who was born in Bodmin. Opposite St Guron's Well, on the wall of the *Cornish Guardian* offices, a memorial plaque marks 'Q's birthplace.

The right fork at the top of Turf Street leads to the 160ft Beacon, a pleasant picnic area with fine views. The 144ft obelisk at its summit commemorates General Walter Raleigh Gilbert who was given a baronetcy by Queen Victoria for his distinguished service in India.

At the top of St Nicholas Street are the War Memorial and The Keep where the Duke of Cornwall's Light Infantry Regimental Museum is housed. There is no charge for admission and even for those with little interest in military matters there is much to catch the eye among the collection of guns, standards, medals and regimental

Lanhydrock —
the gatehouse

Lanhydrock —
the house, gardens
and church

memorabilia which covers 250 years.

From here, Halgavor Road leads down to moorland where a Mock Mayor's Court was held in medieval times. The name, translated from the Cornish, means 'fine for tin streaming and keeping goats' (therefore Goats' Moor). The latest OS map retains the old name in the area south of Bodmin and is marked 'Halgavor Moor' (SX 072652).

Beyond Halgavor Plantation lies Lanhydrock — about $2^1/_2$ miles south-east of Bodmin. Here is everything that most visitors could wish for to enjoy a day of varied pleasure in and around the estate. It is a seventeenth-century house largely rebuilt after a fire in 1881, superbly sited above the Fowey valley and Respryn Bridge. There are thirty-six rooms open to view in the house alone.

Respryn Bridge was one of the most important in Cornwall during the Civil War and was held for King Charles when Royalists were encircling the Parliamentarian troops at Lostwithiel in 1644. Four

A view of Bodmin Moor from Alex Tor

years later, however, although Cromwell's victory was not generally celebrated in Cornwall, Lord Robartes, who owned the estate and had made his fortune from tin, wool and banking, planted an avenue of trees at Lanhydrock and so proclaimed his allegiance to the Roundhead cause.

The Long Gallery was untouched by the fire and in this 116ft room the magnificent plaster ceiling depicting scenes from the Old Testament is still in perfect condition. The many acres of garden and woodland given to the National Trust — the latest as recently as 1970 by the 8th Viscount Clifden — are particularly beautiful with fine shrubs, formal gardens and woodland walks. They include Brownqueen Wood which was the monks' deer park when Lanhydrock belonged to St Petroc's Priory before the Dissolution. The gatehouse (1651) and church are also interesting. There are open-air theatre and other events in summer and a music festival in November.

Two other holiday attractions also lie in this direction. One is the Forestry Commission's Silvermine Trail or Bluebell Walk, reached by taking the Fletcher's Bridge turning at the first junction beyond Carminow Cross. At that point, in the fields lies Castle Canyke, one of the chain of Celtic Iron Age settlements serving prehistoric tin-streamers and later used on the Ireland to Brittany trade route across mid-Cornwall. The second is Bodmin Farm Park, well signposted after the A38 Liskeard Road. This is a place of family entertainment where donkey rides, a nature trail, friendly farm animals and a collection of old farm tools provide enjoyment for most members of the family.

The area south-west of Bodmin along the A389 is equally fascinating. **Lanivet**'s Panda Inn sign puzzles most people who see it for the first time. But the explanation is simple — the bamboos which thrive in this valley went to the London Zoo to feed Chi-Chi, that most important animal. A chapel tower rising mysteriously behind a charming slate-hung house is another of this village's curiosities. It is, in fact, the remains of St Benet's Abbey, a leper hospital in 1411 and a Courtenay mansion in the sixteenth century. Now it is an excellent licensed restaurant where meals are served in the old gatehouse.

The lane opposite the Panda Inn leads to the old Bodmin-Truro coach road — a straight up-and-over way with fine views at the top. Just beyond the farmstead of Mount Pleasant, as this road joins the A30, a lane on the right leads off into a mass of narrow byways of peace and quiet. Through Lower Woodley and Ruthernbridge, with its ancient packhorse bridge, the lane climbs beside a wildlife sanctuary, past peaceful farms, numerous little unnamed bridges and on to the old granite cottages clustering round **Withiel** church. In June a festival of flowers and music tempts visitors to linger in this remote village with its many footpaths branching away from the church.

A short distance on the right along the Roche road is another byway — this one leads to the tiny village of **St Wenn**. The church is another high and lonely place but is of special interest because of its sundial warning over the porch. Even on a bright day in summer, this place remains solemn. 'Ye Know Not When' say the letters on the face of the old time-keeper. The country all round here is green and uncluttered and the lanes meander across the valley past Rosenannon to St Breock Downs and the prehistoric longstone or, in the brilliance of furze and heather, to Nanstallon, Dunmere and Bodmin.

Bodmin is where one of Cornwall's ancient customs used to be celebrated and is occasionally revived. This was the Bodmin Riding, a horseback procession in July, when guildsmen rode to the priory, received garlands and, after a church service proceeded to take part in various sporting events. The revivals have been held in a more

PLACES OF INTEREST IN AND AROUND BODMIN

St Petroc's Church
Largest parish church in Cornwall.

Gilbert Monument
Beacon
High above Bodmin a memorial 144ft high was erected to Sir Walter Raleigh Gilbert.

Duke of Cornwall's Light Infantry Regimental Museum
The Keep
Cornwall's premier military museum.

Bodmin Gaol
Cardell Road
A chilling exhibition of prison life with pillory, stocks, dungeon and execution block, well presented and maintained. Shop and restaurant.

Lanhydrock
2¹/₂ miles SE Bodmin
(National Trust)
A seventeenth-century house,
largely rebuilt after fire in 1881. The gatehouse (1651) and north wing are unaltered. Good restaurant facilities.

Castle Canyke
Iron Age hill fort sited between Padstow and Fowey near Bodmin beside lane off B3268 from the Regimental Museum

The Candle Shop
Dunmere Road, Bodmin
Cornwall's largest selection of candles.

Bodmin Farm Park
Fletcher's Bridge
Ideal for children, with nature trails and friendly farm animals.

Pencarrow
Off the A389 and B3266 at Washaway
Historic Georgian mansion owned and occupied by the Molesworth-St Aubyns. Refreshments.

sober vein than those of former times which were probably to honour pagan gods and subsequently accompanied by the wild revelry customary on such occasions.

Along Dunmere Road (A389 to Wadebridge) on the edge of an industrial estate, is the Candle Shop, small but worth visiting. Cornwall's largest selection of candles are made here and include such unusual items as 'fruit salad' candles which make interesting Christmas gifts. This establishment is only open from May to September.

Farther along the road to **Washaway** is a sign to Pencarrow, one of the few fine mansions open to the public and still lived in by the owners. It stands in a perfect setting of 50 acres of formal and

A Celtic cross on Bodmin Moor — one of the many ancient remains in this area

woodland gardens cared for by the owners, the Molesworth-St Aubyns. The house is at the end of a mile-long drive (which was cut through an ancient British encampment) past fine rhododendrons, camellias and hydrangeas — all under the shelter of towering beech trees. It was probably built about 1771, but the estate has actually been in the family since the reign of Elizabeth I. The owners are often about the grounds and always have a welcome for visitors, which is something that should put it at the top of anyone's itinerary.

Not many people would choose to live in a prison but when such a place is one of the most unusual museums in the country and the work on site means being in charge of a restaurant and shop as well as the collection of exhibits, the picture might look different. Bodmin Gaol on Cardell Road is the home of Denise and Terry Gilhooly whose enthusiasm for the accurate presentation of history is evident even at

The fifteenth-century bridge at Helland

the entrance to this award-winning place where models of inmates 'stare' at you from narrow windows.

The prison is almost 200 years old and was built because Launceston Gaol, apart from being too small and delapidated, was not central enough. Former days are made very real now by the skilful use of models and properties from the Royal Shakespeare Company while clever lighting and sound effects have been incorporated to recreate startling scenes. At strategic points round the prison complex large information boards not only explain the numerous tableaux but also give background details about life in the gaol at the relevant periods.

One intriguing story, still shrouded in secrecy tells that the Crown Jewels and the Domesday Book were stored here for safety during World War I. The idea was that if an invasion were to take place the treasures could easily be taken to Falmouth and shipped to the secure haven of America. No-one knows just how true the story is but in spite of all doubt, local people accept it as a fact.

Since its closure, Bodmin Gaol has been used for purposes varying from manufacturing engineering products to a nightclub. Now its present use as a museum is probably better suited to its structure, although the château-like main gates are so handsome that they seem almost a misrepresentation of the tragic events once enacted within the walls.

It is easy enough to reach the centre of Bodmin Moor by driving straight along the A30. Much more interesting is the route through lush valleys which make the Moor itself seem even starker by comparison when it is reached at last. Opposite the Hole in the Wall public house on the A30 ringroad, Pool Lane leaves the town through Berry Lane and quickly away from the general hustle and bustle. The high land here gives views over the River Camel as does the village of **Helland**. This small place has a church with one of Cornwall's oldest memorials and an old mill house with a delightful herb garden. Deep in the valley below is an early fifteenth-century bridge in fine condition (probably because it is away from main roads).

For centuries, every donkey in Cornwall was known as the miner's friend but there are few to be seen here today. Memories of former days are still alive at Helland Bridge — nearby there is a place where these gentle animals were once kept. It is called Donkeys' Pool.

Not far from the Longstone crossroads on the B3266 is Colesent. Although this is a dead end it is worth the short detour to see the woods below and possibly the Bodmin-Wenford railway at work.

There are views from here over the Camel but motorists will have to make other choices. One way is through the tiny hamlet of **Merry Meeting** — a place to visit just for the name, though it is quiet and charming. Up-river lies **Wenford Bridge**, so small that many pass it by, but for many years, until his death in 1983, it was home and workshop to the internationally-famous potter Michael Cardew. Still active in his eighties he had enough energy to create works of art envied by many and right up till his death his enthusiasm and fascination for the craft of pottery remained undiminished.

There is a pleasant walk from here down the railway track to **Dunmere**. It is a 7-mile stretch but even a short distance is relaxing. Avoid Monday, Wednesday and Friday, however, if you plan to enjoy this walk, because on those days china clay wagons use the track, keeping alive what is thought to be Cornwall's oldest mineral railway.

Moorland travel consists very much of criss-crossing rivers or avoiding them altogether. From Wenford Bridge it is a question of taking the short route south on the east of the Camel and passing china clay works, then crossing the De Lank River to **Blisland**. Much has been written about this village because it looks so different from every other one in Cornwall. Granite cottages, the Manor House and the old inn are set round what is almost a village green. The dedication of the church to St Protus and St Hyacinth is rare. So is the building's beautiful interior with its breathtaking rood screen, restored in 1896 in pre-Reformation style and one of the finest in Britain.

Away from the village, on Pendrift Common, is Jubilee Rock. It is 700ft above sea level and so the views from here are excellent. In 1809 a Lieutenant Rogers made a place for himself in history by carving this great boulder with coats of arms of royalty and noble families as well as various symbols of agriculture and industry.

From Blisland, beside the Manor House, two other roads twist to the north and climb higher to moorland, where visitors can find a place to picnic and get a different view of the Camel before taking the Bradford road to **Kerrow Downs**, a wild area, but not like Stevenson's 'naked moor' because the boulders and heathers provide a low landscape that is so characteristic of Cornwall's moorland regions. There is an old clapper bridge at **Bradford** and it is tempting to sit beside it and think of the days when it was busy with sheep, shepherds and wool merchants with their packhorses laden for market.

There is another clapper bridge at **Dulphy** which carries the narrow road over boulder-strewn moorland to **St Breward** which, at 720ft above sea level, is Cornwall's highest village. This whole area was more thickly populated by prehistoric man than anywhere else in the region. Hut circles, stripple stones, stone circles and the unexcavated King Arthur's Hall are all within walking distance. There is plenty of scenery here to fire the imagination. Like Luxulyan, this is another granite village, solidly built against all weather. The stone for the houses and cottages came from nearby De Lank quarries which also sent granite to London's Blackfriar's Bridge, the Wolf Rock Lighthouse, Eddystone and Beachy Head Lighthouses, too, as well as harbours and other buildings in distant parts of the world.

There are various ways from here to Roughtor including several moorland paths. The quickest for motorists is to drive down the steep hill into the woods at **Tuckingmill** and turn either left or right. The latter route, which passes eventually through **Watergate**, is for those prepared to brave some very narrow but lovely lanes. The more straightforward road over the Gam Bridge goes right along the B3266

PLACES OF INTEREST ON BODMIN MOOR BETWEEN THE A30 AND A39

Blisland Church
Edge of Moor
Dedication to St Protus and St Hyacinth. Village green not often seen in Cornwall. Main feature of church is rood screen.

Roughtor
Charlotte Dymond Memorial
3 miles SE Camelford

Memorial to young girl murdered by sweetheart; he was hanged at Bodmin.
Bronze Age remains.

Crowdy Reservoir
Off A39 Camelford-Bude road
Walks all round but for other pursuits permits are needed.

near to Michaelstow, but at **Valley Truckle** just before Helstone, turns to Watergate and the moor again. Truckle is a misformation of Tucking with its wool trade associations.

Roughtor, sometimes spelt Rowtor, is understandably popular and in the season the small car park is rarely empty. Here Forestry Commission woods are pleasing to the eye in this barren treeless locality. Near the stream is a monument marking the spot where the unfortunate eighteen-year old Charlotte Dymond was murdered in 1844 by her lover who was hanged at Bodmin for his crime. The National Trust own 174 acres of the land about Roughtor which, rising to 1,300ft, is the second highest point in Cornwall. It was a Bronze Age settlement and remains include hut circles and enclosed fields with signs of lynchet cultivation. This tor, was given to the Trust in 1951 by Sir Richard Onslow, as the 43rd (Wessex) Division memorial to its men who died in World War II. The bronze tablet is set within foundations of the ruined chapel of St Michael.

The signpost at the crossroads along Jubilee road past Roughtor Farm points to Davidstow. About a mile along is Crowdy Reservoir which shines a deep aquamarine on bright summer days. There are opportunities here for windsurfing, and birdwatching from a special hide, but permission must first be obtained from the South-West Water Authority.

The sudden flatness of the road through Davidstow Woods is a strange contrast to much of the countryside. Crossing a deserted airfield it skirts the northern edge of Bodmin Moor along softer lanes

Altarnun church

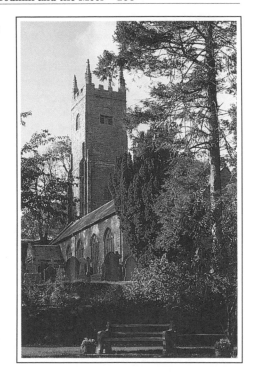

leading to **Altarnun**. Here the old Launceston to Bodmin road used
to carry coaches over the picturesque fifteenth-century bridge in the
centre of this tiny village, the heart of Cornwall's largest parish. Beside
it is the Cathedral of the Moor, a handsome building dedicated to St
Non, mother of the Welsh St David. The church is as fine inside as out,
with seventy-nine Tudor bench ends and massive piers, each pillar
made from a single piece of moorstone. Northey Burnard's slate
carvings in the churchyard are said to equal the best in Europe. There
are home-made teas available here before moving on to Five Lanes,
the A30 and Trewint, famed for its associations with John Wesley. A
Burnard carving of Wesley's head should be noticed on the façade of
the Methodist chapel at Altarnun.

Isbell Cottage, **Trewint**, lies in a lane which runs parallel to the A30
and it was here that Wesley stayed six times with the hospitable

Elizabeth and Digory Isbell, conducting services from the stone porch and on one occasion baptising one of their babies. He journeyed to Cornwall in an endeavour to bring people back to the Anglican church which he begged them never to forsake. But events took quite a different turn, resulting in the establishment of the Methodist movement which caused the great eighteenth-century schism in the Church of England. After some time the Trewint rooms fell into decay but in 1948–50 they were restored to their eighteenth-century style. Now a special service is held annually here on Wesley Day, 24 May — others on Sunday afternoons during July and August.

The highest place in Cornwall, **Brown Willy** (1,375ft), lies behind Jamaica Inn, an eighteenth-century coaching stage made famous by Daphne du Maurier's novel of the same name, in the tiny hamlet of **Bolventor**. The hill is reached only by footpaths, as the nearest road stops at Codda, about a mile in from the A30. The source of the River Fowey is between nearby Maiden Tor and Buttern Hill.

Opposite Jamaica Inn there is a road which leads to one of Cornwall's mysteries — **Dozmary Pool**. In the midst of nowhere it seems, this area of water is reminiscent of lines by R.L. Stevenson about 'a naked moor, and a shivering pool.' In 1533 Dozmary was reported to be fourteen fathoms deep but no one knows how it exists as no stream flows into it and it drains no part of the moor. One legend says that there is an underground connection with the sea, possibly because the name means 'drop of sea'. It has a strange unearthly beauty and an exhilarating brilliance that attracts people whether they want to solve its riddles or not. Two legends remain very firmly associated with this interesting place. One about King Arthur and Excalibur, another how the villain Tregeagle lost mansion and parklands beneath these waters and was condemned to empty Dozmary using only a limpet shell with a hole in it.

A short distance away at **Colliford** beside a new reservoir is the Colliford Lake Park Complex where many endangered species of animals can be seen in the 60-acre conservation area. Of different interest is the twelfth-century Cornish Long House, a single-storey dwelling with a thatched roof and cob walls typical of the period — a rare sight in the region.

Walkers can cross the moor to **Temple**, but motorists have to return to the A30 and drive towards Bodmin, turning left on to the old

PLACES OF INTEREST ON THE CENTRAL MOORLAND

Altarnun Church
Off A30 at Five Lanes
Known as the Cathedral of the
Moor, this handsome building
rises beside a packhorse bridge in
the village, once on the coach
route from Launceston to Bodmin.
Slate memorials in churchyard
carved by Northey Burnard,
unusual jester and fiddler on pew
ends in church.

Isbell Cottage
Trewint
Off A30
A place of pilgrimage for Methodists. John Wesley stayed here
several times during his evangel-
ist journeys to Cornwall. On 24
May open-air services are held
here. This cottage is not a
museum but has many treasures.

Jamaica Inn
Bolventor
Now popular restaurant. Buildings
genuinely Georgian but spoilt
inside with simulated Tudor. Still
retains some old-world charm.

Dozmary Pool
2 miles from Bolventor turn off A30
A place of mystery first used by
Neolithic man — hundreds of
artifacts have been found here.
Associations with King Arthur and
Tregeagle.

Colliford Lake Park Complex
Near Dozmary Pool
A delightfully sited area of 60
acres with many endangered
species and twelfth-century
Cornish Long House. Lakeside
walks, pets corner, picnic areas.
Refreshments, restaurant.

coach road to this hamlet. From the china clay works at Hawk's Tor
there is a track which leads through Temple. It was the old way for
tinners who, having won their ore from that great granite outcrop,
guided laden packhorses down the Warleggan valley to the harbour
of Lostwithiel. The simple church stands on the site of a house built
by the Knights Templars as a hospice for pilgrims on their way to the
Mount. It was that foundation which eventually put it outside episcopal
jurisdiction to become Cornwall's Gretna Green with an unsavoury
reputation. That extra-legal status continued till about 1744.

To explore the southern area it is advisable to start from Bodmin
where the A38 dips into the Glynn valley woods; there has been a
considerable amount of road widening here recently but it is still
delightful, especially in spring and autumn. The road runs close to the
River Fowey and provides easy access for fishermen.

Trethevy Quoit

At the far end of this valley, from Doublebois, narrow, bouldery lanes, colourful in spring, climb to the quiet grey village of **St Cleer** which has several interesting features, its handsome church tower, and the roadside holy well carefully restored by Captain Rogers in 1864 as a memorial to his grandfather, the Reverend John Jope, vicar of St Cleer, 1776–1844.

From St Cleer, the road leads to Trethevy Quoit, an ancient monument standing in a field at the back of some cottages — seeming to guard them. It is a megalithic chamber, 7ft long and about 9ft high. The shape is that of a capstone supported by five uprights. It is believed to have been constructed some 4,000 years ago by Bronze Age people for use as a burial chamber for their tribesmen. These huge granite slabs were probably taken from the moor but it is not yet known what method was used to place such great weights into position.

Across the road from here is the Trequoit Pottery, a small workshop with free parking and a good display of original stoneware.

Beyond the Crow's Nest hamlet more narrow lanes climb up to open moorland below Caradon Hill. In this landscape of deserted

The Cheesewring

mines, **Pensilva** seems to be at the top of its own quiet world. Yet in the mid-nineteenth century it and the surrounding villages were so crowded that they looked more like the mining camps of Colorado and the far West. Today the moors are for sheep and those who enjoy walks away from roads. It is a pleasant, easy path up to Caradon where, as well as views to Brown Willy, Plymouth and Dartmoor, there are blueberries to pick in summer.

North of Pensilva are **Caradon Town** and **Linkinhorne**, once both busy mining centres, but the former is now only a handful of houses. Linkinhorne church, set in its frame of trees, has an unusually handsome granite tower and fine wall paintings rediscovered as recently as 1891 and representing the Seven Works of Mercy and the Seven Deadly Sins. Here, too, is Daniel Gumb's memorial. He was a unique Cornishman who lived with his wife and children in a house built under a granite slab near the Cheesewring on the moor. But he was no idler. He taught himself mathematics and the works of Euclid

The Hurlers Stone Circles, near Minions

Terverbyn Bridge over the River Fowey, near St Neot

in order to study astronomy, working out the more complicated geometric problems on rocks. His carvings can still be seen by those with really keen eyes.

Beyond Coad's Green on the B3257, a narrow lane on the left

PLACES OF INTEREST ON THE MOORLAND EAST OF THE RIVER FOWEY

St Cleer Well
In 1858 water flowed from here but only into a muddy pool to which villagers brought their cattle. Captain Henry Rogers, RN bought the land because of the chapel ruins on it, later restoring it in memory of his grandfather.

Trethevy Quoit
Near St Cleer
A handsome prehistoric burial chamber of five standing stones and a capstone. There is free access at all times.

Cheesewring
Near Minions
Not a prehistoric monolith but a natural formation of rock weathered to this shape. The nearby quarry is used by the Royal Navy to train men in abseiling.

The Hurlers Stone Circles
Near Minions

These ancient megaliths have given rise to the usual legends of men turned to stone for playing on Sunday. They are, in fact, excellent examples of three Neolithic or very early Bronze Age stone circles. Excavation at the nearby Rillaton Barrow revealed a gold cup, now in the British Museum.

King Doniert Stone
Common Moor
A finely preserved wayside monument to King Doniert with a clearly defined pattern of interlacing on both cross shafts. Probably of the ninth century.

Siblyback Reservoir
1 mile through Common Moor
An extensive recreational area with space for walks and relaxation even for those without Water Authority permits.

leads downhill to Trebartha and East Moor. From Trebartha Barton, a lane ends in lonely moorland high among prehistoric hut circles. There are paths everywhere and numerous places to explore — **Smallacombe Downs** being particularly exciting with its views over King Arthur's Bed and the River Fowey on the far side.

Twelve Men's Moor is here, too, an ancient tin-streaming area known for seven centuries by that name. History records that in 1284 the prior of Launceston granted a lease there to twelve hard-working tinners. Among them were men with names that deserve to be recorded, such as Boglawoda, Cada, Foth, Trewortha and Broda. The road from Berriowbridge to Henwood, so busy in the past, is wooded and delightful, climbing up again to moorland. It is so peaceful yet so full of memories, with old engine houses and mine chimneys.

At **Minions**, parts of an old mineral railway track can still be seen and in numerous places nearby there are Neolithic and Bronze Age monuments. Paths from this hamlet lead to the Cheesewring where, until the 1950s, quantities of silver-grey granite were quarried and sent to Liskeard and Looe to be exported. Today the place serves a different purpose. It is used by naval apprentices learning the disciplines of abseiling into the 150ft quarry. But the main fascination of this place for most people is the strange stone formation called the Cheesewring. It is the remains of a cairn where large thick oval slabs balance precariously. The rocks, about 22ft high and 17ft in diameter have been formed by nature and weathered over the years to the fantastic shape that remains.

Beside Minions is **Caradon** — its modern television mast at the top of the 1,210ft hill. On the right, past the houses is a notice to The Hurlers Stone Circles. These strangely-shaped stones have, not unnaturally, given rise to local legends. Whatever the legend says, the facts are that these shapes suit their environment and add to the feeling of Cornwall's past that lingers still on Bodmin Moor.

At Common Moor, a lane on the right leads to Siblyback Reservoir, one of the best recreational reservoirs in Cornwall. Those who want to fish or sail need permission from the South-West Water Authority but otherwise there are walks and picnic areas for the general public.

There is another English Heritage site, King Doniert Stone, at the roadside just beyond Common Moor. Here, however, are actual historical records carved on two granite monoliths. One is inscribed with the Latin words *Doniert Rogavit Pro Anima* — 'Doniert prayed for his soul'. Doniert is thought to have been Durngarth, King of Cornwall in the latter half of the ninth century.

Redgate lies at the crossroads where there is a signpost to the hamlet of **Draynes** (originally Drayness) — its bridge probably the first over the Fowey. It was recorded in 1362 and carries a very ancient track from Caradon to Bodmin. Here a car park is close to the footpath which leads through dense beech woods to the Golitha Falls. The water cascades for over half a mile of twisting cataracts and the Fowey is seen in majestic splendour. The pronounciation is 'Goleetha' which means obstruction.

The Draynes to **St Neot** road is undulating, sloping steeply to this

The Golitha Falls

remote village. High beside the road stands the church dedicated to
a kindly dwarf. The interior is famous for its well preserved fifteenth-century and early sixteenth-century stained glass conveying the impressive beauty of pre-Reformation windows. They tell the story of the Christian religion from the Creation but the windows of St Neot and St George were later additions. Look for the five historic crosses in the churchyard.

Although there is little now to indicate a busy industrial past, St Neot and the Loveny valley were much involved with the wool trade as well as silver, copper, tin and slate. A short distance down the wooded valley are the Carnglaze Slate Caverns, known to have been worked from ancient times. Visitors taken round on guided tours can see another aspect of the Cornishman's skill when confronted with the need to 'win' any substance from under the surface. One of the

PLACES OF INTEREST ON THE MOORLAND WEST OF THE RIVER FOWEY

Golitha Falls
3 miles N Dobwalls
Here the River Fowey cascades through deep woodland over shelves of smooth rock once obstructing its path. Parking facilities by the road at the entrance to the Falls. The path starts across the road and entrance is free. Toilet facilities.

St Neot Church
2 miles N A38 Glynn valley
Rare dedication to a pious dwarf. Probably a Cornish hermit and one who loved animals as suggested by the windows.

Seventeen stained glass lights are priceless, dating from the sixteenth century.

Carnglaze Slate Caverns
Near St Neot
Underground slate caverns of unknown extent though work has been done here for over 200 years. Startling lake.

Pantersbridge
2 miles E of St Neot
Interesting double bridge over two streams which carried the old coach road from Liskeard to Bodmin.

surprises is the great lake, a sight as dramatic as the Blue Grotto on Capri.

The road back to the moor leaves St Neot and climbs to Goonzion Downs and Pantersbridge — a name with a double meaning, appropriate for a double bridge. A charter of 1241 mentions a place on the high road to Bodmin called Pontiesu, named by the Knights Templars as 'Jesus Bridge' or Pontjesus and later corrupted to Pantersbridge. It has charm in its own right, and the second roadway, which eventually took the increasing traffic from Liskeard to Bodmin, is something that adds to its character.

Due north is a farm track to **Warleggan** — one of the names Winston Graham used in his *Poldark* books. The village is today a desolate, ghostly place, almost deserted, perhaps because the last resident vicar, disapproving of the congregation, locked them out of the church and afterwards preached to cardboard figures.

The way back to Bodmin passes through **Mount** and **Cardinham**. Here, two ruined castles and echoes of the ancient nobility still remain.

9 NORTH CORNWALL

Robert of Mortain established **Launceston** as Cornwall's northern gateway and ancient capital when he built his strategic keep
in about 1067 at the top of precipitous slopes overlooking the Tamar.
He probably built Polston Bridge at the same time, thus re-routing the
ancient pilgrim way from Kilkhampton. The first charter of Launceston's Borough Archives proudly calls the new road *Via Regalis
Cornubiensis* — The 'Royal Cornish Way'.

Ownership of land was still a feudal matter in Norman times,
especially in the case of Polston Bridge. Estates in Cardinham were
only given conditionally — the condition being that when the Earl of
Cornwall crossed the Tamar at this point, the Lord of Cardinham
would meet him and, bearing his riding cloak, stay with him for 40 days
or as long as he was in Cornwall. This ancient feudal custom still holds
good, though today's dues are different. Prince Charles, who is Duke
of Cornwall, went to Launceston in 1973 and received his rights from
the Lord-Lieutenant. They were a brace of greyhounds called Whisky
and Soda.

English Heritage is responsible for the upkeep of Launceston
Castle which is a fine monument overlooking the town and the surrounding countryside. A cylindrical keep and ruined curtain walls are
all that remain, but it is still worth a visit if only to understand its
importance as a strategic site.

Immediately below, in Castle Street, is Lawrence House Museum,
a handsome period house full of exhibits relating to the history of the
town and neighbouring places. It is one of Cornwall's finest museums
— its moulded plaster ceilings are particularly fine. A steep road —
with one-way traffic down — leads to the parish church past the
Cornish Cobblers, a shoe-repairer's with a difference. The only ☀
leather used comes from the Grampound Tannery where the Crog-
gan brothers prepared skins for Tim Severin to sail his curragh, *St*

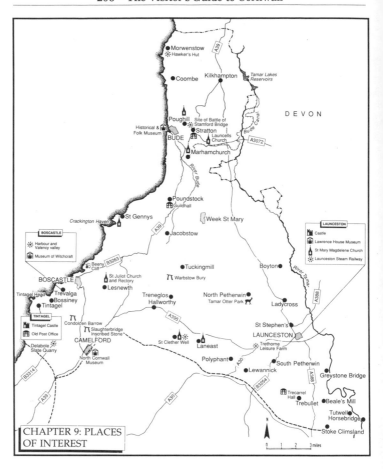

CHAPTER 9: PLACES
OF INTEREST

Brendan, successfully across the Atlantic.

The church of St Mary Magdalene was built under tragic circumstances by Sir Henry Trecarrel who owned an estate a few miles south of the town. While engaged on building his manor house there, he lost both his wife and little son and, grief-stricken, gave up all thought of completing his home and devoted his life to building the church and all matters concerning it. Particularly notable is the superbly carved granite exterior with not an inch of this particularly hard stone undec-

Launceston Museum

orated. The motifs vary from prayers and angels to roses, pomegranates and coats of arms — those of Trecarrel and Kelway are on the upper storey of the south porch. The church was probably completed by Kelway who, it is believed, married one of Trecarrel's daughters.

Streets in Launceston are short, and, although Southgate is two roads away, it is, in fact, reached in a minute. This handsome Norman

PLACES OF INTEREST IN AND AROUND LAUNCESTON

Launceston Castle
A fine ruin overlooking the town. It was the chief seat of Robert of Mortain, brother of William I. Views are impressive.

Lawrence House Museum
Castle Street
A period building given to the National Trust in 1964 to preserve the character of the street. The moulded plaster of the ceilings is exceptional. It is let to the local Borough Council as a museum.

St Mary Magdalene Church
Built in 1511–24 by Sir Henry Trecarrel after the loss of his wife and son. Probably unique in having a granite exterior so elaborately carved. Monuments of interest inside.

Trecarrel Hall
S of Launceston
The banqueting hall is one of the most spectacular domestic buildings of its period in Cornwall.

Shutta Farmhouse
Near Stoke Climsland
Sixteenth-century building. Not open to the public.

arch, all that remains of the walled town defences, has been widened to accommodate increasing traffic. Above the arch and up a flight of extremely steep steps are rooms with a history, as they were originally for soldiers on guard duty and later housed the town's criminals.

Visitors who see Launceston on market day will be very much aware of the White Hart Hotel with its sturdy door. Historians believe that not only the door but the entire doorway, complete with columns, may have been rescued from the chapel of the castle, possibly when the stronghold fell to Cromwell in 1646.

This pleasant town is a good holiday centre for studying the old packhorse bridges crossing the Tamar, Kensey and Inney Rivers and the neighbouring picturesque valleys where quiet corners of country-side are still to be found. The Tavistock A384 road from Launceston leads immediately to leafy lanes, some unusually narrow for motorists used to motorways. This way lies Greystone Bridge (1439) described by Cornwall's historian, Charles Henderson, as 'the fairest bridge in the two shires which it links together ... for beauty of situation and perfection it has no superior in the Western Counties'. Today, it is frightening to watch juggernauts roll across but in spite of everything the structure stands firm. This proves the skill of medieval builders who were paid with indulgences — the conscience money of sinners who repented, hoping to buy their way to Paradise.

The sharp slate hedges of this area are screened by ferns and the lanes meander peacefully by remote places like **Lawley Bridge** and **Beale's Mill**, with its newly restored well, to **Tutwell** and **Horsebridge**. After **Greystone**, the Tamar winds through some of the finest inland scenery in Cornwall, mainly woods once belonging to the great Benedictine house of Tavistock. The name Horsebridge has no animal origin but is a corruption of Hautes Brigge, then Hawte Brig. The flat wide meadows on either side are a great contrast to the wooded valleys of the upper and lower Tamar.

Since 1337, **Stoke Climsland** and much of the surrounding land has been Duchy of Cornwall property, including the church patronage. The first duke, the Black Prince, was a good landlord, much concerned with the responsibilities of his estates and in 1354 he gave six oaks from this deer park (now a farm) towards the construction of Stoke church. This old building stands central to the village which is high above rolling pasturelands and rural countryside and there is a quiet contentment about the lane running between it and the village shop opposite. Low beams and small cool windows are part of the charm of this cottage, also one of the oldest post offices in the country. Little can have changed here since it held the important position as an early Penny Post receiving house in 1839. Formerly, it had been a dwelling for workers attending to church repairs.

A footpath opposite the church leads to Duchy Home Farm land where many prize-winning cattle are now bred. At the left of the road towards Kelly Bray is Shutta, which many miss because it is set a good way back. This is a privately owned sixteenth-century farmhouse which incorporates some interesting features of local history such as a huge granite bowl used for cider making and doors from Whiteford, one of Cornwall's oldest manors. Seven entrances, fifty-two doors and 365 windows were built into Whiteford. Nothing remains of it apart from the name of a nearby farm, the doors here, others on Duchy property and some Adam chimney pieces in Buckingham Palace.

About a mile north of Bray Shop (B3257) a lane leads to the quiet countryside of **Trebullet**. Trebullet comprises two hamlets — Lower Trebullet is near Trecarrel Bridge, from which a steep lane leads to the other group of houses not named on the map. A left turn at the crossroads in their midst goes to Trecarrel Hall. Charles I stayed at the hall on his way to do battle at Liskeard. The bridge is not one he crossed — that was swept away by floodwaters in 1847. Visitors may see Sir Henry's great banqueting hall at Trecarrel. He built it to last — the great beams on its cradle roof are as strong as when they were first lifted there. This might have been another Cotehele but for the two deaths that changed everything. The chapel is also here, with its gallery where the lord of the manor and his lady attended Mass. Perhaps the saddest sight is the pile of great stones lying by the farm gate where they were left almost 500 years ago.

The B3254 runs back to Launceston through the broad open fields of **South Petherwin**. Close by is Botathan farmhouse which witnessed scenes of ghosts and exorcism in the seventeenth century.

The hilltop church at **Lewannick** is built of a stone which is not seen in many other parts of Cornwall. It is dark green and was quarried at **Polyphant** village across the A30. The almost circular churchyard indicates a very early Christian site, possibly fifth century AD. Here are two 'gravestones' with inscriptions in Latin and Ogham (an ancient British alphabet which consists of only twenty letters). Today people go blackberrying among the neglected stone outcrops. A visit to this place is worthwhile.

Not many visitors go along these lanes to **Laneast**, though Sir John Betjeman called the church an unspoiled version of Altarnun. A Norman foundation, it was reconsecrated in the fifteenth century when the thirty-eight pew ends were carved. Today it is very much loved and cared for, with fresh flowers to scent the building. John Couch Adams was born in the parish of St Sidwell's Laneast in 1819 and a black tablet on the wall names him the greatest astronomer since Newton. It also recalls his discovery of the planet Neptune. Truro cathedral also has a memorial to him and in Launceston Museum there is a bust by the sculptor Northey Burnard.

There are walks from here to **St Clether**, but for the motorist the road runs along a ridge, dropping a little to the church, its holy well, a small hall and one house. There is a serenity, too, which draws people to this remote place. The Lord's Prayer in Cornish is to be

PLACES OF INTEREST NEAR LAUNCESTON

St Clether Well
¹/₄ mile NW of church
Lovely setting above the river in an isolated field. The well building is the largest in Cornwall with chapel and stone altar.

Warbstow Bury
3 miles N A395 Launceston-Camelford road (SX 201909)
An impressive prehistoric defensive earthwork: fortress, double-walled and two gateways protecting barrows. King Arthur is said to be buried there.

Trethorne Leisure Farm
Piper's Pool A395

Ideal for young children with animals to see and ponies to ride.

Tamar Otter Park
North Petherwin
Otters, deer, waterfowl, peacocks and owls. Tearoom and shop.

Launceston Steam Railway
Below the castle
Travelling for 1¹/₂ miles through the Kensey valley on the trackbed of the old North Cornwall Railway. Victorian locomotives pull coaches which allow passengers to enjoy the scenery. Museum of Vintage Transport.

found in the church, and there is a stained glass window of the saint.

As you drive along the A395, stop at Trethorne Leisure Farm near Piper's Pool. Youngsters enjoy it here.

Sheep are very much part of the landscape round Launceston, especially north of this road at **Treneglos** hamlet, where the old Cornish 'trev' is no more than a triangular green beside a church and two or three houses. It is almost as high as nearby **Wilsey Downs** where there are walks to prehistoric tumuli. Celtic tribes were forced to seek safety and live above the wooded valleys — Warbstow Bury, north from Wilsey and Treneglos is a good example of this and ranks with Castle-an-Dinas and Chun Castle as one of Cornwall's largest ancient sites. Choose this place for a picnic and walks on a sunny day.

From this expanse of fields and farms, the lane plunges deeply down between hedgerows not despoiled by harsh council machines to **Tuckingmill** near Canworthy Water on the River Ottery. Fleeces from farms on the high ground once kept the local woollen mills busy and villagers in full employment. Now the cottages are quiet, those beside the river reflecting on their changed position in life.

The road from South Wheatley to **North Petherwin** is narrow and undulating but wooded and pleasant. After much study, St Paternus came to this place in the sixth century and the small churchtown remains apart from the main group of houses at Petherwin Gate in a typically Cornish manner. There is a poignant memorial here to three sisters — Susanna, Margaret and Ann who died young about 350 years ago.

The Tamar Otter Park is nearby and in the 23 acres of this, the first branch of the Otter Trust, there are eight otters. Deer run wild and, as well as six owl aviaries, there are peacocks and numerous water fowl.

Boyton, once a thriving town, has now shrunk to a hamlet. It stands on high ground overlooking the Tamar and part of the old Bude Canal. The parish is proud of Agnes Prest of Northcott, a Protestant martyr, burned at Southernhay in Exeter in 1557 for refusing to accept the doctrine of transubstantiation. She shares a memorial with Thomas Benet outside Maynard School in that city and Boyton is still hoping to have her remembered in her parish church — so far un-

successfully. There are numerous walks here, some on high ground and others close to and even along parts of the sadly long-defunct Bude Canal.

Motorists returning to Launceston pick up the B3254 road at **Ladycross**, probably once associated with Tavistock Abbey, and return to Launceston over the Yeolmbridge. This is Cornwall's oldest

and most perfectly finished bridge, the only one with a ribbed vault and pointed arches, similar to that of the north gate of Launceston Castle.

On the hill north of the River Kensey and level with Launceston Castle is St Stephen's, once a collegiate establishment and conse-crated in 1259 which makes it the mother church of Launceston. The original borough of St Stephen's grew up round the monastery below the present church and from it Launceston's old name originated — Lanson or Dunheved. There are arguments for both but the former is more Celtic as it comes from Lan Stephen's ton, *lan* being Cornish for holy ground. Today, this area of the Kensey valley keeps a little of its past — a packhorse bridge, slate-hung cottages overlooking the mill complex and a toll house, where Launceston's wealth once lay. The building of St Thomas was formerly the chapel of St Stephen and stands as the lone reminder of Launceston's pre-Conquest religious past.

In the Kensey valley, the Launceston Steam Railway will take you back into history as Victorian locomotives pull their coaches through

$1\frac{1}{2}$ miles of beautiful scenery along the trackbed of the old North Cornwall Railway. Among the museum's many exhibits is a restored 1905 Robey horizontal steam engine.

The rest of north Cornwall can be divided into two sections, each with a character of its own. **Camelford**, about 16 miles north-west of Launceston along the A395, can be a base for seeing King Arthur country. Motorists driving north from Wadebridge on the A39, approach this quiet market town through the lovely Allen valley, a route starred with primroses and bluebells in spring.

A peaceful place now, Camelford was once a lively pocket borough, busy with wool and cloth-making as indicated by the nearby hamlet of Valley Truckle (Cornish for tuckingmill). Sheep have always been plentiful here — not camels as the town hall's weathervane would suggest. That is the practical result of the way medieval heralds worked this animal into the town's arms, a play on the name of the river. Well signposted from the A39 and worth a visit, is the North Cornwall Museum and Gallery. This exhibition opened in 1973 in an old coach house to display a collection of items reflecting rural life in north Cornwall. A section of the building has been constructed to resemble a typical moorland cottage interior and in addition, changing craft and painting exhibitions are held throughout the season. Those who have seen it are not surprised to learn that it has been featured on both television and radio as well as being given the Pilgrim Trust Award for the best small museum in Britain.

The westward coast roads from Camelford all pick up the B3314 where **Delabole**, between 2 and 3 miles away, is well signposted. The village is clean and attractive but the focal point is the slate quarry which has been producing fine slate for many centuries. Pack saddle donkeys were first used to remove the rock: horses were next and now lorries provide the transport. The great quarry is 500ft deep and over $1\frac{1}{2}$ miles round. Richard Carew included it in his 1602 Survey of Cornwall, John Wesley wrote about it in the eighteenth century and Eden Phillpotts made it the subject of his novel *Old Delabole* (1914). The skills they all admired are still practised today and masons produce items such as church altars and fine flooring, memorial stones and plant holders. The name of the local inn has strong links with the quarry, being known as the Bettle and Chisel. After learning about the names of various slate tiles — Ladies, Countesses,

Delabole Slate Quarry

⌐(PLACES OF INTEREST AROUND CAMELFORD)⌐

North Cornwall Museum and Gallery
The Clease, Camelford
Privately-owned collection showing rural life of the locality. Opened in 1974 in an old coach house and including a reconstructed moorland cottage interior.

Delabole Slate Quarry
Follow AA signs from Camelford One-and-a-half miles round and 500ft deep, it spans 400 years of industrial history. See work in progress from the viewing platform and visit showroom where uses of slate are displayed.

Duchesses, Queens, Rags and Imperials — it is interesting to see them on the old cottages and walls for many miles round about.

Northwards along the B3266, the road crosses the high plateau of Waterpit Down, pleasant with extensive views and the ubiquitous sheep. A roadside cross here is a tenth-century stone carved with interlaced ornamentation. It has weathered considerably since it was set up as a pilgrims' waymarker. A maze of narrow lanes leads eventually to **Lesnewth**, very remote but once an important place where Cornish kings and chieftains held court (*Lis* means court/palace and *Noweth/Newith,* new). The church of St Michael is securely built into the hillside opposite a farm and easily missed as the roof is at road level.

Walkers will find that several paths lead away from this unusual churchtown into the lovely Valency valley but motorists have to cross the latter for the B3263 Boscastle road at the head of the valley, partly owned by the National Trust. The drop down to St Juliot's church is steep but typical of roads in this area. The building was in a ruinous condition when novelist Thomas Hardy arrived in 1870 to inspect it and draw up plans for its restoration. This he did and it was re-opened 2 years later. Lovers of Hardy's works will know how the famous man returned again and again to court the rector's sister Emma Gifford at St Juliot Rectory and how she persuaded him to leave architecture for literature and later married him in 1874. Beeny Cliff, Buckator, Penally and Pentargon are among the places he loved and incorporated in his second novel, *A Pair of Blue Eyes.* There is a nature walk, mostly alongside the little river, from the church of St Juliot down to the harbour.

PLACES OF INTEREST CONNECTED WITH THOMAS HARDY

St Juliot Church
Head of Valency valley
Dedicated to St Julitta, this isolated building was restored by Thomas Hardy. The brass and ruby oil lamps he installed are in Wellington Hotel, Boscastle.

St Juliot Rectory
This figured largely in the time when Hardy was working there — especially as he stayed at the rectory and returned to court the rector's sister, Emma.

Beeny Cliff, N Boscastle
Loved by Hardy and Emma — she sketched it and he wrote from there.

Boscastle Harbour
Hardy's poem *Moments of Vision* describes the cliff outline of Penally Point, the northern arm of the harbour — resembling the neck, head and beak of a bird of prey. Opposite the bathing pool.

Valency Valley
Five miles long, some National Trust. Still lovely and unspoilt.

At **Boscastle**, the original inner harbour was built by Sir Richard Grenville in 1584; with 61 acres of adjoining cliffs, it is National Trust property. There is an information centre open in the summer in the Old Smithy. It is hard to believe that it was once Launceston's port for shipping slate, corn and tanning bark. Cargoes of food and coal were imported here. Today, few would care to negotiate even a small motor yacht between the sharp, twisting rocks of this narrow inlet, but local boatmen who know the dangers, take visitors out to see a different view of the cliffs, especially the one some call King Arthur's Head.

Steep, heather and gorse-clad cliffs and a narrow strip of water make Boscastle. Little enough, but it is very popular and no doubt the Museum of Witchcraft adds to its appeal. Matters of the past, perhaps, but there are those who say that the black power is still very potent in the area, and agree with the notice on the door of the museum — 'These things happen today'.

The Valency valley runs inland for 5 miles. In spring it is a delight — in autumn, unbelievably beautiful. About 132 acres of it are National Trust property and this includes Sentry Ground, the ancient sanctuary ground of Minster church. Nearby Forrabury Common is a unique survival of Celtic land tenure in long rectangular plots known as 'stitches'.

The cliff walks from here to Tintagel are nothing less than splendid,

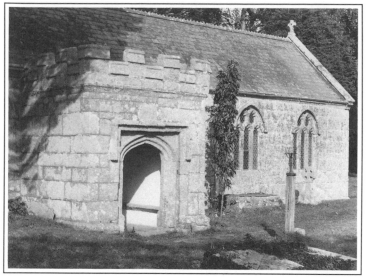

The church at St Juliot

especially on a fine spring day when there is a profusion of wild flowers
and a mass of sea birds. In June, puffins can be seen on Long Island
but not, alas, without binoculars. Rocky valley, the walk from these
cliffs to **Trevalga**, is one of exceptional beauty. In fact a day spent
here would not be wasted. Motorists climb out of Boscastle to pass
Trevalga and arrive at Trethevy (the head of Rocky valley) along the
B3263. Walk down the valley to the cliffs and look for the maze: two
rare labyrinth pattern carvings.

Behind Trethevy Manor, beside the B3263, a narrow lane climbs
high above Bossiney Haven giving fine views of a great coastal sweep
of cliffs. It is the way to St Nectan's Glen, Valency valley in miniature,
and St Nectan's Kieve (great bowl). This is a beautiful valley walk
leading back to the main road.

Bossiney village is now a quiet hamlet but in 1584 it was the
centre of a 'rotten' borough whose MP was Sir Francis Drake. Long
before that, Bossiney Court was mentioned in the Domesday Book.
It stands on ground once owned by the first Duke of Cornwall, the
Black Prince.

The cliffs at Tintagel

It is difficult to know where Bossiney ends and **Tintagel** begins because of recent buildings. Many suggest that Tintagel should be avoided as commercialism spoils the memory of King Arthur. Perhaps there are too many gift shops here but there is also much to enjoy. In the centre is the Old Post Office, one of the National Trust's most picturesque properties. This small fourteenth-century stone house with an ancient slate roof of fairy-tale curves was built on the plan of a medieval manor with a large hall. It is called the Old Post Office because it was the letter receiving office for the district, opened by the GPO in 1844, and is now restored as such.

A dusty, easy slope (a Land Rover is also available for those who prefer it) takes visitors to the foot of **Tintagel Head**, which is Duchy of Cornwall property. On this magnificent promontory are the well preserved remains of a Celtic monastery as well as the ruins of one of the Black Prince's castles.

English Heritage has charge of another castle — on the land overlooking the narrow division between cliff and headland. This is the remains of a medieval stronghold built by Earl Reginald of Cornwall. On the other side of the valley is King Arthur's Castle Hotel, an outstanding place built to accommodate holidaymakers flocking here as a result of Alfred Tennyson's Arthurian poetry. Even in 1897,

PLACES OF INTEREST IN AND AROUND TINTAGEL

Tintagel Old Post Office
(National Trust)
A small fourteenth-century stone house built as a medieval manor. The irregular slate roof is picturesque. Opened in 1844 as the district letter receiving office.

Worthyvale Manor
Near A39
Arthur is said to have fought Mordred here and both died. In 823 Egbert, later first king of all England, defeated the Celts. An inscribed stone lies on the river bank. The Manor, farm trail and trout farm only open for those on self-catering holidays here. No casual visitors.

Tintagel Castle
Cliff-side remains of a medieval castle built on prominent site in mid-twelfth century by Reginald, Earl of Cornwall. English Heritage.

Condolden Barrow
(SX 0091871)
Prehistoric barrow believed to be associated with Queen Iseult.

Museum of Witchcraft
Boscastle Harbour

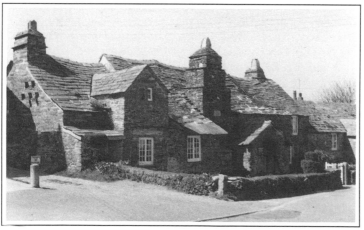

The Old Post Office, Tintagel

this building was thought to detract from the spirit of the area and the 14 acre headland was eventually bought for the National Trust as a memorial to the Poet Laureate. Away from the village is the church of

PLACES OF INTEREST IN BUDE

Bude Historical and Folk Museum
Old Forge
Lower Wharf
There is considerable emphasis on shipwrecks and lifeboats in this excellent local museum.

Bude Canal
A remarkable piece of engineering in being the longest tub boat canal in Britain — and with inclined planes — but it was a project devised before engineers had power and the materials to make it successful. Today, Sir Thomas Acland's brilliant scheme is a place of recreation for visitors.

Ebbingford Manor
Off Vicarage Road
Dates from the twelfth century, not open to the public.

St Materiana. It is a fine Norman building and should be visited when walking along the Glebe Cliff, which has a viewpoint with wheelchair access.

After leaving Tintagel by the B3263, there is a lane to the left beyond Penpethy Farm which is worth exploring. For archaeologists, the lonely mound of Condolden Barrow is an intriguing monument, as some people believe Queen Iseult to be buried there. Hardy wrote it into his play *The Famous Tragedy of the Queen of Cornwall.*

Across the B3266 at **Slaughterbridge** is Worthyvale Manor, an ancient and beautiful place with a farm trail and trout farm on an estate crowded with history, now unfortunately only open to those enjoying self-catering holidays at the manor. It was recorded in the Domesday Book of 1086, but was important even before that, for King Arthur is said to have led his Celtic forces into battle against Mordred where the lane crosses the River Camel. Both were killed and a large stone inscribed in Latin still lies on the river bank, giving the name Slaughter-bridge an irrevocable link with the past even though historians consider it to be merely legendary. Later, however, in 823, another decisive battle took place in Worthyvale fields when the Saxon leader Egbert was victorious and later became the first king of all England.

Those who live in **Bude** do not consider their pleasant town to be at all remote or forgotten, but in the far north of Cornwall, it is an area with its own special character and quite different from any other part of the Duchy. A friendly, attractive place offering a warm-hearted welcome to visitors.

The entrance lock of the Bude Canal, alongside the beach at Bude

In the 1830s, Sir Goldworthy Gurney built the toy-like castle beside the beach. Today it houses the offices of the town council who maintain the building, keep the gardens colourful and have transformed the former gardener's shed into a café and information area. Adjoining this, the old forge beside the canal has become the town's

Historical and Folk Museum displaying a wide variety of exhibits.

The musem is appropriately sited on the lower wharf facing the Bude Canal which was built in 1826 by Sir Thomas Acland. This canal was almost unique in Britain, as it was not primarily built to carry goods to the coast, but to transport huge quantities of shell sand inland to sweeten the acid soil and so improve large areas of otherwise unproductive land. The original 30-mile stretch from Bude to Launceston carried barges fitted with wheels and these were hauled up inclines by stationary steam engines. Bude, however, did not become a canal port. It developed into a quality holiday resort and visitors now park their cars beside the canal and watch raft races. They may also fish there because it is regarded as one of the finest coarse-fishing waters in the West. A $2^1/_2$-mile stretch of quiet level walking along the tow path is not only pleasant but of special interest for lovers of wildlife. About half a mile along, a bird hide has recently been erected.

Ebbingford Manor, the town's oldest house, dating from the twelfth century, is off Vicarage Road which runs beside the canal. This small but charming building was at one time home of the Arundells, who were related to Henry VIII and Lord Baltimore, the founder of Maryland. It is not open to the public.

It is hard to believe that wrecks were a terrifying commonplace in the early days of the nineteenth century, for the pleasures of Bude, which include golf and twelve tennis courts for visitors, are only for relaxation. There is safe saltwater swimming in the pool, while beyond the castle are sands and surf comparable to those of South Africa and Australia!

Marhamchurch lies south of Bude and across the A39 through high banked hedges and narrow climbing lanes. It is an unusual rectangular village set on a ridge and seems to be keeping watch over the surrounding farmland. Its wide central road leads to the Norman church, low and square near the war memorial. The solid fifteenth-century oak door is always open and is one of its interesting features, as is the encased sanctuary knocker. A former rector, Brother Peter, came from the Girondist House of the Holy Cross at Bordeaux and was the incumbent of Marhamchurch in 1458. His service here was apparently so happy that after his death his ghost returned to the old rectory, where he has apparently often been seen, even in this century.

The north Cornish coast

Village celebrations are the same here as at all other churches with Celtic origins — their feast day usually follows the church festival. The tradition at Marhamchurch is a rare one. On Revel Day — after 12 August — Father Neptune crowns a local school-girl who then rides through the village on a white horse.

The narrow lanes to the south are undulating and delightful, with the high views showing the agricultural nature of the region. Conservationists will like to visit Goscott Farm, just south of **Week St Mary**. This is a stock-rearing farm where the owners work to retain the traditions of the countryside.

Jacobstow church, embraced by trees in a roadside dell, is easily missed and the unspoiled hamlet is charming because of its very solitude. Nearer the coast the wooded lanes are lost in high open fields again.

Wainhouse Corner is a junction on the A39 where the way leads to the fearful cliffs of **Crackington Haven** and for a considerable distance, north and south, the coastal footpath crosses National Trust land. This tiny cove was a harbour for colliers in the eighteenth and nineteenth centuries and their captains must have been intrepid sailors to navigate here. **Cambeak** promontory on the southern arm of Crackington Haven stretches into the sea like a great lizard and

The Gildhouse, Poundstock

gated paths lead to Trevigue, a sheltered farm providing good teas. Cars may be left here for a further walk to High Cliff. This is Cornwall's highest coastal point and the views are typical of this northern area.

Northwards, on the cliff out of the Haven stands **St Gennys** church. It is almost alone in its fold of green fern on the cliffside and ornamental cherry trees give it a fairy-tale look in spring. One of the treasures here is the altar tabernacle, a splendid piece of church furniture. Handsomely embroidered kneelers also add to the glory of this Celtic church where prayers have been said since St Gennys established his humble cell on these cliffs.

The road to **Millook** is narrow, steep and badly cambered in places but it can be negotiated with good brakes and the use of bottom gear. Once safely out of the valley, the wide road past the Common falls away to a startling panorama across Widemouth Bay and north to Morwenstow.

Inland from this striking coast lies **Poundstock** church, Gildhouse

PLACES OF INTEREST NEAR BUDE

Goscott Farm
S of Week St Mary
A stock rearing farm where every care is taken to encourage and retain indigenous plants and all wildlife.

Poundstock Church
Dedicated to the dwarf hermit, St Neot, this building is beautifully sited in a dell away from the main road. Murals and exceptionally handsome bench ends are among the interesting features. Beside the churchyard the Gildhouse of

stormy history is used for parochial church meetings.

The Tree Inn
Stratton
Here giant Anthony Payne was born. Huge and faithful servant of Sir Bevil Grenville especially at the Battle of Stamford Hill.

Battle of Stamford Hill 1643
The site is near Stratton. In the field there a plaque on the wall commemorates the place where Cromwell's army was routed.

and lych gate. Gentle enough now, it was not so in the fourteenth century when local villains were commissioned as Collectors of Subsidies and lawbreakers wielded more power than good citizens. Affairs reached a climax in 1357, however, when armed men swarmed into the church as a priest was celebrating Mass, killed him at the altar and desecrated the vestments and sacred vessels. It was not long before the killers were caught and punished and Poundstock returned to peace again. It still retains much of its medieval beauty. The Gildhouse served many purposes: poorhouse, school, substitute church and today, a meeting place for the parochial church council. The windows are original and worth studying.

The spectacular sands of **Widemouth Bay** stretch away almost endlessly. Once they were dreaded by sailors but now visitors can enjoy adventure holidays here and learn canoeing, and wind-surfing.

Cornwall has not revealed all its treasures yet — there is much to see between Bude and Morwenstow. Some say that this area is the best of all. The A3072 road goes to **Stratton** which, though it has fallen below Bude in status, was important in Roman times. Its character, however, is quite different. It is rightly proud of Anthony Payne, the Cornish giant who was born at The Tree Inn, and died there too. This huge man weighed 532lb. His portrait by Kneller is in Truro Museum. He devoted his life to the service of his master, Sir

The Tree Inn, Stratton

Bevil Grenville, whose troops defeated the Roundheads at the Battle of Stamford Hill in 1643. A plaque on the wall at Stamford Hill marks the site.

Away from the main road, but worth seeing, is **Poughill** (pronounced 'Puffle') church, dedicated to St Olaf, a Dane. There are two large wall representations of St Christopher, repainted by Frank Salisbury and a Tazza Cup and Paten, beautifully shaped and richly decorated. The clock in the tower has a memorial tablet which is rarely seen but worth mentioning. It says of Sir Goldsworthy Gurney: 'His inventions and discoveries in Steam and Electricity made communication by land and sea so rapid that it became necessary for all Britain to keep uniform clock time.'

Those following the coastal walk will have increasingly fine views especially near Stowe Barton where the road dips into the Coombe valley. This handsome farm was built on the site of Sir Richard Grenville's home, unfortunately pulled down in 1739: today only the stables remain.

The bridge at **Coombe** carries a tablet — now very weathered —

which commemorated King William IV's contribution to its building. In the early days of the nineteenth century, the ford here was a danger to the lives of men and animals so the Reverend R.S. Hawker of Morwenstow appealed to the king for financial help and eventually a bridge was built. Duckpool is a good place to swim and the National Trust cliff, Steeple Point, affords an ideal vantage point for walkers. The nearby Coombe valley is also Trust land. The cottage at the entrance to this valley is of special interest though people rarely notice the cross-shaped window above the door. Here Hawker spent his honeymoon and began writing *Trelawney*, the poem which is now considered to be Cornwall's anthem.

As the road climbs out of this valley, it continues north past the dish aerials of the Government's Composite Signals Organisation Station — an imposing sight. Beyond is **Morwenstow**, which is almost the end of Cornwall but is full of history and known as Hawker country. For over 40 years, till 1875, this famous parson-poet was vicar here. Wrongly styled an eccentric, he startled his fellow churchmen by righting many wrongs and frequently risking his life to rescue ship-wrecked sailors and give Christian burial to the bodies of the drowned. In the churchyard is what might be considered a memorial to his brave dedication — the figurehead of the *Caledonia*, wrecked on the rocks below in 1842, leaving only one man alive. Petitioner for his parishioners' cause at a time of dire poverty, and restorer of the harvest festival, Robert Stephen Hawker's achievements will long be remembered. He wrote fine poetry in a hut on the clifftop, now National Trust, and his unique vicarage chimneys modelled on church towers, can just be glimpsed in the woods below the church.

The Bush Inn, a few hundred yards away from the churchtown, is unusual in retaining the traditional sign, the sign of a bush, once given to all taverns to signify where drinks were sold. It is an old inn where the Morwenstow Union Friendly Society probably met in the late eighteenth century. It had a thatched roof until a few years ago, but now that has gone and some of its charm has disappeared as well.

The end of Cornwall is reached where Marsland Mouth lies below Marsland Cliff — the scene of many shipwrecks in days of sail — but the lane turns inland to **Woolley**, where there is not an end but a beginning. For among the marshes at Woolley Barrows, Cornwall's River Tamar, which marks the boundary with Devon, has its source.

The lych gate at Kilkhampton church

The A39 road south, which was the pilgrim highway to St Michael's Mount, goes to **Kilkhampton**. The church here is worth a visit because it has a splendid lych gate, good pew ends and numerous Grenville monuments.

From the B3254, the road leads to the Tamar lakes with fly-fishing on the Upper, coarse on the Lower and walks, picnics and much else to enjoy in beautiful surroundings. The first of these reservoirs was created in 1820 when Lower Lake was built to feed the now obsolete

PLACES OF INTEREST NORTH OF BUDE

Hawker's Hut
Vicarage Cliff, Morwenstow
(National Trust)
Perched on the edge of the cliff
overlooking the fearful rocks
where so many ships foundered
and whose men he saved, Parson
Hawker built his shelter. Access

by footpath from churchyard gate.

Launcells Church
In a wooded valley beside St
Swithin's Well, this is one of the
gems of Cornwall. Encaustic tiles,
box pews and a medieval mural.

Bude Canal.

In high summer, the lanes all round here are heavy with honey-
suckle and in their midst is **Launcells** church. One expert called it
unique in Cornwall, and though out of the way, it is worth searching
for. Embraced by trees and waterside meadows, time has left
Launcells untouched. More than sixty superbly carved bench ends, a
medieval mural depicting the sacrifice of Isaac and rare fifteenth-
century encaustic tiles on the chancel floor are all here. These
treasures, as with others in Cornwall, are not easily located, but when
discovered they are a source of delight to any visitor who has come
to the Royal Duchy for a truly different holiday.

FURTHER INFORMATION

ACCOMMODATION

Cornwall offers a wide range of accommodation from luxury hotels to camp sites. There are too many to list here but details can be obtained from the Cornwall Tourist Board or Information Centres.

ANIMAL AND BIRD RESERVES AND PARKS

Bodmin Farm Park
Fletcher's Bridge, Bodmin
Off A38 Bodmin-Liskeard road at Fletcher's Bridge signpost
☎ Bodmin (0208) 20074
Open: mid-May-September, daily (except Saturday) 10am-6pm. Last admission 5pm. Nature trail, children's activities, refreshments, gifts.

Goonhilly Downs Nature Reserve
The Lizard
Apply to warden Ray Lawman
☎ Mullion (0326) 240808

Goscott Farm
S of Week St Mary
☎ Week St Mary   (0288) 84434
Farm walks.

Gweek Seal Sanctuary
Gweek Wollas Farm, Gweek
☎ Mawgan (0326) 22361
Open: daily 9.30am-6pm Easter-end September. 9.30am-4.30pm

October-Easter. Feeding twice daily 11am and 3.30pm approx.
Ten pools, hospital, aquarium, woodland walks, rides, shop, video, safari train.

Lelant Bird Reserve
Open viewing at Hayle estuary beside A30 and A3074.

Mousehole Bird Hospital
☎ Penzance (0736) 7313867 before visiting.

Newquay Zoo and Leisure Park
See *Visitor Centres*

Padstow Tropical Bird and Butterfly Gardens
Fentonluna Lane, Padstow
☎ Padstow (0841) 532262
Open: all the year 10.30am-8pm in summer, 5pm in winter. Refreshment terrace open in summer. Gift shop. Parking on link road B3276.

Paradise Park
$1/_4$ mile on B3302 from A30 at Hayle
☎ Hayle (0736) 753365
Open: 10am-6pm, May to September and 10am-4pm October to April

Peloe Dairy Farm
☎ Praze (0209) 831284
Near Praze-an-Beeble
Open: daily in summer except Saturday, 11am-6pm.
Video, assault course, trail, displays, tractor-trailer rides. Refreshments, shop.

St George's Island Bird Sanctuary
Privately owned but for information
☎ Looe (05036) 2255

Tamar Otter Park
North Petherwin
Open: April-October 10.30am-6pm.
Otters, deer, waterfowl, peacocks
and owls.

Trethorne Leisure Farm
See *Visitor Centres*

ANNUAL EVENTS

These are the best known of the
wide variety of events, in date
order, which take place every year.
The numerous carnivals, music
festivals and regattas are widely
advertised in local papers:

Towednack Cuckoo Feast: 28 April
*Black Prince Boat Festival at
    Millbrook:* Mayday
Padstow 'Obby 'Oss: 1 May
Helston Flora Day: 8 May
Royal Cornwall Show, Wadebridge:
    second week in June
Old Cornwall Society Bonfires:
    Midsummer Eve
Bodmin Ridings: July
Stithians Show: second Monday in
    July
St Mellion Cherry Pie Feast: July
*St Endellion Music and Drama
    Festival:* end of July
Scilly Water Sports: beginning of
    August
*RAF St Mawgan International Air
    Day:* mid-August
*Oyster Boat Race, Falmouth to
    Fowey:* end of Falmouth Regatta
    Week in August. Working boats
    only
Crying the Neck, Helston: last
    Friday in August

Cornish Gorsedd: first Saturday in
    September. Various venues.

BOATING

Most resorts have boat trips:
information about these and boats
for hire is best found locally, usually
near the pier or quay.

BUILDINGS OPEN TO THE PUBLIC

Details are correct at time of
publication but they are subject to
modification from year to year.
Check locally beforehand.

Antony House (NT)
2 miles NW of Torpoint, 16 miles
SE of Liskeard, 15 miles E of Looe
☎ Plymouth (0752) 812191
Open: April-October, Tuesday,
Wednesday, Thursday, Bank
Holiday Monday, also Sundays in
June, July and August, 1.30-
5.50pm. (Last tour of house 5pm.)

Cornish Mine Engines (NT)
On A3047 at Pool, near Camborne
☎ Redruth (0209) 216657
Open: April-end of October, daily
(including Good Friday) 11am-6pm
or sunset if earlier (last admission
half an hour before closing).
Two engines, one on either side of
the A3047.

Cotehele (NT)
2 miles E of St Dominick, 4 miles
from Gunnislake (turn at St Anne's
chapel), 1 mile W of Calstock by
footpath (6 miles by road)
☎ Liskeard (0579) 50434
Open: April-end of October, garden
and mill daily, house closed Friday,
11am-5.30pm (last admission 5pm).

Shop, licensed restaurant and video-viewing. Historic *Shamrock* also on view.

Egyptian House (NT)
6 Chapel Street, Penzance
☎ Penzance (0736) 64378
NT shop on ground floor.
Open: January to end of March 9am-5pm except Wednesdays.
April-December Monday 9am-5pm.

Godolphin House
Near Helston (between villages of Townshend and Godolphin Cross).
☎ Germoe (0736) 762409
Open: May and June, Thursday 2-5pm; July-September, Tuesday and Thursday 2-5pm.

Guildhall
Saltash
Contains interesting regalia which can be seen in the mornings when the caretaker is present.
Enquiries to Town Hall, Fore Street.
☎ Saltash (0755) 54846

Isbell Cottage
Trewint (Wesley's Cottage)
On A30 between Bodmin and Launceston
Methodist shrine in N Cornwall.
Open daily — admission free.

Lanhydrock (NT)
2$^1/_2$ miles SE of Bodmin, follow signposts from either A38 Bodmin-Liskeard or B3268 Bodmin-Lostwithiel.
☎ Bodmin (0208) 3320
Open: April-end of October, daily 11am-5.30pm (5pm on October). House closed Mondays except Bank Holidays
Shop and refreshments. Wooded walks round house and down to River Fowey at ancient Respryn Bridge. Open-air events in summer.

Lawrence House (NT)
9 Castle Street, Launceston
☎ Launceston (0566) 773277
Open: April-end September
Monday to Friday 10.30am-4.30pm.
Open some Bank Holidays.
Includes Launceston's local history museum. Free but visitors invited to contribute to museum expenses.

Mary Newman's House
Culver Street
Saltash (nr Town Quay)
☎ Plymouth (0752) 82211
House and garden open in season
Thursday 12 noon-4pm, Saturday 10am-4pm and Bank Holidays.

Mount Edgcumbe House and Country Park
Cremyll, near Saltash
☎ Plymouth (0752) 822236
Open: House and Earl's Garden April-October Wednesday to Sunday and Bank Holidays 11am-5.30pm. Country park and formal gardens open daily all year. Restaurant, special events in summer.

Pencarrow
Washaway, Bodmin
4 miles from Bodmin, 3 miles from Wadebridge, near junction of A389 and B3266
☎ St Mabyn (0208) 84369
Open: House and tearooms, Easter-mid-October Sunday to Thursday, 1.30-5pm. Bank Holiday Mondays and June-September 11am-5pm. Gardens open daily during the season.

Prideaux Place
Padstow
☎ Padstow (0841) 532411
Open: Easter Saturday for 2 weeks.
Mid-May to September Sunday-Thursday 1.30-5pm. Bank Holidays

11am-5pm. Closed May Day.
Terrace tearoom and gift shop.
Opera and drama in evenings.

St Michael's Mount (NT)
$^1/_2$ mile S of Marazion (A394).
Access on foot at low tide, or by
ferry.
☎ Penzance (0736) 710507
Occasional special charity open
days at certain weekends, when NT
members are also asked to pay for
admission.
November-end March, Monday,
Wednesday and Friday by guided
tours only as tide, weather and
circumstances permit (no regular
ferry service). April-October daily
10.30am-5.45pm. Last admission
4.45pm.
Shop and restaurant April-October.

Tintagel Old Post Office (NT)
☎ Camelford (0840) 770256
Open: April-October daily including
11am-5.30pm. Closes 5pm in
October. Shop.

Trecarrel Hall
Near Trebullet, $3^1/_4$ miles S of
Launceston, between A388 and
B3254
☎ Mrs Burden, Coads Green (0568)
82286 to view.

Trelowarren
Mawgan-in-Meneage, near Helston
From Helston take A3083 Lizard
road, then left on to B3293,
signposted Trelowarren
☎ Mawgan (0326) 22224
Open: House open during August.
Home of Vyvyan family. Craft
exhibitions during season. Restau-
rant, shop and woodland walk.

Trerice (NT)
3 miles SE of Newquay via A392
and A3058 (turn right at Kestle Mill)

☎ Newquay (06373) 875404
Open: April-October, Wednesday to
Monday11am-5.30pm. (5pm in
October.) Shop and restaurant.

Trevithick's Cottage
Lower Penponds, Camborne
May be visited on application —
just call.

CASTLES

Launceston
Beside A388
☎ Launceston (0566) 2365

Pendennis
Pendennis Point, Falmouth
☎ Falmouth (0326) 316594
Open: April-September daily 10am-
6pm, October-March Tuesday-
Saturday 10am-4pm.
Wheelchair access in grounds, part
of keep and shop. Parking for
coaches. Restaurant April-
September. Education area, toilets,
tape tour, various events in season.

Restormel
Lostwithiel
☎ Bodmin (0208) 872687
Open: April-September daily 10am-
6pm.
Parking, toilets. Refreshments
locally.

St Catherine's
Fowey
(free access)

St Mawes
At the end of A3078 in St Mawes
☎ St Mawes (0326) 270526
Open: As Pendennis Castle.

Tintagel Castle
Tintagel Head
☎ Camelford (0840) 770328
Open: As Pendennis Castle.

Carn Brea Castle, Redruth is an ancient monument now a licensed restaurant. Approach road from Carnkie village off B3297. Reservations:
☎ Redruth (0209) 218358
Open: for all year for coffee, lunch and dinnner.
This restored building stands on a hill that was a fort 2,000 years before Stonehenge was built.

Ince and Caerhays Castles
Privately owned and occasionally open to the public. See local press for details.

Doyden Castle
Can be seen on a cliff walk from Port Quin along the coast to The Rumps. It is owned by the National Trust and let as a holiday home.

CRAFT WORKSHOPS

The variety and range of craft workshops can only be indicated here. Smaller ones are to be found in unexpected out-of-the-way places.

Miscellaneous
Barbican Centre
Battery Road, Penzance
Open: daily April-October 10-5.30pm, November-Christmas 10.30am-5pm.
West Country brass rubbing centre.

Creftow
6 Church Strret,
Helston (opposite museum)
Open: daily 10am-4pm except Wednesdays and Saturdays.

The Candle Shop
Dunmere Road
Bodmin
☎ Bodmin (0208) 73258

Open: Easter-September Saturday, Sunday 11am-6pm. October-Christmas Saturday 10am-3pm. Otherwise 10am-6pm daily.

Cornwall Crafts Centre
Trelowarren
Mawgan-in-Meneage
☎ Mawgan (0326) 22366
Exhibitions held through the year. Trelowarren House is also used for conferences, concerts and retreats, all with an artistic or religious basis.

Ironcraft
Calcraft Products
Wheal Arthur, Gunnislake
Signposted on Gunnislake to Tavistock road out of Calstock
☎ Tavistock (0822) 832648

Glass
Merlin Glass
Pavlova Mill
Station Road, Liskeard
☎ Liskeard (0579) 342399
Glassmaking Monday, Tuesday, Thursday, Friday 8.30am-4.30pm. Lunch 12noon-1pm. Shop and showroom Monday-Friday 9am-5pm, Saturday 9am-4pm.

Knitwear and Textiles
June Upton
Anvil Cottage,
Porkellis, Helston TR13 0JT
☎ Truro (0326) 40638
Spinning, dyeing and knitting.

Ann Sagin (knitwear designer)
Nancarris Mill, Constantine
☎ Falmouth (0326) 40687

Sharon Verry (textiles)
Higher Polgear Farm House, Nine Maidens, Redruth
☎ Redruth (0209) 860931

Leathercraft
St Eval Leather Crafts
Downhill, St Eval, Wadebridge

³/₄ mile from St Eval church
(SW 861690)
☎ St Mawgan (0637) 4357
Open: Monday to Friday 9am-
4.30pm. After 4.30pm by appointment only. Handmade leather
goods and reproductions of
medieval leather vessels.

Ceramics
Ginnie Bamford
Sloop Craft Market, St Ives
☎ Penzance (0736) 796051

Bob Berry
Coldharbour Studios,
Towednack, St Ives
☎ Penzance (0736) 798316
Specialists in Japanese Raku ware.

J. & S. Chown of Hayle
Hope Farm, Gwithian Road,
Connor Down, Hayle
☎ Camborne (0209) 713361
Bone china you can afford.
Open: 9am-5pm Monday-Saturday,
appointments preffered.

Fosters Pottery
Tolgus Hill, Redruth
☎ Redruth (0209) 215754
Open: summer 9am-5pm week-
days, all year 10am-12noon
Saturdays.
Large showroom. Refreshments.

Helland Pottery
Paul Jackson, Helland, Bodmin
☎ Bodmin (0208) 75240

Kernewek Pottery Ltd
Newquay Road,
Goonhavern, Perranporth
On A3070 Redruth to Newquay
road
☎ Truro (0872) 573505
Specialists in contract pottery made
to customers own requirements.

Leach Pottery
The Pottery Cottage, St Ives
☎ Penzance (0736) 796398
Showroom open in usual trading
hours.

St Nectan's Pottery
St Nectan's Glen, Trethewy,
Tintagel
In farm courtyard on B3263 midway
between Tintagel and Boscastle.
Workshop open daily in season.

Trequoit Pottery
Trethevy Quoit, Darite, Liskeard
☎ Liskeard (0571) 45978
Parking, showroom, admission free.

Silversmith
Les Freke
Oakcroft, Treknow, Tintagel
☎ Camelford (0840) 770928

GARDENS

Boconnoc
4 miles NE Lostwithiel, signposted
on A390 between Taphouse and
Lostwithiel
Open: one Sunday only, usually
day before Spring Bank Holiday.
See press. Park and garden only.

Glendurgan Gardens (NT)
Helford River, 4 miles SW of
Falmouth, ¹/₂ mile SW of Mawnan
Smith on road to Helford Passage
☎ Falmouth (0326) 250906
Open: March-end October,
Tuesday-Saturday10.30am-5.30pm
(last admission 4.30pm). Closed
Good Friday, open Bank Holiday
Mondays.

Penjerrick Gardens
1 mile south of Budock Vean
☎ Falmouth (0326) 250074
Open: Wednesday and Sunday in
season, 1.30-4.30pm.

Probus Demonstration Gardens and Arboretum

On the A390 just outside Probus
☎ Truro (0872) 74282 and ask for the gardens
Open: October-April Monday-Friday 10am-4pm, May-September daily 10am-5pm.

Trebah Garden

On the Helford river
☎ Falmouth (0326) 250448
Open: all year 10.30am-5pm.
Gardens shop March-October.
Magnificent, sub-tropical and steeply wooded 25 acres. Play area for children, plants for sale, dogs on lead. Access to beach — peaceful and beautiful.

Trelissick Gardens (NT)

4 miles S of Truro, on both sides of B3289 above King Harry Ferry
☎ Truro (0872) 862090
Open: March-end October, Mondays-Saturdays 11am-5.30pm.
Plants and souvenirs at garden shop. Refreshments open 12noon-5.30pm. Everything closes at 5pm March and October.

Trengwainton Gardens (NT)

2 miles NW of Penzance, $1/_2$ mile W of Heamoor on Penzance to Morvah road (B3312) and just E of Penzance-St Just road (A3071)
Open: March-end October, Wednesday-Saturday and Bank Holiday Monday, 11am-5.30pm.
Teas sometimes available at Trengwainton Farm.

Tresco Abbey Gardens

Isles of Scilly
☎ Scillonia (0720) 22849
Open: daily throughout the year.
Snack bar open in summer.

Trewidden

Buryas Bridge
Penzance (entrance off Land's End road A30)
☎ Penzance (0736) 62087
Open: Monday-Saturday all year.
For charity openings see local press.

Trewithen Gardens

Grampound Road, Probus, adjoining Demonstration Gardens on A390
☎ St Austell (0726) 882418
Open: March-end September Monday-Saturday 10am-4.30pm.
Nursery and plant shop with picnic and children's play areas. House tours, free car parking.

LIFEBOAT STATIONS

A number of these are open to the public depending on weather conditions. Lifeboats: Coverack, Falmouth, Fowey, Lizard, Cadgwith, Newquay, Padstow, Penlee, Port Isaac, St Agnes, St Ives, St Mary's (Isles of Scilly), Sennen Cove.

LIGHTHOUSES

An important feature of this sea-girt region, these masterpieces of engineering, some built locally, provide a circle of safety round the Western Approaches. Four are open to the public:

The Lizard
☎ The Lizard (0326) 290431
Open: when fine in season, 10am-4pm.

Pendeen, St Just-in-Penwith
☎ Penzance (0736) 788418
Open: in season 10am-lighting up time, weather permitting.

St Anthony, Roseland Peninsula
☎ Portscatho (0872) 580213
Now automatic but visitors may be
fortunate to find Mr Ellis at home to
show them round.

Trevose Head, Padstow
☎ Padstow (0841) 520494
This lighthouse is about to be
automated, so check to confirm if
open.

ARCHAEOLOGICAL SITES

(including industrial archaeology)

Bant's Carn Burial Chamber and Ancient Village
1 mile N of Hugh Town, St Mary's,
Isles of Scilly (SV 911124)
Bronze Age burial chamber about
40ft in diameter with entrance
passage and outer and inner
retaining walls. Nearby village huts
were occupied in the mid-Roman
period (English Heritage).

Botallack Mine Ruins
Can be seen from the cliff at end of
footpath walk from Botallack village
on B3306.

Cadsonbury
Near New Bridge, 2 miles SW of
Callington (SX345675)
An important univallate hill fort at
the crown of a steep lonely hill in
the River Lynher valley. Not yet
excavated, but probably of early
Iron Age. There is footpath access
from the New Bridge to Clapper
Bridge road. (National Trust.)

Carn Brea
Carnkie
Redruth
Neolithic hill fort, promoted as a
World Heritage Site.

Carne Barrow
Pendower Beach 1 mile SW Veryan
and 5 miles SW Tregony
Walk from car park behind beach at
Pendower or in valley at Carne.
(National Trust.)

Carn Euny Ancient Village
1¹/₄ miles SW of Sancreed
Remains of Iron Age settlement.
Open: any reasonable time.

Castle-an-Dinas
Free access by footpath from minor
road from St Columb ESE to A30
towards Roche.

Chapel Carn Brea
3 miles NE Land's End between
A30 and B3306.
Access on foot from byroad to east
of hill which connects A30 with
B3306. Reputed to have widest sea
view visible from the mainland of
British Isles, 657ft above sea level.
(National Trust.)

Chysauster (English Heritage.)
Gulval Downs (SW472350)
Well preserved remains of an Iron
Age village with rooms arranged
around an irregularly-shaped
courtyard.
Open: daily April-September 10am-
6pm. Toilets, car park.

Condolden Barrow
Free path access from lane leading
from B3263 Tintagel road joining
B3314 road towards Camelford.

Cornish Beam Engines
Pool
See *Buildings*

Gwennap Pit
Busveal, off A393 Falmouth-
Redruth road.
Open to view.

Helsbury Castle

Just off the B3266 about 2 miles from Michaelstow in Camelford direction.
Iron Age earthwork.

The Hurlers Stone Circles

$1/2$ mile NW of Minions
(ŠX255714)
Three large stone circles in a line, none of the monoliths exceeds 6ft in height. Early Bronze Age flints have been found here and the monument is considered one of the best of its type in the south-west. (English Heritage.)

Killifreth Engine House

Beside B3298 St Day-Scorrier road.

Kit Hill Mining Monument

Free access at all times along a road winding up through heather to a car park at foot of monument, an 85ft stack. Miners used to hold their Stannary Parliaments here.

Lanyon Quoit

Free access — it lies beside the minor road from Madron NW to north coast road B3306 at Morvah.

Men-an-Tol

Bosullow Common
West Penwith
Standing stones reached by footpath from Bosullow Common.

Men-Scryfa

Bosullow Common
West Penwith
Inscribed stone.

Merry Maidens

Beside B3315 Newlyn-Treen road.
Free access from road.

Mulfra Quoit

Mulfra Hill
West Penwith

Chambered tomb reached by footpath from midway along Treen-Chyandour road.

Nine Maidens and Hangman's Barrow

Near junction of B3297 Wendron-Redruth road and B3280 Praze-an-Beeble-Redruth road.
Standing stones.

The Rumps

Pentire Point, north of the Camel estuary (SW935811)
One of the best examples of an Iron Age promontory fort. Three lines of defensive ramparts cut off the 6-acre headland, one entrance serving the whole. Wheel-turned Iron Age pottery has been found here. (National Trust.)

St Breock Standing Stone

On St Breock Downs reached from St Breock church at Wadebridge. Easily visible from road.

St Piran's Round

Perranporth (SW779545)
This impressive Iron Age fortification, also called Piran or Perran Round, is an adaptation made in the Middle Ages for a *plen-an-gwary* or open-air theatre-in-the-round. High, terraced banks round the huge amphitheatre serve for players and audience.

Tregonning Hill

Take the landward cross road at Ashton (near Helston) on A394
Access by car or on foot.
Crowned by fortifications of Castle Pencaire. China clay first found here.

Trencrom Hill

3 miles S of St Ives
(SW518362)

Well preserved Iron Age site of 64 acres, stone-walled and enclosing hut circles. Of legendary interest as the home of Giant Trecobben who played bowls with his brother on St Michael's Mount. One of the bowls remains as Bowl Rock on the Lelant-Towednack road which runs below on the north side. (National Trust.)

Treryn Fort (Treen Cliff)
4 miles SE of Land's End (SW398222)
Perhaps Cornwall's best known cliff fort. The 36 acres include Logan Rock. The area has a five-line complex of fortifications. (National Trust.)

Trethevy Quoit
1 mile NE of St Cleer (SX259688)
A closed megalithic chamber used for burials, 7ft long and 9ft high. Five standing stones supporting a huge capstone. Open any reasonable time. (English Heritage.)

Warbstow Bury
2 miles N of Hallworthy A396 (SX201908)
A magnificent Celtic Iron Age fort with a double wall and two gateways, one of Cornwall's largest. Some claim that King Arthur lies in one of the graves of this great barrow.

MUSEUMS AND GALLERIES

This list excludes those buildings open to the public that have museums associated with them or other places that have special displays and are listed elsewhere.

Archibald Thorburn Museum and Gallery
See **Forest Railroad Park** entry under *Steam Railways*.

Automobilia
The Old Mill, St Stephen, St Austell 4 miles off A30. Signposted from Summercourt on A3058
☎ St Austell (0726) 823092
Open: October-May 10am-4pm, June-September 10am-6pm. Last admission 5.30pm.
Audio-visual presentation, home-made food, free parking.

Barbara Hepworth Museum and Sculpture Garden
Trewyn Studio and Garden, Barnoon Hill, St Ives
☎ Penzance (0736) 796226
Open: July and August 10am-6.30pm. Sundays 2-6pm. April-June, September 10am-5.30pm. Closed Sundays. October-March 10am-4.30pm. Closed Sundays. Administered by the Tate Gallery, London.

Bodmin Gaol
Cardell Road, Bodmin
☎ Bodmin (0208) 76292
Open: daily 10am-6pm.

Bude Historical and Folk Museum
The Old Forge, Town Wharf, Bude
☎ Bude (0288) 353576
Open: Easter-September daily 11am-4pm. Maintained by local council

Butter Market Museum
The Old Butter Market, Church Street, Helston
Open: Monday to Saturday 10.30am-1pm, 2-4.30pm (closed Wednesday 12 noon).

Camborne Museum
Public Library, The Cross,
Camborne
Open: 3-5pm weekdays (except
Thursday), 10am-12noon Saturday.
Admission free.
Mining exhibits, early coins and
photographs.

Camborne School of Mines Museum
On A3047 midway between
Camborne and Redruth
Open: all year Monday to Friday,
excluding Bank Holidays 9am-
4.30pm. Admission free.

Dairyland
Tresillian Barton,
Summercourt, Newquay
On A3058 Newquay to Summer-
court road
☎ Newquay (0872) 510246
Open: Easter week and May-
September 10.30am-5.30pm. April
and October 12noon-5pm.
Working farm with one of Europe's
most modern milking parlours and
country life museum. Facilities for
disabled. Picnic area, farmyard and
playground. Free parking.

Delabole Slate Showroom
North Cornwall. B3314 to Delabole
then follow AA signs
☎ Camelford (0840) 212242
Open: Monday to Friday 8am-5pm,
except Bank Holidays.
Museum is probably re-opening.

The Duke of Cornwall's Light Infantry Regimental Museum
The Keep, Bodmin
☎ Bodmin (0208) 72810
$1/_4$ mile S of town centre on B3269
Open: Monday to Friday 9.30am-
12.30pm, 2-4.30pm. Closed on
Bank Holidays. Parties at other
times by arrangement.

Falmouth Maritime Museum
Bell's Court in centre of town
Open: Monday-Saturday April-
October 10am-4pm, November-
March 10am-3pm.

Fowey Town Hall Museum
Trafalgar Square, Fowey
Open: Easter weekend, Spring
Bank Holiday-September, week-
days 10.30am-12.30pm, 2.30-
4.30pm.

Guildhall Museum
Fore Street, Lostwithiel
☎ Bodmin (0208) 872380
Open: Easter week, then mid-May
to September. Guided tours.

Isles of Scilly Museum
Church Street, Hugh Town,
St Mary's
☎ Scillonia (0720) 22337
Open: daily except Sundays April-
October 10am-12noon, 1.30-4.30pm.
Also Whitsun-September 7.30-9pm.
Winter Wednesday 2-4pm.

Lanreath Mill and Farm Museum
Churchtown, Lanreath, Looe
$1/_2$ mile off B3359 midway between
Taphouse and Looe
☎ Lanreath (0503) 220218
Open: Sunday-Friday. Demonstrations 2-4pm — Sunday: eggcraft;
Monday: corn dollies; Tuesday:
patchwork/quilting; Wednesday:
spinning; Thursday: leather; Friday:
lace.

Mid-Cornwall Craft Centre Galleries
Biscovey
☎ Par (0726) 812131
Open: 10am-5pm, Monday-
Saturday, all year, except Christ-
mas and New Year.
Arts and crafts on display and sale.

Military Vehicle Museum
Lamanva, Penryn
Signed on the Penryn-Gweek road
near Argal reservoir
☎ Falmouth (0326) 72446
Open: in season daily, but may be
moving to Flambards, Helston.

Museum of Methodism
Carharrack Methodist Church,
Carharrack
Open: all year Tuesday-Thursday
10am-12noon. Enquiries to
playgroup next door.
Displays relate to Wesley's visits to
Cornwall and later Methodism in
Cornwall.

Museum of Witchcraft
Boscastle Harbour
Open: Easter-September 10am-5pm

Nautical Museum
(opposite Admiral Benbow)
Chapel Street, Penzance
☎ Penzance (0736) 68890
Open: 10am-5pm during season.

Newlyn Orion Art Gallery
24 New Road, Newlyn, Penzance
☎ Penzance (0736) 63715
Open: all year, Monday-Saturday
10am-5pm.

**North Cornwall Museum and
   Gallery**
Camelford
☎ Camelford (0840) 212954
Open: April-September 10.30am-
5pm, daily except Sundays.

Old Guildhall Museum
Higher Market Street, East Looe
☎ Looe (05036) 3709
Open: Easter-end September
10.30am-5pm.
Exhibits include stocks, pillory,
prison cells, paintings, china,
smuggling displays.

**Paul Corin Magnificent Music
   Machines**
St Keyne Station just off B3254
☎ Liskeard (0579) 343108
Open: daily Easter-October
10.30am-5pm.

**Pendeen Crafts and Mining
   Museum**
Boscaswell
Open: shop hours in season.

Penryn Local History Museum
Town Hall, Penryn
☎ Town Clerk, (0326) 37086
Open: Monday to Friday 9am-
12.30pm, 2-5pm.

Penwith Art Gallery
Back Road West, St Ives
☎ Penzance (0736) 795579
Open: Tuesday-Saturday 10am-
1pm and 2.30-5pm all year.

**Penzance and District
   Museum and Art Galley**
Morrab Road, Penzance
☎ Penzance (0736) 63625/63405
Open: all day Monday-Friday.
Saturday 10.30am-12.30pm.

Perranzabuloe Museum
Ponsmere Road, Perranporth
☎ Truro (0872) 573368
Open: May-Sept Monday to Friday
11am-1pm, 2-5pm.

**Royal Institution of Cornwall
   Museum and Art Gallery**
River Street, Truro
☎ Truro (0872) 72205
Open: daily 9am-1pm, 2-5pm.
Restaurant 10am-4.30pm.

St Agnes Parish Museum
Penwinnick Road, St Agnes
☎ St Agnes (0872) 552181
Open: daily April-October 10.30am-
5pm, also evenings July, August.

St Ives Museum
Wheal Dream, St Ives — behind
Smeaton's Pier
☎ Penzance (0736) 796005
Open: Monday to Friday 10.30am-
5pm in summer. Maritime history.

Shire Horse Farm and
Carriage Museum
Lower Grylls Farm,
Treskillard,
Redruth
☎ Camborne (0209) 713606
Leave Camborne bypass at Pool
turning, A3047, across traffic lights,
turn right over railway bridge, follow
signposts to Carriage Museum
Open: daily 10am-6pm Easter to
September. Free wagon rides,
picnic area, farmhouse teas.

Trinity House National
Lighthouse Centre
Old Buoy Store,
Wharf Road,
Penzanze
☎ Penzance (0736) 60077
Open: daily March-October.
Has world's finest collection of
lighthouse equipment.

Valhalla Museum
Tresco
Isles of Scilly
☎ Scillonia (0720) 22818
Open: 10am-4pm all year.
Ships figureheads.

Wayside Museum
Zennor
On B3306 Land's End-St Ives road
at Zennor
Open: 9.30am to dusk daily May-
October.
Mining, fishing, quarrying, agricul-
tural and craft implements,
domestic utensils, old mill and open
hearth. Admission free.

Wheal Martyn China Clay
Museum
Carthew St Austell
Follow signposts to Carthew on
A391 2 miles N of St Austell
☎ St Austell (0726) 850362
Open: daily April-end October
10am-6pm. (Last admission 5pm.)
Complete nineteenth-century clay
works. Working waterwheels,
wagons, locomotives, craft pottery
and introductory slide programme.

NATURE TRAILS

Most nature trails in Cornwall and
the Isles of Scilly are laid out by the
Forestry Commission, the National
Trust or the South-West Water
Authority.

Cardinham Woods
Off A38 Bodmin to Plymouth road 2
miles E of Bodmin
(SX099664)
Forestry leaflet available.

Coombe Valley
On coast road 3 miles W of
Kilkhampton and 5 miles N of Bude
(SS213117).
Two trails laid out by National Trust.
Booklet from local bookshops.

Deerpark Forest
Off Taphouse to Looe road B3359
near Herodsfoot
(SX197603)
Forestry Commission leaflets
available.

Duchy Nurseries
Lostwithiel
Turn off A390 on edge of Lostwithiel on Liskeard side and drive up a
narrow lane to immaculately-kept
nurseries. Nature trail opposite.
☎ Bodmin (0208) 872665

Halvana Forest Trail
Off A30 from Five Lanes
(SX213788)
Leaflet available.

Lanhydrock (National Trust)
2¹/₂ miles SE of Bodmin, overlooking River Fowey. Follow signs from
either A38 Bodmin-Liskeard or
Bodmin-Lostwithiel roads.
☎ Bodmin (0208) 73320
For opening times see *Buildings*.

Mineral Tramways Project
Kerrier Groundwork Trust has
details of all walks and picnic areas.
☎ Redruth (0209) 211364 between
9.30am-5pm, Monday-Friday.

Silvermine Trail
A public walk, marked on OS 1in
map between B3254 Liskeard-Looe
road and the B3359 Middle
Taphouse-Polperro road.

St Clement Wood
Near Malpas, 2 miles SE Truro,
beside Tresillian River.

St Mary's
Isles of Scilly
Two nature trails at Holy Vale and
the Moors.

Tehidy Country Park
Many acres of woodland with
various walks and display panels
for guidance.
Free access at all times. Best from
B3301 at North Cliffs/Reskajeage
Downs.

Trelissick (National Trust)
4 miles S of Truro on both sides of
B3289
☎ Truro (0872) 862090
For opening times see *Gardens*.

RESERVOIR RECREATION

Reservoirs provide a wide range of
opportunities for enjoyment. Most
are open for fishing; on some it is
possible to sail, canoe or even
water ski. Many are superb places
for a picnic, and to sit and watch
the ever-changing scene of water,
boats, fishermen and birds, or to
stroll through some of Cornwall's
most beautiful scenery. Not all the
reservoirs are open for every
facility, but each year sees a
broadening of those available. In
this way it is hoped to increase the
areas of peace and quiet for pure
enjoyment of the countryside. For
information regarding permission
and permits apply to:

Information Office
Recreation,
South-West Water Authority,
Peninsula House,
Rydon Lane,
Exeter, EX2 7HR
☎ Exeter (0392) 219666

Argal-College
Off B3281 Penryn to Constantine
road. Birdwatching, stocked trout
fishing (fly only), coarse fishing,
picnicking, toilets and walking.

Colliford Lake Park Complex
Bodmin Moor
☎ Cardinham (0208) 82335
Lakeside walks, picnic areas, rare
breeds park, pets corner. Restau-
rant (evenings only), refreshments.

Crowdy
Off A39 Camelford to Bude road.
General access, birdwatching and
natural trout fishing.

244 • The Visitor's Guide to Cornwall

Porth
Off A3059 Newquay to Wadebridge road
Birdwatching and coarse fishing only.

Siblyback
Between A30 Bodmin to Launc-eston road and A38 Bodmin to Liskeard road. Picnicking, walking, toilets, play area, refreshments kiosk, birdwatching, sailing, boardsailing, canoeing, water skiing and stocked trout fishing (fly only).

Stithians
Between A394 Falmouth to Helston and A393 Falmouth to Redruth roads.
Birdwatching, sailing and boardsail-ing, canoeing, rowing, water-skiing and natural trout fishing (fly only).

Tamar Lakes
Off A39 at Kilkhampton
Picnicking, walking, toilets, birdwatching, refreshment kiosk, sailing, boardsailing, canoeing. Natural trout and coarse fishing at Lower Lakes.

RIDING AND PONY-TREKKING

The following are some of the licensed riding establishments offering riding and trekking holidays.

Chiverton Riding Centre, Silverwell, near Truro
☎ Truro (0872) 560471

Old Mill Stables, Lelant Downs, Hayle
☎ Hayle (0736) 753045

Sunrise Riding Centre, Henwood, Liskeard
☎ Liskeard (0579) 62895

Tall Trees Riding Stables, Davidstow, Camelford
☎ Otterham Station (0840) 6249

SPORTS CENTRES

Carn Brea Leisure Centre
(or Pool Leisure Centre)
Station Road, Pool, Redruth
Just off the A3047 Camborne-Redruth road at mini-roundabout.
☎ Camborne (0209) 714766
Open: 9am-10.30pm daily.
Largest leisure centre in Cornwall.
Coaching courses in various sports.
Parking space for 400 cars.

Climbers Club
The Count House, Bosigran, Pendeen, St Ives
☎ Penzance (0736) 796960

Cornish Gliding & Flying Club
Perranporth Airfield
☎ Truro (0872) 572124

Cornish Leisure World
Carlyon Bay, St Austell
☎ Par (0726) 814261

Cornwall Flying Club
Bodmin Airfield, Cardinham
☎ Cardinham (0208) 82419

Polykth Recreation Centre
Two minutes' drive from St Austell Station
☎ St Austell (0726) 61585
Open: 9am-10pm. Pool opening times of pool relate to school holidays.

STEAM AND OTHER RAILWAYS

Forest Railroad Park
$1/_2$ mile N of A38 at Dobwalls
(between Liskeard and Bodmin)

☎ Dobwalls (0579) 20325
Open: daily April-October 10am-
5.30pm (last admission 4.30pm).
Café, picnic areas, toilets, car park.
A theme park based on the
American railways in miniature —
most extensive in Europe. Model
layouts, loco shed. Also visit
Archibald Thorburn Museum
on same site, open as above.

Lappa Valley Railway and Leisure Park
St Newlyn East, Newquay
5 miles from Newquay. Follow
signs to St Newlyn East then
special signs to railway
☎ Mitchell (0872) 510317
Open: daily 10.15am-5.30pm
during season.
Car park, buffet, licensed restaurant, old engine house and chimney
stack of disused East Wheal Rose.
Two-mile round trip in roomy
carriages.

Launceston Steam Railway
Kensey valley, Launceston
☎ Launceston (0566) 75665
Open: Sundays and Tuesdays until
Whitsun 2-5pm. Whitsun-September
daily except Saturdays.
October, Sunday and Tuesday 2-
5pm. Santa specials on December
weekends.
Picnic facilities, museum, car park,
refreshments at station buffet.

Mevagissey Model Railway and Museum
Meadow Street, Mevagissey
☎ Mevagissey (0726) 842457
Open: summer 11am-5pm (9pm in
high season). Winter, Sundays only
2-4pm.
One of the world's most unique
collections of model railways
(nearly 1,500 items).

TOURIST INFORMATION CENTRES

These are run by local authorities
with the assistance of the Cornwall
Tourist Board.

Cornwall Tourist Board
Muicipal Buildings,
Boscawen Street, Truro
☎ Truro (0872) 74555

Bodmin
Shire House, Mount Folly
☎ Bodmin (0208) 76616

Bude
Crescent Car Park
☎ Bude (0288) 354240

Camelford
North Cornwall Museum,
The Clease
☎ Camelford (0840) 212954

Falmouth
28 Killigrew Street
☎ Falmouth (0326) 3123000

Fowey
Post Office, 4 Custom House Hill,
☎ Fowey (0726) 833616

Launceston
Market House Arcade, Market St
☎ Launceston (0566) 772321

Looe
The Guildhall, Fore St,
East Looe (seasonal)
☎ Looe (0503) 62072

Lostwithiel
Liddicoat Road
☎ Bodmin (0208) 872207

Newquay
Marcus Hail
☎ Newquay (0637) 871345

Penzance
Station Road
☎ Penzance (0736) 62207

Perranporth
Ponsmere Road
☎ Perranporth (0872) 573363

St Ives
The Guildhall, Street-an-Pol
☎ Penzance (0736) 796297

Isles of Scilly
Portcressa Bank, St Mary's
☎ Scillonia (0720) 22536

Saltash
Granada Service Area
Carkeel Roundabout
☎ Saltash (0752) 849526

Tolgus Mill
National Gold Centre
Portreath
☎ Redruth (0209) 313001

Victoria
A30 Roche (seasonal)
☎ Fowey (0726) 890481

Wadebridge
Town Hall (seasonal)
☎ Wadebridge (0208) 813725

TRANSPORT

Ferries C=Car, F=Foot
Plymouth (Devonport) to Torpoint
   (C)
Plymouth (Stonehouse) to Cremyll
   (F)
Fowey to Polruan (F)
Fowey to Bodinnick (C)
Padstow to Rock (F)
Falmouth to St Mawes (F)
Falmouth to Flushing (F)
Feock to Philleigh (King Harry) (C)
Penzance to Isles of Scilly

(St Mary's Inter-island launch
services leave for the off-shore
islands shortly after arrival of the
ship at St Mary's. Boatmen's
Association launches leave daily at
10.15am and 2.15pm during
summer.)

Isles of Scilly Steamship Co Ltd
Quay Street, Penzance
☎ (0800) 373307

British International Helicopters Ltd
Heliport, Penzance
☎ Penzance (0736) 64296

Brymon Airways
Newquay Civil Airport
☎ St Mawgan (0637) 860551

Western National Bus Services Ltd
Truro
☎ Truro (0872) 40404

British Rail. For all passenger train
and fares enquiries
☎ Truro (0872) 76244

VISITOR CENTRES

Carnglaze Slate Caverns
South from St Neot towards A38
☎ Liskeard (0579) 320251.
Open: Easter-September.

Cornish Leisure World
Crinnis Beach
Carlyon Bay, St Austell
☎ Par (0726) 814261
Open: daily Easter-September.
1³/₄ miles sandy beach, large car
park, general beach facilities,
restaurants, miniature railway,
nightclubs.

Cornwall Aero Park &
Flambards Victorian Village
Helston
☎ Helston (0326) 564093

Open: mid-April to November every day 10am-5pm; late July to early September extended opening; park closes 8pm.

Delabole Slate Quarry
Follow AA signs from Camelford
☎ Camelford (0840) 212242
Open; 8.30am-4.30pm weekdays, not Bank Holidays.
Showroom open monday-Friday 8am-5pm, except Bank Holidays. The uses of slate are displayed.

Golitha Falls Centre
Between St Cleer and St Neot, slightly SW of Siblyback Lane. Free entry.

Goonhilly Downs Visitor Centre
The Lizard
7 miles from Helston on B3294 Helston-St Keverne road
☎ Helston (0326) 22333
Open: 10am daily Easter-October. Working models of dish aerials and satellites, audio-visual display, restaurant and shop.

Minack Open-air Theatre
New exhibition of Minack history. For opening times
☎ Penzance (0736) 810694

Newquay Zoo and Leisure Park
Trenance, Newquay
5 minutes from town centre on the Edgcumbe road/Trevemper road
☎ Newquay (0637) 873342
Open: daily from 10am April-October. Café. Attractions include boating lake, squash and tennis courts, miniature railway.

Poldark Mine
Wendron
3 miles N of Helston on B3297 (Redruth road)
☎ Helston (03265) 573173

Open: daily April-November 10.30am-5.30pm, July & August 10am-6pm. Last admission 4pm. Tin mine, museums, historic engines, restaurant, shop, children's play area. Route for mildly disabled.

Royal Navy Air Station
Culdrose
South of Helston on A3083
Public viewing enclosure open all year, car park, picnic area. Fleet Air Arm Museum and shop open: week before Easter-end October 9.30am-6pm. Refreshment bar and toilet facilities when shop is open.

St Agnes Model Village and Leisure Park
☎ St Agnes (0872) 552793
Open: daily April-October 10am-6pm; July to mid-September 10am-10pm.
One admission price covers Cornwall in Miniature, Land of Make-Believe, large models of prehistoric animals, circus, haunted house and 7 acres of beautiful gardens. Café, gift shop, shooting gallery. Suitable for wheelchairs.

St Austell Brewery Visitor Centre
☎ St Austell (0726) 66022
Open: late May. Please telephone for brewery tour.

Trethorne Leisure Farm
Piper's Pool (A395)
☎ Piper's Pool (0566) 86324
Open: Easter-autumn. Special rates OAP and children.
Animals, pony rides.

Trinty House National Light-house Centre
Old Bouy Store
Wharf Road, Penzance
☎ Penzance (0736) 60077

Open: March-October daily.
One of the few national museums outside London, this exhibition has an audio-visual theatre, illustrates the history of the lighthouse, shows how they were built and how the keepers lived.

YACHTING AND SAILING CLUBS

Cargreen, Saltash
☎ Saltash (0752) 8433169

Falmouth
Port Pendennis, Falmouth Harbour
☎ Falmouth (0326) 374043

Flushing
New Quay, Flushing
☎ Falmouth (0326) 374043

Fowey Gallants
Alan Toms
New Quay House,
Polruan
☎ Fowey (0726) 832335

Helford River
☎ Manaccan (0326) 23460

Looe
☎ Looe (0503) 62559

Mylor
Mylor Yacht Harbour, Falmouth
☎ Falmouth (0326) 374391

Penzance
Albert Pier, Penzance
☎ Penzance (0736) 64989

Porthpean
St Austell
☎ St Austell (0726) 66266

Rock Sailing Club
☎ Trebetherick (0208) 862709

St Mawes
☎ St Mawes (0326) 270686

Saltash
Clubhouse , Waterside
Saltash
☎ Saltash (0755) 55988

Scillonian
c/o Harbour Master
St Mary's,
Isles of Scilly
☎ Scillonia (0720) 22718

YOUTH HOSTELS

Youth Hostels Association (England and Wales)
Trevelyan House
8 St Stephen's Hill
St Albans, Herts AL1 2DY
☎ St Albans (0727) 55215

Hostels at:
Boscastle
Palace Stabs
☎ Boscastle (0840) 250287

Coverack
Parc Behan
☎ St Keverne (0326) 280467

Falmouth
Pendennis Castle
☎ Falmouth (0326) 311435

Mevagissey
Boswinger
☎ Mevagissey (0726) 844074

Newquay
Alexandra Court
Narrowcliffe
☎ Newquay (0637) 876381

Padstow
Tregonnan
Treyarnon Bay
☎ Padstow (0841) 520322

Perranporth
Droskyn Point
☎ Truro (0872) 573812

St Just in Penwith
Letcha Vean
☎ Penzance (0736) 788437

USEFUL ADDRESSES

British Horse Society
Hon. Secretary: Mr S. Milln
Bosinver Farm, St Austell,
Cornwall, PL26 7DT
☎ St Austell (0726) 72128
Pony-trekking and riding holidays.

British Tourist Authority
Information Centre
Thames Tower, Blacks Road,
Hammersmith, London
☎ 081 846 9000

Camping Club of Great Britain and
    Ireland
Greenfields House, Westwoodway,
Covenrty CV4 8JH
☎ 0203 694995

Caravan Club Ltd
East Grinstead House
East Grinstead,
Sussex RH19 1UA
☎ East Grinstead (0342) 410258

Cornwall Birdwatching and
    Bird Preservation Society
Tregarrick,
St Mawgan-in-Pydar,
Newquay
☎ Newquay (0637) 860309

Council for the Protection of Rural
    England
25 Buckingham Palace Road,
London SW1 0PP
☎ 071 976 6433

Cyclists Touring Club
69 Meadrow
Godalming, Surrey GU7 3HS
☎ Godalming (0483) 426994

English Heritage
(Historic Buildings and Monuments
    Commission)
Fortress House
23 Savile Row
London W1X 2HE
☎ 071 222 9251

Isles of Scilly Information Office
Town Hall
St Mary's
Isles of Scilly TR21 0LW
☎ Scillonia (0720) 22536

National Trust
36 Queen Anne's Gate
London SW1H 9AS
☎ 071 222 9251

National Trust
Cornwall Information Office
The Estate Office
Lanhydrock Park,
Bodmin, Cornwall PL30 4DE
☎ Bodmin (0208) 74281

South-West Arts
Bradninch Place,
Gandy Street,
Exeter, EX4 3LS
☎ Exeter (0392) 218188

South-West Water (Cornwall
    Division)
Dowrglann, Stennack Road
Holmbush Industrial Estate
St Austell
☎ St Austell (0726) 66766

West Country Tourist Board
Trinity Court
37 Southernhay East
Exeter EX1 1QS
☎ Exeter (0392) 76351

INDEX